Books by
JOHN HOLT

HOW CHILDREN FAIL

HOW CHILDREN LEARN

THE UNDERACHIEVING SCHOOL

WHAT DO I DO MONDAY?

FREEDOM AND BEYOND

ESCAPE FROM CHILDHOOD

INSTEAD OF EDUCATION

NEVER TOO LATE

TEACH YOUR OWN

TEACH YOUR OWN

A Hopeful Path for Education

John Holt

LIGHTHOUSE BOOKS

27A Sydney Street   Brightlingsea   Essex   England

ACKNOWLEDGMENTS

Excerpt from "Pumping Polysyllabism" reprinted with permission from *Mother Jones* magazine, © 1977, The Foundation for National Progress.

Excerpt from *The Fort Lauderdale News,* July 1, 1979, used by permission.

Excerpts from ACTING OUT: Coping With Big City Schools by Roland Betts, Introduction by John Holt: Copyright © 1978 by Roland Betts. Introduction Copyright © 1978 by John Holt. By permission of Little, Brown and Company.

Excerpt from TRAVELS AROUND AMERICA by Harrison E. Salisbury: Copyright © 1976 by Harrison E. Salisbury. Used with permission from publisher, Walker and Company.

Excerpt from the *Cape Cod Times,* June 22, 1979, used by permission.

Excerpts from AMERICAN HOME ACADEMY © 1979 Dick & Joyce Kinmont. Used by permission.

Excerpts from "Good Samaritans at Age Two" by Maya Pines: Reprinted from *Psychology Today* Magazine. Copyright © 1979 Ziff-Davis Publishing Company. Used by permission.

Excerpts reprinted from the April 1980 *Home Educator's Newsletter,* A publication of The National Association of Home Educators. Used by permission.

Contents

My sister, when her older children would begin to play lovingly but too roughly with their year-and-a-half-old sister, used to say to them, "Careful! That's a person!"

It is, in fact, nothing short of a miracle that the modern methods of instruction have not yet entirely strangled the holy curiosity of inquiry; for this delicate little plant, aside from stimulation, stands mainly in need of freedom; without this it goes to wrack and ruin without fail. It is a very grave mistake to think that the enjoyment of seeing and searching can be promoted by means of coercion and a sense of duty. To the contrary, I believe that it would be possible to rob even a healthy beast of prey of its voraciousness, if it were possible, with the aid of a whip, to force the beast to devour continuously, even when not hungry, especially if the food, handed out under such coercion, were to be selected accordingly.

ALBERT EINSTEIN

Introduction

This book is about ways we can teach children, or rather, allow
them to learn, outside of schools—at home, or in whatever other
places and situations (and the more the better) we can make
available to them. It is in part an argument in favor of doing it,
in part a report of the people who are doing it, and in part a
manual of action for people who want to do it.

Many events, some public, some personal, some in my own
mind, led me to write this book. It began in the late 1950s. I was
then teaching ten-year-olds in a prestige school. I was also spending a lot of time with the babies and very young children of my
sisters, and of other friends. I was struck by the difference between
the 10s (whom I liked very much) and the 1s and 2s. The children
in the classroom, despite their rich backgrounds and high I.Q.'s,
were with few exceptions frightened, timid, evasive, and self-
protecting. The infants at home were bold adventurers.

It soon became clear to me that children are by nature and from
birth very curious about the world around them, and very energetic, resourceful, and competent in exploring it, finding out about
it, and mastering it. In short, much more eager to learn, and much
better at learning, than most of us adults. Babies are not blobs, but

true scientists. Why not then make schools into places in which children would be allowed, encouraged, and (if and when they asked) helped to explore and make sense of the world around them (in time and space) in the ways that most interested them?

I said this in my first two books, *How Children Fail* (1964) and *How Children Learn* (1966). They were soon widely read, and translated in many other countries. Along with others saying much the same thing, I found myself busy as a lecturer, TV talk show guest, etc. Many people, among educators, parents, and the general public, seemed to be very interested in and even enthusiastic about the idea of making schools into places in which children would be independent and self-directing learners. I was even asked to give a course on Student-Directed Learning at the Harvard Graduate School of Education. For a while it seemed to me and my allies that within a few years such changes might take place in many schools, and in time, even a majority.

When parents told me, as many did, that they were dissatisfied with their children's schools, I urged them to form committees, hold meetings, and organize public support for school reform, pressuring school boards and if need be electing new ones. In a few places, parents actually did this.

At first I did not question the compulsory nature of schooling. But by 1968 or so I had come to feel strongly that the kinds of changes I wanted to see in schools, above all in the ways teachers related to students, could not happen as long as schools were compulsory. I wrote about this in an article, "Not So Golden Rule Days," which appeared first in the *Center Magazine* of the Center for the Study of Democratic Institutions, and later in my third book, *The Underachieving School.* Since compulsory school attendance laws force teachers to do police work and so prevent them from doing real teaching, it would be in *their* best interests, as well as those of parents and children, to have those laws repealed, or at least greatly modified. In the article, I suggested some political steps or stages in which this might be done.

In such ways many of us worked, with great energy, enthusiasm, and confidence, for this kind of school reform. As people do who are working for change, we saw every sign of change, however small, as further proof that the change was coming. We had not yet learned that in today's world of mass media ideas go in and out of fashion as quickly as clothes. For a while, school reform was in fashion. There is no way we could have known that it was only fashion. One only finds out later what is fashion and what has lasting effect.

There were signs, even then. I had been one of a number of speakers invited to Minneapolis, a liberal city in a liberal state, to talk to a large conference of Minnesota teachers. At my meeting there were perhaps seven hundred. After my talk, during the questions, which had seemed friendly, a stout woman, thin pressed-together lips turned way down at the corners, said in a harsh angry voice, "What do you do with the children who are just plain lazy?" The entire audience burst into loud applause. I was startled and shocked. When the applause died down, I replied as best I could, and the meeting resumed its normal polite course. Later, I pushed aside the awkward memory of that little incident. I did not want to hear what it was plainly saying, that for a second the silent majority had spoken, and said, "Children are no damned good."

In my travels I was often invited to visit schools and classes by people who said, "We've read your books, we think they're wonderful, and we're doing all the things you talked about." Well, they usually were, but not in the way they meant—they were doing all the mistaken and harmful things that I described in the books and had once done myself. People also talked to me with great enthusiasm about innovative programs. But these were always paid for with federal money, and as time went on, it always turned out that when the federal money stopped, so did the program. People might feel badly about losing these wonderful programs. But pay for them with local money, their own money? It was never considered.

When I went to places to talk I was always met at the airport by two or three people. Usually, we were friends from the start. They had read my books, saw things much as I did. We always had a good time together, talking about the things we agreed on, sharing success stories, horror stories, hard luck stories. They always made me feel so at home that by lecture time, I assumed that with a few exceptions the people there must all be like my friends. Only slowly did I realize that the people who brought me in to speak were almost always a tiny minority in their own school or community, and that my task was to say out loud in public what people were sick of hearing *them* say, or even what they had been afraid to say at all. They hoped that if people heard me—famous author, guest on the "Today" show, etc.—they might pay attention.

From many such experiences I began to see, in the early '70s, slowly and reluctantly, but ever more surely, that the movement for school reform was mostly a fad and an illusion. Very few people, inside the schools or out, were willing to support or even tolerate giving more freedom, choice, and self-direction to children. Of the very few who were, most were doing so not because they believed that children really wanted and could be trusted to find out about the world, but because they thought that giving children some of the appearances of freedom (allowing them to wear old clothes, run around, shout, write on the wall, etc.) was a clever way of getting them to do what the school had wanted all along—to learn those school subjects, get into a good college, etc. Freedom was not a serious way of living and working, but only a trick, a "motivational device." When it did not quickly bring the wanted results, the educators gave it up without a thought and without regret.

At the same time I was seeing more and more evidence that most adults actively distrust and dislike most children, even their own, and quite often especially their own. Why this should be so, I talked about in my books, *Escape From Childhood* and *Instead of Education.* In a nutshell, people whose lives are hard, boring, painful, meaningless—people who suffer—tend to resent those who seem to suffer less than they do, and will make them suffer if they can. People who feel themselves in chains, with no hope of ever getting them off, want to put chains on everyone else.

In short, it was becoming clear to me that the great majority of boring, regimented schools were doing exactly what they had always done and what most people wanted them to do. Teach

children about Reality. Teach them that Life Is No ⌐
them to Shut Up And Do What You're Told. Please don ⌐
derstand me on this. People don't think this way out of pu⌐
meanness. A man writing, sympathetically, to a radical paper,
about life in small towns in Iowa, where in order to pay their debts
many full-time farmers have to do extra work in meat-packing
plants—as he says, "shoveling lungs"—says, "The work ethic has
been ground into these folks so thoroughly that they think anyone
who doesn't hold down, continually, a full-time *painful* job is a
bum." They don't want their kids to be bums. Back To The Basics,
for most of them, is code for No More Fun and Games In School.
Most of them don't care particularly about reading, as such. They
read little themselves—like most Americans, they watch TV.
What they want their child to learn is how to *work*. By that they
don't mean to do good and skillful work they can be proud of.
They don't have that kind of work themselves, and never expect
to. They don't even *call* that "work." They want their children,
when their time comes, to be able, and *willing,* to hold down
full-time painful jobs of their own. The best way to get them ready
to do this is to make school as much like a full-time painful job
as possible.

Of course, they would be glad to see their children go to a
"good" college, become lawyers, doctors, corporation executives,
part of that world of wealth and power they see every day on TV.
But this is like winning the lottery. You may hope for it—about
the only hope you've got—but you don't plan on it. Anyway, most
people know by the time their children finish second or third grade
that they are not going to win the big prize. What's left is that
full-time painful job. To get them ready for that is what most
schools are for, always were for.

Just the other day, this truth was once again thrust in my face.
Taking a cab to the airport, I fell into conversation with the driver,
a cheerful, friendly man. He asked me where I was going and what
I did. I said I wrote books about children, schools, and education,
and also published a little magazine about people teaching their
children at home. He said he didn't think that was a very good
idea, and went on to talk about schools and what was wrong with

them. As soon as I reached the airport, I wrote down all I could remember of his words. The fragments I quote here give a fair picture of the whole.

Early in our talk he said,

> Seems to me the students are directing the teachers these days, instead of the other way round. . . . When I was a kid, if I'd ever talked back to a teacher, I would have got a face full of knuckles. (Laughed.) Then I would have had to hope to God he didn't tell my father about it.

Print can't convey the approval, even the *pleasure,* with which he said this. I rarely meet people who have this faith in violence to solve problems. When I do, they scare me. I thought in the cab, "What have I got myself into now?" During the ride, I said little, tried once or twice without success to change the subject, and at the end said nothing at all. He did all the talking, getting angrier and angrier. Yet when we reached the airport he said good-bye and wished me a good trip, in the most friendly way. I looked at him as we parted. In the city I see many faces that look angry, brutal, and cruel. He did not look that way at all.

After saying the words quoted above, he said, "God help any of my children if they had ever talked back to a teacher," with such ferocity that it froze the tongue in my mouth. Yet I wonder now what he would have done if they had, and whether in fact he had actually ever done it. Suppose one of his children had claimed to be the victim of a teacher's injustice. My guess is that he would have told them to forget about justice, that the teacher was the boss, and that their job was to do whatever he said.

This thought recalled a scene in Frederick Wiseman's film *High School,* in which a student and a disciplinary vice-principal were arguing. The student, wearing glasses, good at using words, obviously not a poor kid, was stubbornly insisting that he hadn't done something he was accused of doing, and therefore, that he shouldn't be punished for it. The vice-principal, a big man, a former athlete and probably once a poor kid, was just as stubbornly trying to explain to the student that it didn't make any difference whether he had done what he was accused of or not; the people in charge had *decided* that he did do it, and there was nothing for him to do but take his punishment—"like a man," he said, implying that only crybabies and troublemakers whine about justice. Theories about what was true, or fair, were beside the point. In the real world, Authority had declared him guilty and he was going to be punished, and he might as well accept it.

Later in our conversation the driver spoke admiringly of Catholic schools, saying,

> I know a guy who had a couple of high school kids who were kind of wild. He sent them to Saint——School. There, if a kid talked back to one of the priests, he'd deck him, right then and there, no questions asked. (He laughed approvingly.)

I know well and on the whole believe all the conventional arguments about the futility and destructiveness of violence. None of them would have made the slightest dent on this driver. For in our conversation he told me that all six of his children had gone to college, earned the money for it themselves, and made it through. One had finished at the top of her class of 170 at a school for dental technicians. Another was trying to get into medical school, but (so the driver said) had not yet been able to, because he was not black or Puerto Rican or Mexican. (He talked a long time, and very bitterly, about this.) But in any case, here he was, driving a cab, and here were his six children, all college graduates, on their way to higher levels of society. Here was all the proof he needed that his threats and toughness worked. Not for a moment would he ever have considered the possibility that his children might have done what he wanted not so much because they feared his fist as because they valued his good opinion.

We must be clear about this. It is not because he is cruel himself that this father, like many others, insists that the schools be harsh and cruel to his children. It is because he believes that this is how the world really works, that only by being tough on kids can we help them to live better than we do, working at good jobs instead of waiting on tables and driving crummy cabs. Nor is it only working-class people who take this harsh view of life. Let me tell again a story I told in an earlier book. A boy in one of my fifth grade classes was the son of a middle executive in a large corporation, perhaps not extremely wealthy but certainly in the top 5 percent in income. In the two or three years before the boy came to my class he had done poorly in his studies and had been a behavior problem both at school and at home. Expert "help" had been called on, and had not helped. In my less rigid class the boy found many things to do that interested him, became the class chess champion, did much better in his studies, particularly math, which he had always hated, and became much better behaved, both at school and at home. His mother, a gentle and soft-spoken woman, came to see me one day after school. She said how pleased she and her husband were that their son was doing so much better in his schoolwork, and was so much more pleasant and easy to live with. She told me how much he enjoyed my class, and how much he talked about all the interesting things that went on in it. Then she paused a while, frowning a little, and finally said, "But you know, his father and I worry a little about how much fun he is having in school. After all, he is going to have to spend the rest of his life doing things he doesn't like, and he may as well get used to it now."

As long as such parents are in the majority, *and in every social class they are,* the schools, even if they wanted to, and however much they might want to, will not be able to move very far in the directions I and many others have for years been urging them to go. These parents do not want their children in or anywhere near classes in which children learn what interests them most, for the satisfaction and joy of doing it. They want their children to believe what countless teachers and parents have told me: "If I wasn't *made* to do things, I wouldn't do anything." They don't want them to think that the best reason for working might be that the work itself was interesting, demanding, and worth doing. For the real world, as they see it, doesn't run that way and can't be made to run that way.

While the question "Can the schools be reformed?" kept turning up "No" for an answer, I found myself asking a much deeper question. Were schools, however organized, however run, necessary at all? Were they the best place for learning? Were they even a good place? Except for people learning a few specialized skills,

I began to doubt that they were. Most of what I knew, I had not learned in school, or in any other such schoollike "learning environments" or "learning experiences" as meetings, workshops, and seminars. I suspected this was true of most people.

As time went on I began to have more and more doubts even about the word "learning" itself. One morning in Boston, as I walked to work across the Public Garden, I found myself imagining a huge conference, in a hotel full of signs and posters and people wearing badges. But at this conference everyone seemed to be talking about *breathing*. "How are you breathing these days?" "Much better than I used to, but I still need to improve." "Have you seen Joe Smith yet—he certainly breathes beautifully." And so on. All the meetings, books, discussions were about Better Breathing. And I thought, if we found ourselves at such a conference, would we not assume that everyone there was sick, or had just been sick? Why so much talk and worry about something that healthy people do naturally?

The same might be said of our endless concern with "learning." Was there ever a society so obsessed with it, so full of talk about how to learn more, or better, or sooner, or longer, or easier? Was not all this talk and worry one more sign that there was something seriously the matter with us? Do vigorous, healthy, active, creative, inventive societies—Periclean Greece, Elizabethan England, the United States after the Revolution—spend so much time *talking* about learning? No; people are too busy *doing* things, and learning from what they do.

These ideas led into my book *Instead of Education* where I tried to make clear the distinction between *doing,* "self-directed, purposeful, meaningful life and work" and *education,* "learning cut off from life and done under pressure of bribe or threat, greed and fear." Even as I wrote it I planned a sequel, to be called *Growing Up Smart—Without School,* about competent and useful adults who during their own childhood spent many years out of school, or about families who right now were keeping their children out.

During the late '60s and early '70s I knew a number of groups of people who were starting their own small, private, alternative schools. Most of them did not try to start their own school until after years of trying to get their local public schools to give them some kind of alternative. When they finally decided to make a school of their own, they had to persuade other parents to join them, reach some agreement on what the school would be like, find a place for it that the law would accept and that they could afford, get the okays of local fire, health, safety, etc., officials, get enough state approval so that their students would not be called truants, and find a teacher or teachers. Above all, they had to raise money.

One day I was talking to a young mother who was just starting down this long road. She and a friend had decided that they couldn't stand what the local schools were doing to children, and that the only thing to do was start their own. For many months they had been looking for parents, for space, for money, and had made almost no progress at all. Perhaps if I came up there and talked to a public meeting. . . .

As we talked about this, I suddenly thought, is all this really necessary? I said to her, "Look, do you really want to run a school? Or do you just want a decent situation for your own kids?" She answered without hesitation, "I want a decent situation for my own kids." "In that case," I said, "Why go through all this work and trouble—meetings, buildings, inspectors, money? Why not just take your kids out of school and teach them at home? It can't be any *harder* than what you are doing, and it might turn out to be a lot easier." And so it soon proved to be—a lot easier, a lot more fun.

In talking with young families like these, I found that what they most needed was support and ideas from other families who felt the same way. For this reason, I began publishing a small, bi-monthly magazine called *Growing Without Schooling,* in which parents could write about their experiences teaching their children at home. Some of the material in this book first appeared in that magazine. (See Appendix for more information.) Of this material, some is quoted from books, magazines, news stories, court decisions, etc. Some was written by me. Much of it comes from letters from parents. The letters quoted here are only a small part of the letters we have printed in the magazine, which in turn are only a very small part of those that people have sent us.

The ones quoted here are of course some of the best, but many others that we might have printed are just as good. I have had to break up many of these letters so as to fit the parts under different chapter headings. This may have caused a loss of some of the impact and flavor of the originals, which were often very long and covered many topics. Still, what we have quoted will give some idea how affectionate, perceptive, and eloquent most of these letters are. Reading the mail sent to *Growing Without Schooling* has been one of the great rewards of doing this work. I hope readers of this book will enjoy these letters as much as I have.

1

Why Take Them Out?

Why do people take or keep their children out of school? Mostly for three reasons: they think that raising their children is their business not the government's; they enjoy being with their children and watching and helping them learn, and don't want to give that up to others; they want to keep them from being hurt, mentally, physically, and spiritually.

First, before some unschoolers tell you in their own words why they took their children out of school, two questions: (1) How many such people are there? (2) What kind of people are they?

Good short answers to these questions would be (1) nobody knows and (2) all kinds.

The reason no one knows or can find out how many families are teaching their own children is that many of these people, fearing with good reason that if the local schools knew they were teaching their own children they would make trouble for them, are doing this in secret. Sometimes they simply hide their children from the local schools, don't even let them know they exist. Sometimes they tell the local schools, perhaps truthfully, perhaps not, that they have registered their children in some private school. Sometimes they have registered their own home as a school, which in many states is easy to do. Sometimes they and a few other families register as a church-related school. There is simply no way to tell how many such people there are. Thus, there is no way to tell how many of the registered private schools in any state are schools as most people understand that word, i.e., special buildings with specialized hired teachers, and how many are disguised homes with the parents doing the teaching.

Dr. Raymond Moore, author of the books *Better Late Than Early* (New York: Reader's Digest Press, 1945) and *School Can Wait* (Provo, Utah: Brigham Young University Press, 1975), who has a great interest in these matters and is in touch with many home-schooling families, thinks that there may be as many as thirty thousand families teaching their own children. I would say somewhat less, unless the children taught under the Calvert and Seventh-Day Adventist programs are included, which would make the figure much higher. At any rate, these families are a small minority. How fast is this figure likely to grow? My guess is that as long as our political temper remains about what it is, that is, if we don't get into a war and turn ourselves into an armed camp, the number of people teaching their own children will grow rapidly. For as far into the future as I can see, however, most children will be going to some school, i.e., some special place where they are taught by paid teachers.

Who are these home-schooling families? Again, it is hard to tell. Only a minority of them read *Growing Without Schooling,* not all of those who read it write to us, and those who write talk mostly about their children, not about their background or work or income. Most of our subscriptions and letters come from rural or star routes, small towns, or low- to middle-income suburbs. I have traveled enough so that I know the names of the wealthy suburbs of many large American cities, and I know that we get almost no mail or subscriptions from these. We also get very little mail from the cities themselves.

What about income, education, race? The little evidence we have suggests that the average income of home-schooling families is close to the national average. We have had almost no correspondence with people who, judging by their addresses, writing paper, businesses, etc., were obviously rich. Many families who write us have incomes well below the national average; they have chosen to live in the country or in small towns on very modest incomes, supporting themselves by small-scale farming, crafts, small businesses, etc. Some home-schooling mothers are on welfare. As to educational background, my guess is that most of the families who read *GWS* have been to college. Some of our most successful home-schooling families, however, have not been beyond high school. I suspect that a somewhat higher percentage of the people now using church-based correspondence schools have not been to college. As to race, I have no way even of guessing. A few of our readers and subscribers have Hispanic surnames. Other than that I know nothing, except, as I say, that so far we have had little contact with people in cities.

In sum, we are so far talking about a group of Americans, probably mostly white, more rural than urban, otherwise quite average in everything except stubbornness, courage, independence, and trust in themselves and their children.

THE INCOMPETENCE OF SCHOOLS

One reason people take their children out of school is that they think they aren't learning anything. In an article in the March 1978 issue of the *Radcliffe Quarterly* I pointed out that, with few exceptions, schools are appallingly *incompetent* at their work, even as they define it, having found it easier to blame all their failures on their students.

When I began work at the Colorado Rocky Mountain School, my first teaching task was to tutor an otherwise bright and capable seventeen-year-old whose school skills were at about second grade level. High-priced specialists in his hometown had pronounced him "brain damaged." In spite of the label, he wanted to read, write, and figure like everyone else, wanted me to help him, and thought I could help him.

Not having studied "education," I had never heard of "brain damage." But it was clear to me that whatever those words might mean, it was my responsibility and duty to find out what was keeping this boy from learning and to figure out something to do about it. I soon learned that he had a very precise and logical mind, and had to understand one thing thoroughly before he could move on to the next. What had stopped his learning almost at the start of his schooling was that he had not been able to understand fully many of the things that teachers were telling him about reading, arithmetic, spelling, etc., and either could not ask the right questions to find out what he needed, or else could not get answers to the questions he asked. Some of his questions I could answer right away; others kept me thinking and wondering for many years. But even though I did not solve all his problems, my conviction that they *could* be solved may have been help enough. A few years later he wrote me from an army post, telling me what books he was reading—serious, adult books. He had clearly solved his problem himself.

What I had tried to be is what I would now call a *serious* teacher. I was not willing to accept fancy excuses as a substitute for doing what I had undertaken to do—help children learn things. When, as often happened, they did not learn what I was teaching, I could not and did not blame it on them, but had to keep trying new ways of teaching it until I found something that worked. As *How Children Fail* makes clear, this often took a long time, and I failed more than I succeeded. Another book about serious teaching is James Herndon's first book, *The Way It Spozed To Be* (New York: Simon & Schuster, 1968), a very funny, truthful, and in the end sad story about his first year's painful but successful struggles—for which he was then fired—to help students that the rest of his inner-city school had long since given up on.

One reason that so few schools are any good at their work is that they are not serious. "Good" schools and "bad," private and public, with only a few exceptions they have always run under the rule that when learning happens, the school takes the credit, and when it doesn't, the students get the blame. Where in earlier times the schools might have said that some kids were bad, stupid, lazy, or crazy, now they say they have mysterious diseases like "minimal brain dysfunction" or "learning disabilities." Under whatever name, these remain what they always were—excuses for the schools and teachers not doing their job.

For further evidence of the incompetence of schools, we have this quote from the Chicago *Tribune* (1977):

> It has been ten years in the making, but Chicago school officials now believe they have in place a complete sweeping program to teach children to read—a program that may be the pacesetter for the nation. . . . For some years, a Board of Education reading expert, Bernard Gallegos, has been putting together a package of the reading skills children need to learn in elementary school. At one point, Gallegos' list topped 500 elements. It has since been reduced to 273 over grades 1 through 8.

This might be rather comic if it were not so horrifying. Five hundred skills! What in the world could they be? When I taught myself to read, I didn't learn 500 skills, or even 273; I looked at printed words, on signs, in books, wherever I might see them, and puzzled them out, because I wanted to know what they said. Each one I learned made it easier for me to figure out the next. I could read before I went to school, but insofar as that school taught reading, they did it by what we might call the Spell-and-Say method—"*c, a, t,* cat." Most people who read, above all those who read well, were never taught 273 separate skills. And by what process was that list of 500 cut down to 273?

It's worth noting that the first of these skills is to repeat two- and three-syllable words. In practice, this is probably going to mean that all children, including black, Hispanic, Asian, or from other non-WASP groups, are going to have to pronounce these words "correctly," i.e., the way the teacher pronounces them. Children who can't, don't, or won't talk like middle-class North American white people will almost certainly be branded as not being "ready" to move to the next of the 273 steps. We can expect the schools to spend years trying to teach many of these children to talk "right," so that they can then begin teaching them to read. This, in spite of the fact that the world is full of people who read English fluently, though they speak it in a dialect or with an accent that few Chicago teachers (or few Americans) could understand.

As I write, it is about three years since that story was printed. I don't know whether the Chicago schools ever put that scheme into practice, or if they did, whether they are still using it. One thing is sure—if Chicago children are learning to read better than children anywhere else, it has been a well-kept secret.

Some years ago I heard from a teacher in another large city who, being serious, had over the years *found* a way to help children who had never read before become good readers. She had just been fired, because when the school board adopted some new reading program and ordered all teachers in the city to use it, she sensibly and responsibly refused to scrap her reading program that worked. This no doubt happened in Chicago; the best reading teachers were probably asked to change their methods or be fired. The children must be so busy trying to learn how to pass 273 reading tests that they have no time to read, and what's worse will soon not even want to. Indeed, as in many other schools, quite a few children who *can* read are probably held back because they can't pass some of the 273 tests. Then, ten years or so from now, we will read in the papers about some great *new* plan.

A teacher who had been doing some substitute teaching in a private elementary school, wrote to *GWS:*

> I found myself . . . in third grade for four days. The two teachers team teach and so I had to team teach. Both are old-fashioned types who push math and reading workbooks. I almost went wild. I couldn't figure out the questions and answers (I refuse to use the teacher's answer book) and the kids were frustrated and in pain sitting still. By the second day I could see these kids never had time to think, let alone read as a pleasure—just word-grabbing, mind-reading workbooks. In their room were paperbacks, *Charlotte's Web* and many more goodies not yet touched, because apparently the kids "can't read well enough yet." I went to the . . . principal and said I couldn't continue unless the reading time while I was there became silent reading. She agreed to it but was not very happy about me, I could easily sense. I told the kids new rules, "If you don't know a word and are really bothered by it, signal and I'll come whisper in your ear. No sounding it out, no vowels, no syllables, no questions, just the word." Very few asked after the first few minutes. But they asked for silent reading twice a day.

James Herndon makes much the same kind of report in his book *How to Survive in Your Native Land* (New York: Simon &

Schuster, 1971). When he and one or two other teachers stopped asking the children questions about their reading, stopped grading them, stopped tracking them, and *just let them read,* they very soon read much better, even those who had been very poor readers. But his school and fellow-teachers refused to learn anything from this experience.

Another familiar complaint is that students can't write. An article entitled "Pumping Polysyllabism" from the August 1977 issue of *Mother Jones,* suggests that the students may not always be the ones to blame:

> Two Chicago English professors have found that a good way to improve your grade on a term paper is to use what they call "verbose, bombastic" language.
>
> Professors Joseph Williams and Rosemary Hake say they took a well-written paper and changed the language a bit. They kept the ideas and concepts the same, but wrote two different versions—one in simplified, straightforward language and another in verbose language, loaded with pedantic terms.
>
> They then submitted the two papers to nine high-school teachers; they were surprised to find that all nine gave the verbose papers nearly perfect scores but downgraded the straightforward essays as too simple and shallow.
>
> The professors then submitted the same two papers to ninety more teachers and came up with similar results. Three out of four high school teachers and two out of three college professors gave higher marks to pompous writing.

THE CIVIL LIBERTIES OF CHILDREN

I don't want to and am not going to make this just a collection of bad stories about schools. The arguments against compulsory schools go much deeper. Some of them I expressed in a letter to the American Civil Liberties Union:

> Though the courts have not yet agreed, compulsory school attendance laws, in and of themselves, seem to me a very serious infringement of the civil liberties of children and their parents, and would

be so no matter what schools were like, how they were organized, or how they treated children, in other words, even if they were far more humane and effective than in fact they are.

Beyond that, there are a number of practices, by now very common in schools all over the country, which in and of themselves seriously violate the civil liberties of children, including:

1. Keeping permanent records of children's school performance. This would be inexcusable even if there were nothing in the records but academic grades. It is nobody's proper business that a certain child got a certain mark in a certain course when she or he was eight years old.

2. Keeping school records secret from children and/or their parents, a practice that continues in many places even where the law expressly forbids it.

3. Making these records available, without the permission of the children or their parents, to whoever may ask for them—employers, the police, the military, or other branches of government.

4. Filling these records, as experience has shown they are filled, with many kinds of malicious and derogatory information and misinformation. These may include not just unconfirmed teachers' reports of children's misbehavior, but also all kinds of pseudopsychological opinions, judgments, and diagnoses about the children and even their families. For examples, see *The Myth Of The Hyperactive Child,* by Peter Schrag and Diane Divoky (New York: Pantheon Books, 1975).

5. Compulsory psychological testing of children, and including the results of these tests in children's records.

6. Labeling children as having such imaginary and supposedly incurable diseases as "minimal brain dysfunction," "hyperactivity," "specific learning disabilities," etc.

7. Compulsory dosing of children with very powerful and dangerous psychoactive drugs, such as Ritalin.

8. Using corporal punishment in school, which in practice often means the brutal beating of young children for very minor or imagined offenses.

9. Lowering students' academic grades, or even giving failing grades, solely for disciplinary and/or attendance reasons. Not only is this practice widespread, but school administrators openly boast of it, though what it amounts to in fact is the deliberate falsification of an official record, a kind of printed perjury.

10. In all of these matters, and indeed in almost any conflict

between the child and the school, denying anything that could fairly be called "due process."

To return once more to compulsory school attendance in its barest form, you will surely agree that if the government told you that on one hundred and eighty days of the year, for six or more hours a day, you had to be at a particular place, and there do whatever people told you to do, you would feel that this was a gross violation of your civil liberties. The State, of course, justifies doing this to children as a matter of public policy, saying that only thus can it keep them from being ignorant and a burden on the State. But even if it were true that children were learning important things in schools and that they could not learn them anywhere else, neither of which I admit, I would still remind the ACLU that since in other and often more difficult cases, i.e., the Nazi rally in Skokie, Ill., it does not allow the needs of public policy to become an excuse for violating the basic liberties of citizens, it ought not to in this case.

Over the years the ACLU has tended to see as a civil liberties matter the right of children to go to school, but not their right not to go. I have been told that a committee of the ACLU is now discussing when and in what circumstances compulsory schooling may be an infringement of civil liberties. In some cases local branches of the ACLU, or ACLU attorneys, have given support to unschooling families. But it would surely be helpful if someday the national organization took a strong position on some of the issues I have mentioned.

A NEW SENSE OF RESPONSIBILITY

Even though many and perhaps most adults today dislike and distrust children, there is at the same time a growing minority of people who like, understand, trust, respect, and value children in a way rarely known until now. Many of these people are *choosing* to have children as few people before ever did. They don't have children just because that is what married people are supposed to do, or because they don't know how not to have them. On the contrary, knowing well what it may mean in time, energy, money, thought, and worry, they undertake the heavy responsibility of having and bringing up children because they deeply want to spend a part of their life living with them. Having chosen to have children, they feel very strongly that it is *their* responsibility to help these children grow into good, smart, capable, loving, trustworthy, and responsible human beings. They do not think it right to turn that responsibility over to institutions, state or private, schools or otherwise, and would not do so even if they liked and trusted these institutions, which on the whole they do not.

We may think of these views as very old-fashioned or very modern. They are probably some of both. Not long ago, Dr. Frank Merrill of Riverton, Utah, expressed them in a letter to us in these eloquent words:

> . . . I am a retired physician with a large family (I personally delivered 14 of my own children and 2 of my 8 grandchildren to date.) I have 9+ years of "higher" education above and beyond "high" school, one college degree in the physical sciences and two professional degrees (most of which has not fit me for a practical avocation nor to teach my children the same—I had to come to that by another route.)
>
> To begin with, I do not register nor allow the registration of the births of my children with any state or federal governmental agency, electing rather to make and keep my own family records and to utilize the services of a private international genealogical organization for deposition of copies thereof for historical and reference purposes.
>
> 1. Although in the past, in my nescience concerning the issues involved, I have allowed my older children to attend public schools, I have come not to see fit to send the younger ones to any school whatsoever for their basic education, electing rather to train them myself in basic communicational skills (I have not yet found a tutor with whom I have been satisfied in this area) and in habits of simple honest and responsible personal conduct, etc., and otherwise encourage them to observe, to search, and to think for themselves.
>
> 2. I have elected not to concern myself whether or not my children or any one of them do well at Stanford's or any other's achievement testing program as being only other means and methods for ranking and filing them; rather, to concern myself with encouraging them in the development of a sense of self-satisfaction

derived from achieving functional adequacy (if not excellence) in avocations of their own unhampered selection thereby ranking and filing themselves in a realistic manner and order.

3. I have come not to feel any obligation to account, with reference to the birthing, the rearing, and the training of my children to any agency other than my God who authorized their inception to begin with, especially and in particular not to those, be they public administrators, "highly educated," or otherwise, who may not have any children of their own issue (or perhaps one or two) and who may be my juniors by a whole generation or more.

4. I have come not to feel obligated to rear and teach my children after any pattern or program devised, pre-scribed (i.e., written beforehand,) or presented (i.e., sent ahead) by someone else or in such a manner as to meet any "standards" set for them by any arbitrary political system. (After all, what "standards" can be set or presumed to be enforced or enforceable by any state or other political agency external to the family itself which will not ultimately be swallowed up by those of the school of life itself when honestly attended?)

My children are well mannered, respectful to their parents, to their elders, to their peers, and to one another, are interested in life in general; they ask many questions which serve as the basis for their instruction one by one, day by day, and they appear articulate beyond their peers without their own family.

The fact that my children exist and that I am their father confers upon me, (and likewise upon every man so situated,) by natural law, an eminent domain, and with that the inescapable original obligation, and, with that, the sole natural right (and authority) to rear and to train them according to the dictates of my own conscience before God; therefore, by what law of justice (if any) can I be required or compelled to allow that obligation to be fulfilled by (or that right to be exercised by) another (which, indeed is not possible —it may only be relinquished and/or abandoned if not deliberately delegated) or to cast the minds of my children into the molds of other men or to rear and instruct them according to the dictates of other men's consciences if I elect not to do so? It is written somewhere: "Render unto Caesar (or the Governor) that which is Caesar's * * * etc.," but I am not Caesar's, neither is my mind, nor are my children, nor are their minds, and for me, and for them, God sets the standards and arranges the program in all things and unfolds it day by day, season by season.

God bless you sir. You may quote me verbatim and share this with the readers of your organ as you please. But if you see fit to do so please do not dismember it as so many publishers are wont to do of contributions made to them for their own purposes.

Judy McCahill, wife of a career officer in the U.S. Navy, shares Dr. Merrill's sense of personal responsibility:

Always, always must we parents and any others who undertake a revolutionary change which seriously affects the lives of others remind ourselves that we do so for selfish reasons. My husband and I began to get cold feet ("sounds like an epidemic," our daughter said) two or three days before school started this year; what urged me to continue with our plans was the thought that I would be very unhappy if I didn't give it a try. It was certainly not that we didn't consider what was best for the children; we believe (and still believe) they would be better off growing up at home than in a classroom. But keeping them home was mostly *my* decision, *my* experiment, *my* act of faith. What I hope is that the children not only will flower more truly in their home environment, but also will be enriched by growing up with parents who are attempting to live their beliefs. I hope that they will learn the true meaning of action, that a wrong seen is a wrong to be righted; a better way seen, one to be taken.

We did not give Colleen (12), Michael (11), Sean (9), Kevin (7) a choice between school and school-at-home. As the excitement in the neighborhood mounted during the week before school started, the boys were disturbed about our decision. But we felt that they had been so completely indoctrinated by our society's trust in schooling that they would never decide "in our favor" if we gave them a choice. If after two or three years of this experiment they are still determined, we will discuss it. [Author's note: As will be seen later, one of the four children did later return to school, when the family were in England.] Living as we do in the heart of our school-going, career-pursuing, achievement-oriented culture, we had to operate this way. We justify it by the fact that we are their parents and, we think, of all the people on earth, wisest when it comes to their upbringing.

The mother of a Muslim family living in this country expresses similar reasons for keeping her youngest children at home:

. . . Like many other families who are schooling their children at home, our main reason for wanting to make this move was a religious one. In our case, however, the religion is Islam, not Christianity. We are a very committed Muslim family, and it is of the greatest importance to us that our children grow up in an atmosphere which is not destructive to their religious orientation and values. For this reason, we are obviously in total disagreement with many social and moral values (or "unvalues") which are being propagated in schools, as well as with the limited educational approaches. Moreover, in our faith religious and other learning is not to be approached as two separate matters since Islam does not acknowledge any schism between "sacred" and "secular" aspects of life.

Our three older children had grown up in public schools, with very serious consequences to their sense of self-worth and the rightness of their values, and above all on the integratedness of their personalities. They passed through the hands of a series of junior high and high school teachers and situations in which religion, and anyone who upholds high moral and ethical values, was viewed with contempt or at least stigmatized as being very, very strange and abnormal. When my son was in the first year of junior high, we had just come back from a year overseas and the boy was feeling very much at odds with the school atmosphere. I went to the principal and expressed my concern about him, saying that he was a very religious youngster with high values. Would it not be possible to form a club or association for youngsters of similar inclinations? The response of the principal was astonishing. He told me he would look into my son's record and behavior and talk with his counselor to see if he was really normal and fit in. Of course, you can imagine how I felt after this encounter, and the club idea naturally died of its own accord although I tried without success to interest other people in the community in it. I felt and still do feel that such an organization would be very important and meaningful to young people who care about religion and values but have no support and are even afraid to voice their opinions under prevailing conditions.

When the fourth child, Y, was old enough for kindergarten, we enrolled him in a Catholic school, hoping it would be in some significant way an improvement over public school. But it was a total disappointment, in no real way different in atmosphere or approach. Thus, toward the end of Y's kindergarten year, seeing that there was no workable solution except to teach the children at home, I went to discuss the matter with the local superintendent of instruction.

Although he made it clear that he is not in favor of home schooling, he was helpful and cooperative. We must, he said, submit a letter to him by early summer, which he would submit to the local school board, who would in turn submit it to the state board of education. My husband and I wrote a very brief statement that "because the religion of our family, Islam, is a complete way of life which requires that religious education go hand-in-hand with secular education, the educational needs of our children cannot be met in a normal school situation." We also mentioned that we might be spending time outside the country and hence needed to have a method of schooling which could be continued wherever we might be residing. Permission for home schooling was given under the understanding that I would be using the Calvert materials, would teach 176 days a year, and would be under the general supervision of the local school principal (i.e., would submit the Calvert tests and confer with her once a quarter, and the child would have to take standard achievement tests and end-of-the-year tests, if any, annually.)

The experience of teaching my children has given me endless new insights concerning the role of parents (especially mothers), both what it is for most of us and what it could and should be, and the nature and meaning of education. I cannot express what a satisfaction it is to see my children growing up with stable, integrated, happy personalities, especially after the struggle of watching the harmful effects of school on the three older children. . . .

PROTECTING CHILDREN FROM HARM

Most people, however, take their children out of schools not so much for philosophical or political reasons as for the more direct and personal reason expressed by the Muslim mother: to prevent the schools from hurting their children, or hurting them any more than they already have. Many parents write to tell a story like this: Their child has taught himself to read, or somehow learned, before he went to school. He finds himself, perhaps in the pre-school, perhaps in one of the early elementary grades, reading from one to three years ahead of his class. Naturally he does not want to do the reading readiness exercises or other workbook tasks that the other children are doing, to "teach" them to do what he already knows how to do. He wants to read the kind of books he is able to read. But when he tries to do this, he gets in trouble. The teacher orders him to do the work the other children are doing, and when he naturally and sensibly says he doesn't want to, or simply doesn't, the teacher punishes him. She may bawl him out in front of other children, take his books away from him, stand him in a corner, shut him in a closet, strike him, give him a failing grade, call him "hyperactive." Quite often such teachers tell the parents of such children that unless the child does the work the other children are doing, he will fail and will have to *repeat the grade,* in spite of reading a year or more ahead of the grade level.

Naturally the amazed parents point out that since the child is reading far ahead of the class, it makes no sense to have him do the work the other children are doing or to fail him for not doing it. This seldom does any good. The teacher says stubbornly that the child has to do what the others are doing. If the parents then go to the principal, the principal usually backs up the teacher. This experience makes unschoolers out of many people who might otherwise have been content to send their children to school.

Other parents tell an opposite story. In these cases the children are not ahead of the grade, but a little behind it. Like the boy I tutored in Colorado, they are having trouble in reading or arithmetic, don't understand something in the workbooks, and so on. They can't do the homework, and are often punished, even beaten, for that. They tell their parents that they don't understand, and that when they ask the teacher for help, the teacher won't help them. The parents—many of whom, to judge from what they say or from the look of their letters, are poor—go to the teacher and ask her please to give their child a little extra help. The teacher then usually says, "I can't be giving special help to your child, I have all the rest of the children to look after." So the child falls further and further behind.

Of course, the parents themselves are in most cases perfectly capable of giving their children the help they need. But they have been told so often by the school not to interfere in the child's learning, not to try to teach the children anything, that they have come to feel as helpless as if they were facing some rare disease.

The teacher won't help; the parents don't think they can. The children, who along with their other problems are probably being teased and laughed at by the other children for being behind, get more and more discouraged. Many of them drop out of school. Many of the parents tell me that when they were children the same thing happened to them.

Many of the letters we receive from parents give similar reasons for unschooling their children:

> Once L turned five last summer, most adults she encountered in the community seemed to say to her a variation of this: "Oh, you're five now. Aren't you lucky? You can go to school in the fall!"
>
> We, her parents, didn't want her to go and said so. But we told her that it was her decision. We also told her we would never force her to go to school. Enchanted with the idea of riding the school bus, L happily decided to go.
>
> She quit, the first time, the second day of school because the teacher (one to 32 children) took a book away from her that she was reading, presumably so she would do a mimeographed pre-reading exercise or other activity the teacher had chosen. I found out later that L disliked pre-reading work. . . . I suspect she understands all too well the ludicrousness of pre-reading when you've been reading for a year.
>
> We gently convinced L to return since she had had only a glimpse of what she was quitting. A few days later, she quit for the second time. We asked for a conference with the teacher and principal. The teacher had by that time had a chance to observe L read. Despite her experience in a long career, where surely she had met five-year-olds who could read, she blurted out, "What am I going to do with you? You'll have to go to the first grade!" L bounced back, "Don't forget, I'm only five years old."
>
> Since L's main complaint was the lack of reading opportunity, the school offered her the option of attending a reading class of "slow" first graders to give her more reading and them inspiration. She bit the bait and returned to school. After a time at school (late November or early December) I noticed that she was reading less at home and not only that, she exhibited nervous behavior and other signs of anxiety when she was reading. Could this be the same child who the previous summer had sat reading for long stretches of time, totally absorbed and happy?

One day L came home from school with a book from the library. She was thrilled. I was never told that Thursday was library day and that the book must be returned the following Thursday. The day came and the book remained at home. L and several other children were punished by not being allowed to go to the library. They were also told to write a page of fives.

Shortly before the Christmas holidays L left school for good. Three months later she did some sight reading which we recorded just for the fun of it. As we listened to it replay, I observed with surprise that she was actually enjoying herself again and showed no signs of anxiety. We're so very happy that she had the sense to get out when she did. Now she often has read several books before the rest of us wake up in the morning. She also reads off and on throughout the day—everything from Spider Man and Tintin to the wonderful picture books we get from the library.

A neighbor child several years older than L comes to play after school sometimes. She's pleasant and cooperative but when she plays "school" with our children, she is "teacher" and changes into a nagging, demanding tyrant. It got so bad that L was refusing to play the game. I finally had to point out to this child that she was reflecting her teacher's behavior and that L had left school to avoid that kind of human contact. This same child could read when she entered school two years ago. She is now "having problems" in reading. One day this same child started lecturing L about school. Wasn't she coming back? And if she didn't, she wouldn't learn anything. L flashed back with, "That's why I left. I wasn't learning anything." She still maintains that is her primary reason for leaving. The other thing she couldn't tolerate was the violence among the children.

Parents frequently tell us that after some time in school their children could no longer do things that they had done well before going to school. A mother, who by the way is single and on welfare, wrote:

> My daughter, 6, has attended schools on and off for a few years and *always* learns more in the "off" times!
>
> After several months in public school her formerly perfect numbers are often backward, probably because of a teacher's remark to her in kindergarten, "If you're such a good reader, why are you poor in Math?"!!

After months of "cooling it" about Math and lots of manipulative counting "games," she's enjoying Math again—but still thinks she's *bad* in Math.

I can see "socialization" creeping into her ways and I want her out of school!

A few months later she wrote:

One day I decided to take L out of school (after several weeks of one or two days per week attendance due to various "complaints" —headache, bellyache, sore throat). I walked into the "open" classroom, with its Science Corner, its Library nook, its Life Science (animals) areas, etc., and felt a wave of uncertainty. "Can I provide as rich and diverse an environment? Will she resent being taken away from her peers?" Then I noticed that I have *never* seen anyone working—independently or in a group—in any of these nifty study areas! Then I noticed that five little boys (excluded from the "group singing") were writing "I Must Behave In Class" ten times on pieces of paper.

That did it!

Many parents have written that their children's physical health improved strikingly once they were out of school. Nancy Wallace wrote from New Hampshire:

The changes that have occurred in Ishmael since we took him out of school have been unbelievable. Gone are the fits of temper that erupted every day around 4 P.M., gone are the headaches, the lines of tension around his mouth, and gone is his depression. He used to complain bitterly that he had no time to read (schools don't *let* you read these days until you've mastered the 1,000 "skills" deemed necessary to learn this "most difficult subject"!), and consequently he read every free second he had outside of school and rarely played. He didn't eat his lunch because it got stale at school, he came home with wet, cold feet acquired at recess, and he barely spoke to us. We had thought, "Ishmael is going through a state, all kids are like this, etc.," but boy were we wrong! These days Ishmael sleeps well, eats well, *laughs, plays, and learns.* He gets his (apparently psychologically necessary) reading done in the morning, does his "schoolwork" happily because we learn about the things he wants to learn about—Indians, dinosaurs, binary numbers—and then he has time to do woodworking, skiing, art, and playing. The school board was worried that he would become a social misfit, but just the opposite has happened.

A mother wrote from Indiana:

Let me tell you what happened to our son after we removed him from a local public school's first grade last November. He stopped wetting his bed, he stopped suffering from daily stomach upsets and headaches and he has not had a cold for six months, although he averaged one cold a month while attending school. He has gained five pounds and has grown almost two inches. And he is *happy!* . . .

My husband and I had become increasingly concerned about the lowered academic standards in the public schools and the increasing availability of drugs—even in the primary grades. We had also watched our older children lose their innate intellectual curiosity by fourth grade, sometimes never regaining this priceless enthusiasm. . . .

We moved to Evansville three years ago. P attended kindergarten '77–'78, in a class of 42 youngsters. He stuck it out because every morning he and five other kindergarteners attended a reading class for half an hour. During this time he was absent from the noise and general chaos of a large class which he so disliked. I began to look into other schools at this time. . . .

[Reading *GWS*], added to our 25-year interest in *Summerhill,* convinced us that not only was it possible to raise a child without formal schooling, but it is the most probable way to insure that child's lasting interest in all that surrounds him. I decided not to register P for first grade, reasoning that the public school would probably assume that we had put him in a private school and vice versa! My husband, however, was uneasy . . . he did not relish the idea of being hauled into court. (His attitude changed during the following weeks.) We decided to let P attend first grade. Maybe he would like it, etc., etc.

After the second week of school we knew that we would have to take him out. There were thirty children in his class. Each Monday morning the paddle, used freely in this southern Indiana city, was removed from the teacher's desk drawer and prominently displayed. In some of the other classrooms in this school the paddle was hung on a nail next to the blackboard. P was so terrified of the possibility of his being paddled and humiliated in front of his friends that he could think of little else. He never would have been paddled, of course, being as frightened as he was of doing something to initiate the wrath of his teachers. [Author's note: In such schools a small child does not necessarily have to *do* something in order to get paddled.] Nevertheless, he refused to be convinced that he had nothing to worry about and in four weeks he had dropped from the top reading group to the lowest.

Some other incidents: (1) He was backed up against the wall of the bathroom by a larger first grader who asked yet another first grade boy, "Want to see me beat up this kid?" P kicked him and escaped. (2) On the playground at lunch time P threw his arms around a boy from the other first-grade class whom he had known the year before in kindergarten and whom he had not seen all summer. Two fourth grade boys saw this display of affection and called P "gay" thereafter, taunting him at school and on the school bus. (3) P fell on the playground, hit his head and wandered back into the classroom to tell his teacher—who told him *never* to come back into the building until the bell rang. When P told her about his head she told him to report it to the playground supervisor. P did not know there was such a person on that crowded macadam square!

The children were not allowed to converse in the lunchroom and the "hostess" wielding the inevitable paddle reminded them what would happen to them if they did. P would come home from school exhausted, irritable, often crying and carrying his lunch—untouched. (This lunchroom situation has been going on for four years despite formal protests from various parents.)

Another mother writes:

J has been set free! He is enrolled at the Santa Fe Community School but is actually learning at home. As soon as the decision was made he seemed to be released from some terrible burden, he immediately began taking charge of his own life and learning, and began to approach everything with the zest and enthusiasm formerly reserved for his own nature study, sports and building projects. For example, he always hated math, and the necessity of doing math homework caused the most unhappy and miserable hours in our household. Now he has set himself the task of getting math and is proceeding to do so with none of the emotional over-tones formerly present.

It's not an easy task for a poor working-class family to attempt this kind of thing—in fact it's a bit terrifying. Yet I feel strongly that working-class kids are most hurt by public schools and most in need of being set free.

A report from the Fort Lauderdale *News and Sun-Sentinel,* July 1, 1979, speaks of similar changes in a child:

... It was the disappearance of a smile, a simple thing, that led Ms. O'Shea, a certified elementary school teacher, to question the value of public education.

"When Kim was little, she was such a happy, laughy little person. When she went to school, that completely changed. She stopped smiling. She went for six months, and she was very unhappy. It was weird. When I went to the school, the teacher kept apologizing for the noise, and I thought, 'There's not any noise. These kids are like little robots.' It wasn't that healthy. So when that day was over, I said to Kim, 'What's the story?' and I looked at her, and I could feel what she felt. And I said, 'Let's give it a try.'

"A lot of people, when we tell them what we are doing," says Ms. O'Shea, "say, 'Well, you're a teacher, so that's OK.' But they don't understand. Anyone can teach. We sell ourselves short; we don't believe in ourselves enough. We think school can do something for us that we can't do ourselves."

She admits her own training in education has not helped that much, because the girls often want to learn things she doesn't know herself. "But I think whenever you want to learn something, you're going to find a way to learn it. If you have the need, the answer is always there, too."

The answers may be unorthodox, but they are available. The girls have gone to adult education classes to learn watercolor painting and nature studies; they recently learned typing and practiced making change while helping in a friend's key shop for a few days; they have taken lessons in diving, judo, and music; their mother teaches them arts and crafts at home, and they use workbooks, magazines and library books for math, reading, and spelling.

In school, Ms. O'Shea contends, much of their time would be

spent in quiet busywork. "Here, if Layne can do two or three division problems, she can do division. I don't sit there and make her do 70. I feel people should be free to explore life. And they can't do that with people telling them what to do all the time. And who decides what they are supposed to learn? That's what I want to know. Putting children into a fixed or six-hour program at school is just squashing them. All the spirit and spunk they have when they are little is just wiped out."

Finally, a mother wrote us, from a "good" school district in Long Island, about how her child in kindergarten ran afoul of the schools' social engineering:

> We sent our daughter to public school kindergarten. . . . When she started she was already reading books (books that I had read in the fourth and fifth grades!) and writing pages and pages of stories in which she sounded out words and wrote them phonetically, without help. She was happy and enthusiastic at first. She loved riding the bus. But her teacher refused to do any academic work with her at her level. . . .
>
> The problem arose because her teacher decided S was backward socially and that she needed to be cured. At first she gently pushed S to be more out-going and "join in more." But when the cure didn't take, the teacher became impatient and in an angry voice asked S why she couldn't "be like everybody else?" S was crushed and angry. She didn't immediately tell us what happened, but she was very angry at home. She was constantly saying she hated people, even people she didn't know, like waitresses in restaurants. She came home from school tired and in a bad mood. She began to say she didn't feel well and didn't want to go to school. We kept her home. . . .
>
> I tried to find out what had happened. S cried when she told us about the pressures her teacher had been putting on her. She seemed ashamed, also, and this hurt me the most. S felt that she had failed her teacher and that was why the teacher had lost patience with her (stopped liking her). . . .
>
> At about this time, S and I and my younger daughter went to visit their grandparents, aunts, uncles, and cousins. They were shocked at the change in S. She was very hostile, even in the loving atmosphere she was in. . . .

When we got back home I found a Montessori kindergarten in which the teacher was very sympathetic. . . . She said she thought S's reading ability would make her an asset to the class! (Her public school teacher had considered it a definite liability and thought it was probably responsible for her "social backwardness"! She had said to S—we later found out—"You'll never have any friends if you just stand there! You have to approach the other children.") To S's delight and surprise many children approached her at her new school and she made three or four friends. Within a few months she was her old self again. . . .

2

Common Objections to Home Schooling

People, especially educators, who hear me talk about home schooling, raise certain objections so often that it is worth answering them here.

Since our countries are so large and our people are from so many different kinds of backgrounds (this was said most recently to me by a Canadian) *don't we need some kind of social glue to make us stick together, to give us a sense of unity in spite of all our differences, and aren't compulsory public schools the easiest and best places to make this glue?*

About needing the glue, he's absolutely right. We do need such a glue, certainly in big diverse countries like the U.S. and Canada, but also in much smaller and more tightly-knit countries, many of whom are also breaking apart under the stresses of modern life. Right now, the main social glue we seem to have here in the U.S. is hatred of "enemy" countries. Except when briefly united in such hatred, far too many of us see our fellow-citizens, even those of our own color, religion, etc., only as our natural enemies and rightful prey, to do in if we can. Indeed, we insist that this way of looking at other people is actually a virtue, which we name "competition." This outlook may have worked fairly well when our country was young, nearly empty, and rich in natural resources but not anymore. For our very survival, let alone health and happiness, we need a much stronger and better social glue than this.

Some kinds of community gathering places and activities might help us form this social glue. But not schools—not as long as they also have the job of sorting out the young into winners and losers, and preparing the losers for a lifetime of losing. These two jobs can't be done in the same place at the same time.

People are best able, and perhaps only able, to cross the many barriers of race, class, custom, and belief that divide them when they are able to share experiences *that make them feel good.* Only from these do they get a stronger sense of their own, and therefore other people's, uniqueness, dignity, and worth. But as long as schools have their present social tasks, they will not be able to give such experiences to most children. In fact, most of what happens in school makes children feel the exact opposite—stupid, incompetent, ashamed. Distrusting and despising themselves, they then try to make themselves feel a little better by finding others whom they can look down on *even more*—poorer children, children from other races, children who do less well in school.

Even if children do learn in school to despise, fear, and even hate children from other social groups, might they not hate them even more if they did not meet them in school? At least in school they see these other groups as real people. Without school, they would know them only as abstractions, bogeymen. This might sometimes be true, but only of those few children for whom the world outside of school was as dull, painful, humiliating, and threatening as school. Most children who learn without school, or who go only when they want to, grow up with a much stronger sense of their own dignity and worth, and therefore, with much less need to despise and hate others.

The important question, how can people learn to feel a stronger sense of kinship or common humanity with others who are different is for me best answered by a story about John L. Sullivan, once the heavyweight prizefighting champion of the world. Late one afternoon he and a friend were riding standing up in a crowded New York City streetcar. At one stop a burly young man got on who had had too much to drink. He swaggered down the center of the car, pushing people out of his way, and as he passed John L. gave him a heavy shove with his shoulder. John L. clutched a strap to keep from falling, but said nothing. As the young man went to the back of the car, John L.'s friend said to him, "Are you going to let him get away with that?" John L. shrugged and said, "Oh, I don't see why not." His friend became very indignant. "You're the heavyweight champion of the world," he said furiously. "You don't have to be so damned polite." To which John L. replied, "The heavyweight champion of the world can *afford* to be polite."

What we need to pull our countries more together are more people who can afford to be polite, and much more—kind, patient, generous, forgiving, and tolerant, able and willing, not just to stand people different from themselves, but to make an effort to understand them, to see the world through their eyes. These social virtues are not the kind that can be talked or preached or discussed or bribed or threatened into people. They are a kind of surplus, an overflowing, in people who have enough love and respect for themselves and therefore have some left over for others.

Children in public schools are able to meet, and get to know, many children very different from themselves. If they didn't go to public school, how would this happen?

The first part of the answer to this question has to be that it very rarely happens *in* public schools. Except in very small schools, of which there are few, and which tend to be one-class schools anyway, children in public schools, other than a few top athletes, have very little contact with others different from themselves, and less and less as they rise through the grades. In most large schools the children are tracked, i.e., the college track, the business track, the vocational track. Even within each major track there may be subgroupings. Large schools may often have a half-dozen or more tracks. Students in one track go to one group of classes, students in another track go to others. Very rarely will students from different tracks find themselves in the same class. But—and here is the main point—study after study has shown that these tracks correlate perfectly with family income and social status, the richest or most socially prominent kids in the top track, the next richest in the next, and so on down to the poorest kids in the bottom track.

In theory, children are assigned to these tracks according to their school abilities. In practice, children are put in tracks almost as soon as they enter school, long before they have had time to show what abilities they may have. Once put in a track, few children ever escape from it. A Chicago second grade teacher once told me that in her bottom-track class of poor nonwhite children were two or three who were exceptionally good at schoolwork. Since they learned, quickly and well, everything she was supposed to be teaching them, she gave them A's. Soon after she had submitted her first grades the principal called her in, and asked why she had given A's to some of her students. She explained that these children were very bright and had done all the work. He ordered her to lower their grades, saying that if they had been capable of getting A's they wouldn't have been put in the lowest track. But, as she found upon checking, they had been put into this lowest track almost as soon as they had entered school.

Even where the schools do not track children by classes, the teachers are almost certain to track them within in their classes. In *Freedom and Beyond* I gave this example:

> An even more horrifying example of the way this discrimination works can be found in the article "Student Social Class and Teacher Expectation: The Self-Fulfilling Prophecy in Ghetto Education," by Ray Rist, in the August 1970 issue of the *Harvard Educational Review*. The kindergarten teacher described, after only eight days of school, and entirely on the basis of appearance, dress, manners, in short, middle class-ness, divided her class into three tracks by seating them at three separate tables, which remained fixed for the rest of the year. One of these tables got virtually all of her teaching, attention, and support; the other two were increasingly ignored except when the teacher told them to do something or commented unfavorably on what they did. Worse yet, the children at the fa-

vored table were allowed and encouraged to make fun of the children at the other two tables, and to boss them around.

Rist followed these children through three years of school, and reported, first, that these children's first and second grade teachers also tracked by tables within their classes, and secondly, that only one of the children assigned in kindergarten to one of the two bottom tables ever made it later to a favored table. And the odds are very good that most elementary school classes have a kind of caste system in action. Even in small and selective private schools, I found that many of my fellow-teachers were quick to label some children good and others bad, often on the basis of appearance, and that children once labeled bad found it almost impossible to get that label changed.

Enough has been written about class and racial conflict in schools, above all in high schools, so that I don't want to add much to it here. Where different races are integrated in schools, even after many years, this usually begins to break down around third grade, if not even sooner. From fifth grade on, in their social lives, children are almost completely separated into racial groups, which become more and more hostile as the children grow older. Even in one-race schools, white or nonwhite, there is class separation, class contempt, and class conflict. Few friendships are made across such lines, and the increasing violence in our high schools arises almost entirely from conflicts between such groups.

So the idea that schools mix together in happy groups children from widely differing backgrounds is for the most part simply not true. The question remains, how would children meet other children from different backgrounds if they did *not* go to school? I don't know. While the numbers of such children remain small, this will be difficult. But as the numbers of such children grow, there will be more places for them to go and more things for them to do that are not based in school. We can certainly hope, and may to some extent be able to arrange, that in these places children from different backgrounds may be more mixed together. Also, people who teach their children at home already tend to think of themselves as something of an extended family, and using the

Directory in *Growing Without Schooling,* write each other letters, visit each other when they can, have local meetings, and so on. I hope this will remain true as more working-class and nonwhite families begin to unschool their children, and it well may; people who feel this kind of affection and trust in their own children tend to feel a strong bond with others who feel the same.

How are we going to prevent parents with narrow and bigoted ideas from passing these on to their children?

The first question we have to answer is, do we have a right to try to prevent it? And even if we think we do, can we?

One of the main differences between a free country and a police state, I always thought, was that in a free country, as long as you obeyed the law, you could believe whatever you liked. Your beliefs were none of the government's business. Far less was it any of the government's business to say that one set of ideas was good and another set bad, or that schools should promote the good and stamp out the bad. Have we given up these principles? And if we haven't, do we really want to? Suppose we decided to give the government the power, through compulsory schools, to promote good ideas and put down bad. To whom would we then give the power to decide *which* ideas were good and which bad? To legislatures? To state boards of education? To local school boards?

Anyone who thinks seriously about these questions will surely agree that no one in government should have such power. From this it must follow that people have the right not only to believe what they want, but to try to pass their beliefs along to their children. We can't say that some people have this right while others do not. Some will say, but what about people who are prejudiced, bigoted, superstitious? We're surely not going to let people try to make their children believe that some races are superior or that the earth is flat? To which I say, what is the alternative? If we say, as many would like to, that people can tell their children anything they want, *as long as it is true,* we come back to our first question—who decides what is true? If we agree, as I think and hope we do, that there is no one in government or anywhere else whom we would trust to decide that, then it follows that we can't give schools the right to tell all children that some ideas are true and others are not. Since any school, whether by what it says or what it does, must promote *some* ideas, it follows that while people who approve of the ideas being taught or promoted in government schools may be glad to send their children there, people who don't approve of those ideas should have some other choice. This is essentially what the U.S. Supreme Court said in *Pierce* v. *Society of Sisters* (See Chapter 13).

One of the reasons why growing numbers of people are so passionately opposed to the public schools is that these schools are in fact acting as if someone *had* explicitly and legally given them the power to promote one set of ideas and to put down others. A fairly small group of people, educational bureaucrats at the state and federal level, who largely control what schools say and do, are more and more using the schools to promote whatever ideas they happen to think will be good for the children, or the country. But we have never formally decided, through any political process, to give the schools such power, far less agreed on what ideas we would like the schools to promote. On the contrary, there is every reason to believe that large majorities of the people strongly dislike many or most of the ideas that most schools promote today.

Even if we all agreed that the schools should try to stamp out narrow and bigoted ideas, we would still have to ask ourselves, does this work? Clearly it doesn't. After all, except for a few rich kids almost all children in the country have been going to public schools now for several generations. If the schools were as good as they claim at stamping out prejudice, there ought not to be any left. A quick glance at any day's news will show that there is plenty left. In fact, there may well be less support today than ever before for the tolerance and open-mindedness that the schools supposedly promote.

If you don't send your children to school, how are they going to learn to fit into a mass society?

If you don't send children to school, how are they going to be exposed to any values other than the commercial values of a mass society?

Educators often ask me these two questions in the same meeting, often within a few minutes of each other. Obviously, they cancel each other out. The schools may in fact be able to prepare children to fit into the mass society, which means, among other things, believing what most people believe and liking what most people like. Or they may be able to help children find a set of values with which they could resist and reject at least many of the values of the mass society. But they certainly can't do *both*.

It seems to be one of the articles of faith of educators that they, and they alone, hold out to the young a vision of higher things. At meetings they often talk as if they spent much of their time and energy defending children from the corrupt values of the mass media and the television set. Where, but from us, they say, are children going to hear about good books, Shakespeare, culture? We are the only ones who are thinking about what is good for them; everyone else is just trying to exploit them. The fact is, however, that most schools are far more concerned to have children accept the values of mass society than to help them resist them. When school people hear about people teaching their children at home, they almost always say, "But aren't you afraid that your children are going to grow up to be different, outsiders, misfits, unable to adjust to society?" They take it for granted that in order to live reasonably happily, usefully, and successfully in the world you have to be mostly like most other people.

In any case, the schools' efforts to sell children the higher culture seldom work, since they obviously value it so little themselves. In my introduction to Roland Betts's *Acting Out* (Boston: Little, Brown, 1978), a frightening account of life in New York City's public schools, I wrote:

> . . . Our big city schools are largely populated, and will be increasingly populated, by the children of the nonwhite poor, the youngest members and victims of a sick subculture of a sick society, obsessed by violence and the media-inspired worship of dominance, luxury, and power. This culture, or more accurately, anticulture, has done more harm to its members and victims, has fragmented, degraded, and corrupted them more than centuries of slavery and the most brutal repression were able to do. Every day this anticulture, in the

person of the children, invades the schools. If the schools had a true and humane culture of their own, which they really understood, believed in, cared about, and lived by, as did the First Street School some years ago, they might put up a stiff resistance, might even win some of the children over. But since the culture of the school is only a pale and somewhat more timid and genteel version of the culture of the street outside . . . nothing changes. Far from being able to woo the children away from greed, envy, and violence, the schools cannot even protect them against each other.

A friend of mine, in his early thirties, is a journalist, generally liberal, sympathetic to the young. Not long ago he visited a number of high schools in the affluent suburbs of Los Angeles where he grew up, talking to the students, trying to find out what they seemed most interested in and cared most about. I asked eagerly what he had found. After a silence, he said, "They seem to be mostly interested in money, sex, and drugs." He was clearly as unhappy to say it as I was to hear it. We would both like to have found out that these favored young people wanted to do something to make a better world, as many did fifteen years ago. But we should not be surprised that young people should be most interested in the things that most interest their elders.

Nor is it fair to blame the schools, as many people do, for the interest of the young in these things. Attacked from all sides, the schools say plaintively, "But we didn't invent these values." Quite right; they didn't. What we can and must say is that to whatever extent the schools have tried to combat these values, they have almost totally failed. In any case, to return once more to my first point, they can hardly claim that they are at one and the same time teaching children to accept and also to resist these dominant values of our commercial culture.

If children are taught at home, won't they miss the valuable social life of the school?

If there were no other reason for wanting to keep kids out of school, the social life would be reason enough. In all but a very few of the schools I have taught in, visited, or know anything about, the social life of the children is mean-spirited, competitive, exclusive, status-seeking, snobbish, full of talk about who went to whose birthday party and who got what Christmas presents and who got how many Valentine cards and who is talking to so-and-so and who is not. Even in the first grade, classes soon divide up into leaders (energetic and—often deservedly—popular kids), their bands of followers, and other outsiders who are pointedly excluded from these groups.

I remember my sister saying of one of her children, then five, that she never knew her to do anything really mean or silly until she went away to school—a nice school, by the way, in a nice small town.

Jud Jerome, writer, poet, former professor at Antioch, wrote about his son, Topher, meeting this so-called "social life" in a free school run by a commune:

> . . . Though we were glad he was happy and enjoying himself (in school), we were also sad as we watched him deteriorate from a person into a kid under peer influence in school. It was much like what we saw happening when he was in kindergarten. There are certain kinds of childishness which it seems most people accept as being natural, something children have to go through, something which it is, indeed a shame to deny them. Silliness, self-indulgence, random rebelliousness, secretiveness, cruelty to other children, clubbishness, addiction to toys, possessions, junk, spending money, purchased entertainment, exploitation of adults to pay attention, take them places, amuse them, do things with them—all these things seem to me quite unnecessary, not "normal" at all (note: except in the sense of being common), and just as disgusting in children as they are in adults. And while they develop as a result of peer influence, I believe this is only and specifically because children are thrown together in school and develop these means, as prisoners develop means of passing dull time and tormenting authorities to cope with an oppressive situation. The richer the families the children come from, the worse these traits seem to be. Two years of school and Topher would probably have regressed two years in emotional development. I am not sure of that, of course, and it was not because of that fear that we pulled him out, but we saw enough of what happened to him in a school situation not to regret pulling him out. . . .

One of our readers gave us a vivid description of what must be a very typical school experience:

> My mother tells me that after the first day in kindergarten I told her that I didn't need to go to school anymore because I knew everything already. Great arrogance? Not really. I knew how to be quiet, how to listen to children's stories, and how to sing. I wanted to learn about the adult world but was restricted to a world which adults believed children wanted. My great pre-school enthusiasm died an early death. . . .
>
> Shame was one of the first lessons that I learned. In the first grade I was told to color a picture of a mother and daughter working in a kitchen. It struck me that if I were to color the entire picture yellow, then it would be different from all the other pictures. When I handed it in to the teacher I expected her to be pleased, if not genuinely excited. She, instead, glared at me for what seemed to be a long time and caused me to feel the deepest shame and self-contempt. . . . I was six years old.
>
> Since spontaneity was dangerous—it conflicted with the teacher's view of how children should act—lying was a valuable survival technique. . . . In first grade, the class was sent to the kindergarten room to do some work without supervision. I used this opportunity to take a plastic doll and stick the head into a plastic toilet in one of the furnished doll houses in the room. No one was sure who did it, but everyone thought it was amusing—except the teacher. She was red with anger (she was a nun, and working-class Catholic schools in the early 1960s were not the most humane institutions) and I feared a severe beating. Suspicion was eventually focused on me and I lied with complete success, at least for me; another boy was blamed for the incident. I wish that I had said, "Yes, I did it, so what." But I was afraid. . . .
>
> Other incidents occurred to other people and were much more serious. I saw a boy of thirteen, seventh grade, try to explain why he did not have an assignment. His crime was that he spoke with indignation. Before he said three words the teacher stopped him and with a who-the-hell-do-you-think-you-are tone of voice called him to the desk and slapped him across the face with a rubber strap which was about 6 to 8 inches long and ¼ inch thick. He cried; they always did when it was in the face. He never did get the chance to explain why he did not have the assignment. I'm not so sure that

he didn't have it. It may have been that he could not find it quickly enough. . . . This teacher, the principal, was a textbook authoritarian. Every violation of her largely unwritten rules would lead her to deliver the same angry statement: "Don't challenge me." She saw challenges in virtually everything even though we would never have challenged her. I'll just give two of her biggest challenges.

Challenge number one involved misbehavior which the teacher present did not see, but the principal looking into the room did. The fifth, sixth, seventh, and eighth grades (it was a small school) were in this room to practice singing. She was furious, talked about challenges, and scolded the student vehemently. Then she proceeded to slap him halfway across the room. She gave him about eight or ten real haymaker slaps. I was standing only a few feet away at the time. . . . One fact about this event showed how much in awe of authority we were: the victim of this violence did not raise his hands to protect his face. When it was over, all I could hear was the boy crying and my own heart beating.

Challenge number two involved the same boy. This time he urinated, or defecated, or both, in his pants. Perhaps he was ill or maybe he had a mental problem. [Author's note: Or perhaps he had merely been denied permission to go to the bathroom, which happens quite often in school.] He didn't do this regularly. He was about twelve years old. Naturally this called for punishment. He was forced to stand in front of each class in the school while the teacher explained to the class his crime. When he came to our classroom the principal named him the school's stinker and told us why. But what I remember most clearly is the pained smile on his face.

There were many incidents of fear and humiliation. Even though there were not many savage beatings, the point is that we lived in an environment where this could happen anytime. And we knew that. I had no clear idea that there was anything wrong with the school; I only had a vague feeling that things didn't have to be the way they were. I wasn't a noble child resisting tyrannical teachers. No, I loved the game of fear and humiliation and played like the masters.

"We can hardly wait to make someone pay for our humiliation, yield to us as we were once made to yield" (*Freedom and Beyond*, p. 114).

I'm not sure when it started, but in the eighth grade a number of us would terrorize some of the timid boys in the school. We would push the victim around, ridicule him, pull his shirt out, spin him around, dust the chalk erasers on his clothes, mess up his hair, and chase him on the playground. It was easy to be friends with these boys when I was alone with them. But when there was a group of us the teasing would begin. *Since we were always in groups* [Author's emphasis], the teasing of these boys, two in particular, was nearly unending. On the playground they had to avoid being seen. One of the boys would go home for lunch and not return until the last minute of recess. We did it without thought and it seemed to be only boyish pranks. It was sadism and I found it to be almost irresistible.

We then started to turn on the group members and practice our arts on the selected victim. I remember coming home with sore sides from laughing so hard at another's humiliation, but I felt empty and actually unhappy. The next day I would do it again. This only stopped when I became the victim. It was pure hell. Everyone you knew devoted all his time to your being humiliated. Any one act was insignificant: slapping an unaware student in the back of the head was popular. But it happened all day long in a multitude of ways. Christmas vacation came and one of my prime torturers transferred to another school. Things cooled off for me, but not for the timid boys or the younger children in the school. We almost had serious violence with the male students several years younger than us.

I don't remember the beginning or the end of this sadistic behavior. I know that I didn't act this way before my last two years in grade school or since then.

This reader's experience is surely not unusual. When I was nine, I was in a public elementary school, in a class in which almost all the boys were bigger and older than I was, most of them from working-class Italian or Polish families. One by one, the toughest ones first, then the others, more or less in order of toughness, they beat me up at recess, punched me until they knocked me down and/or made me cry. Once a boy had beaten me up, he rarely bothered to do it again. There didn't seem to me to be much malice in it; it was as if this had to be done in order to find my proper place in the class. Finally everyone had beat me except a boy named Henry. One day the bigger boys hemmed us in and told us that we had to fight to find who was the biggest sissy in the sixth grade. Henry and I said we didn't want to fight. They said if we didn't, they would beat up both of us. So for a while Henry and I circled around, swinging wildly at each other, the bigger boys laughing and urging us on. Nothing happened for some time, until one of my wild swings hit Henry's nose. It began to bleed, Henry began to cry, and so did I. But the bigger boys were satisfied; they declared that Henry was now the official biggest sissy in the class.

A teacher writes:

> On Friday I was reading *GWS* and intrigued with it as usual. I'm especially interested in the "social life" aspect of schools and the damage it causes. This morning I asked my third graders, "Do you feel that in our school kids are nice, kind to each other?"
>
> Out of 22 kids, only two felt that they saw kindness, and the rest felt most kids are mean, call names, hurt feelings, etc. Frankly I was amazed. I have always felt our school is a uniquely friendly place. . . .

When I point out to people that the social life of most schools and classrooms is mean-spirited, status-oriented, competitive, and snobbish, I am always astonished by their response. Not *one* person of the hundreds with whom I've discussed this has yet said to me that the social life at school is kindly, generous, supporting, democratic, friendly, loving, or good for children. No, without exception, when I condemn the social life of school, people say, "But that's what the children are going to meet in Real Life."

The "peer groups" into which we force children have many other powerful and harmful effects. Every now and then, in the subway or some public place, I see young people, perhaps twelve or thirteen years old, sometimes even as young as ten, smoking cigarettes. It is a comic and pitiful sight. It is also an ordeal. The smoke tastes awful. Children have sensitive taste buds, and that smoke must taste even worse to them than to most nonsmoking adults, which is saying a lot. They have to struggle not to choke, not to cough, maybe even not to get sick. Why do they do it? Because "all the other kids" are doing it, or soon will be, and they have to stay ahead of them, or at least not fall behind. In short, wanting to smoke, or feeling one has to smoke whether one wants to or not, is one of the many fringe benefits of that great "social life" at school that people talk about.

I feel sorry for all the children who think they have to smoke, and even sorrier for any nonsmoking parents who may desperately wish they could persuade them not to. If the children have lived in the peer group long enough to become enslaved to it, addicted to it—we might call them "peer group junkies"—then they are going to smoke, and do anything and everything else the peer group does. If Mom and Pop make a fuss, then they will lie about it and do it behind their backs. The evidence on this is clear. In some age groups, fewer people are smoking. But more children are smoking every year, especially girls, and they start earlier.

The same is true of drinking. We hear more and more about drinking, drunkenness, and alcoholism among the young. Some states have tried in recent years to deal with the problem by raising the minimum drinking age. It doesn't seem to have helped; if anything, the problem only gets worse. One news story sticks in my mind. One night last summer in a town near Boston four high school girls, all about sixteen or seventeen, were killed and another seriously injured in an auto accident. Earlier in the evening they had loaded up their small car with beer and several kinds of liquor and had gone out for an evening of driving and drinking. By the time of the accident, all were drunk. The one survivor was later quoted by the papers as saying, from her bed in the hospital, "I didn't think there was anything wrong with what we were doing; all the kids around here do it."

Of course, children who spend almost all their time in groups of other people their own age, shut out of society's serious work and concerns, with almost no contact with any adults except child-watchers, are going to feel that what "all the other kids" are doing is the right, the best, the only thing to do.

How are we going to prevent children being taught by "unqualified" teachers?

First of all, to know what is meant by "qualified," we have to know what is meant by quality. We could hardly agree on who was or was not a good painter if we did not to a large extent agree on what was or was not a good painting. The question asked above assumes that since educators agree on and understand correctly what is meant by good teaching, they are able to make sound judgments about who is or is not a good teacher. But the fact is that educators do not understand or agree about what makes good teaching. The dismal record of the schools is proof enough of this. Still further proof is that, when charged in court with negligence (see the section "A Doubtful Claim" in Chapter 14), educators defend themselves by saying (with the approval of the courts) that they cannot be judged guilty of not having done what should have been done, because *no one knows what should have been done.* This may be so. But it clearly follows that people who don't know what should be done can hardly judge who is or is not competent to do it.

In practice, educators who worry about "unqualified" people teaching their own children almost always define "qualified" to mean teachers trained in schools of education and holding teaching certificates. They assume that to teach children involves a host of mysterious skills that can be learned only in schools of education and that are in fact taught there; that people who have this training teach much better than those who do not; and indeed that people who have not had this training are not competent to teach at all.

None of these assumptions are true.

Human beings have been sharing information and skills, and passing along to their children whatever they knew, for about a million years now. Along the way they have built some very complicated and highly skilled societies. During all those years there were very few teachers in the sense of people whose *only* work was teaching others what they knew. And until very recently there were no people at all who were trained in teaching, *as such.* People always understood, sensibly enough, that before you could teach something you had to know it yourself. But only very recently did human beings get the extraordinary notion that in order to be able to teach what you knew you had to spend years being taught how to teach.

To the extent that teaching involves and requires some real skills, these have long been well understood. They are no mystery.

Teaching skills are among the many commonsense things about dealing with other people that, unless we are mistaught, we learn just by living. In any community people have always known that if you wanted to find out how to get somewhere or do something, some people were much better to ask than others. For a long, long time, people who were good at sharing what they knew have realized certain things: (1) to help people learn something, you must first understand what they already know; (2) showing people how to do something is better than telling them, and letting them do it themselves is best of all; (3) you mustn't tell or show too much at once, since people digest new ideas slowly and must feel secure with new skills or knowledge before they are ready for more; (4) you must give people as much time as they want and need to absorb what you have shown or told them; (5) instead of testing their understanding with questions you must let them show how much or little they understand by the questions they ask you; (6) you must not get impatient or angry when people don't understand; (7) scaring people only blocks learning, and so on. These are clearly not things that one has to spend three years talking about.

And in fact these are not what schools of education talk about. They give very little thought to the act of teaching itself—helping another person find something out, or answering that person's questions. What they spend most of their time doing is preparing their students to work in the strange world of schools—which, in all fairness, is what the students want to find out: how to get a teaching job and keep it. This means learning how to speak the school's language (teeny little ideas blown up into great big words), how to do all the things schools want teachers to do, how to fill out its endless forms and papers, and how to make the endless judgments it likes to make about students. Above all else, education students are taught to think that what they know is extremely important and that they are the only ones who know it.

As for the idea that certified teachers teach better than uncertified, or that uncertified teachers cannot teach at all, there is not a shred of evidence to support it, and a great deal of evidence against it. One indication is that our most selective, demanding, and successful private schools have among their teachers hardly any, if indeed any at all, who went to teacher training schools and got their degrees in education. Few such schools would even consider hiring a teacher who had only such training and such a degree. How does it happen that the richest and most powerful people in the country, the ones most able to choose what they want for their children, so regularly choose *not* to have them taught by trained and certified teachers? One might almost count it among the major benefits of being rich that you are able to *avoid* having your children taught by such teachers.

In this connection, the following story from the Philadelphia *Inquirer,* November 18, 1979, may be of interest:

> Between 1978 and 1979, public school enrollment in New Jersey fell 3% from 1.38 million to 1.33 million. But enrollment in private non-parochial schools from 1978 to 1979 rose 8.5%, from 14,000 to 15,200. And, while attendance data for parochial schools is not yet available, indications are that it experienced a similar jump.
>
> . . . Rev. Peder Bloom, assistant headmaster of Doane Academy/St. Mary's Hall, an independent Episcopalian school founded in 1837, sees not only a larger, but a more varied clientele applying.
>
> "Any number" of parents are both working to pay tuition bills, he says, and presently *the biggest single occupational parent group is public school administrators* [Author's emphasis], according to private school administrators. It used to be doctors; now they are second. . . .

As we will see in Chapter 13, when a district court in Kentucky challenged the state board of education to show evidence that certified teachers were better than uncertified, the board was unable to produce (in the court's words) "a scintilla of evidence" to that effect. The same thing happened more recently in a Michigan court. It is very unlikely that any other state boards would be able to do so.

In the state of Alaska, hundreds or perhaps thousands of homesteading families live many miles from the nearest town, or even road. The only way they can get in and out of their homes is by plane. Since the state cannot provide schools for these families, or transport their children to and from existing schools, it very sensibly has a correspondence school of its own which mails school materials to these families, who then teach their children at home. Nobody seems to worry very much about whether these families are "qualified," and no one has yet brought forth any evidence that home-taught children in Alaska do less well in their studies than school-taught children, there or in other states. For that matter, many states in the Lower Forty-Eight have laws saying that if children live more than so many miles from the nearest school, or bus route to a school, they don't have to go to school. It would be interesting to find out how many such children there are, and what provisions these states make for their education, and how well these children do in their schoolwork.

Perhaps the leading correspondence school for school-aged children is the Calvert Institute of Baltimore, Maryland. It has been in business for a long time, and for all that time most school districts (I know of no exceptions) have been willing to accept a year of study under Calvert as equal to a year of study in school. Indeed, this assurance that Calvert-taught children would not fall behind has been part of what Calvert offered and sold its customers and clients. These have been, for the most part, American families living overseas: missionaries, military or diplomatic people, people working in foreign offices of American firms, etc. A recent Calvert ad said they have had over three hundred thousand customers. Clearly a very large number of parents have taught and are teaching their children at home, without these children falling behind. But very few of these parents can have been certified teachers.

The same must be true of the Home Study Institute, of Washington, D.C., which has served mostly, but not exclusively, members of the Seventh-Day Adventist Church. I don't know how many families use or have used their materials, but the quality of the materials I have seen, and the range of courses they offer, suggest that this organization, too, serves a large number of people, few of whom can have been or be certified teachers. Yet again, there is no evidence that the students who learn at home from these materials are failures either in school or later in life.

Years ago I read that one or more inner-city schools had tried the experiment of letting fifth graders teach first graders to read.

They found, first, that the first graders learned faster than similar first graders taught by trained teachers, and secondly, that the fifth graders who were teaching them, many or most of whom had not been good readers themselves, also improved a great deal in their reading. These schools apparently did these experiments in desperation. It is easy to see why they have not been widely repeated. Even in those schools that are willing to allow "paraprofessional" adults, i.e., people without teachers' certificates, in their classrooms, the regular teachers almost always insist that these paraprofessionals *not* be allowed to do any teaching. But poor countries have found in mass literacy programs that almost anyone who can read can teach anyone else who wants to learn.

I found in my own classes, as in others I have since observed where children are allowed to talk to each other and to help each other with schoolwork, that many children were very good at teaching each other. There were many reasons for this. Even though I did my best to convince them that ignorance was no shame, they felt much freer to confess ignorance and confusion to each other than to me, since they knew they knew little and wrongly thought that I knew almost everything. Also, they did not have to fear that their friends might give them a bad grade. I had told them that I did not believe in grades, and I think they believed me. But they understood, as I did, that this had little to do with reality; both the school and their parents demanded grades, and I had to give them. Some of them, who really liked me, may have feared that after struggling to teach them something I would be disappointed if they didn't learn it. Indeed this was true, and though I tried not to be disappointed or at least not to show that I was, I never really succeeded. They wanted to please me, and knew when they hadn't.

Learning from each other, they didn't have to worry about this. A child teaching another is not disappointed if the other does not understand or learn, since teaching is not his main work and he is not worried about whether he is or is not a good teacher. He may be exasperated, may even say, "Come on, dummy, pay attention, what's the matter with you?" Since children tend to be direct and blunt with each other anyway, this probably won't bother the learner. If it does, he can say so. Either the other will be more tactful, since he rightly values their friendship more than the effectiveness of his teaching, or the learner will find another helper. And this is another and important reason why children are good at teaching each other. Both child-teacher and child-learner know that this teacher-learner relationship is temporary, much less important than their friendship, in which they meet as equals. This temporary relationship will go on only as long as they are both satisfied with it. The child-teacher doesn't *have* to teach the other, and the child-learner doesn't *have* to learn from the other. Since they both come to the relationship freely and by their own choice, they are truly equal partners in it.

I want to stress very strongly that the fact that their continuing relationship as friends is more important than their temporary relationship as learner and teacher is above all else what makes this temporary relationship work. There is an old rule in medicine (not always obeyed): "First, do no harm." In other words, in treating patients, make sure you do not injure them. The rule is just as true for teaching. Above all else, be sure that in your eagerness to make them learn, you do not frighten, offend, insult, or humiliate those you are teaching. Teachers of animals, whether dogs, dolphins, circus animals, or whatever, understand that very well—it is the first rule in their book. It is only among teachers of human beings that many do not understand and even hotly deny this rule.

It is because they understand this rule, if not in words at least in their hearts, that the kind of parents who teach their own children are likely to do it better than anyone else. Such people do not knowingly hurt their children. When they see that something they are doing is hurting their child, *they stop,* no matter how good may have been their reasons for doing it. They take seriously any signals of pain and distress that their children give them. Of course, the distress signals that children make when we try too hard to teach them something are quite different from the signals they make when something hurts them. Instead of saying "Ow!" they say, "I don't get it," or "This is crazy." It took me years, teaching in classrooms, to learn what those signals were, and still longer to understand how I was causing the distress. But parents teaching at home are in a much better position to learn these distress signals than a classroom teacher. They are not distracted by the problems of managing a class, they know the children better, and their spoken and unspoken languages, and they care about them more. Also, as I have said elsewhere, they can try things out to see what works, and drop whatever does not. Since they control their experience, they can learn more from it.

This is not to say that all families who try to teach their own children will learn to do it well. Some may not. But such families are likely to find home schooling so unpleasant that they will be glad to give it up, the children most of all. A home-schooling mother wrote me that when, simply out of fear of the schools, she began to give her children a lot of conventional schoolwork, they said, "Look, Mom, if we're going to have to spend all our time doing this school junk, we'd rather do it in school." Quite right. If you are going to have to spend your days doing busywork to relieve adult anxieties, better do it in school, where you only have one-thirtieth of the teacher's anxieties, rather than at home, where you have all of your parent's. So far, only one family I know of has given up home schooling as a failure, largely because the parents couldn't control their anxieties. In time, there may well be others. I doubt that there will be many.

We can sum up very quickly what people need to teach their own children. First of all, they have to *like* them, enjoy their company, their physical presence, their energy, foolishness, and passion. They have to enjoy all their talk and questions, and enjoy equally trying to answer those questions. They have to think of their children as friends, indeed very close friends, have to feel happier when they are near and miss them when they are away. They have to trust them as people, respect their fragile dignity, treat them with courtesy, take them seriously. They have to feel in their own hearts some of their children's wonder, curiosity, and excitement about the world. And they have to have enough confidence in themselves, skepticism about experts, and willingness to be different from most people, to take on themselves the responsibility for their children's learning. But that is about all that parents need. Perhaps only a minority of parents have these qualities. Certainly some have more than others. Many will gain more as they know their children better; most of the people who have been teaching their children at home say that it has made them like them more, not less. In any case, these are not qualities that can be taught or learned in a school, or measured with a test, or certified with a piece of paper.

Are there then *no* requirements of schooling or learning? Isn't there some minimum that people ought to know? Could people teach their children who had never been to school themselves? Even if they didn't know how to read and write? I think even then they probably could. A woman told me not long ago, after a meeting, that though she had a degree from Radcliffe and a Ph.D. from Harvard, the most helpful, influential, and important of all the teachers she had ever had was her mother, who had come to this country as an immigrant and who was illiterate not only here but in the country of her birth. And while a consultant to a program to teach adult illiterates to read, I heard about one of the students, a middle-aged woman who had for years concealed her illiteracy from her college graduate husband and her children, whom she used to regularly help with their schoolwork. For many years I told her story to show how cleverly people can bluff and fake. Only recently did I realize that this woman's children would not have come to her year after year for help on their schoolwork *unless her help had been helpful.* She was in short not just a clever bluffer, but a very good teacher.

I don't expect many illiterate parents to ask me how they can take their children out of school and teach them at home. But if any do, I will say, "I don't think that just because you have not yet learned to read and write means that you can't do a better job of helping your children learn about the world than the schools. But one of the things you are going to have to do in order to help them is *learn* to read and write. It is easy, if you really want to do it, and once you get out of your head the idea that you *can't* do it. If any of your children can read and write, they can help you learn. If none of them can read and write, you can learn together. But it is important that you learn. In the first place, if you don't, and the schools find out, there is no way in the world that they or the courts are going to allow you to teach your children at home. In the second place, if you don't know how to read and write, your children are likely to feel that reading and writing are not useful and interesting, or else that they are very difficult, neither of which is true. So learning to read and write will have to be one of your first tasks."

How am I going to teach my child six hours a day?

Who's teaching him six hours a day right now?

As a child, I went to the "best" schools, some public, most private. I was a good student, the kind that teachers *like* to talk to. And it was a rare day indeed in my schooling when I got fifteen minutes of teaching, that is, of concerned and thoughtful adult talk about something that *I* found interesting, puzzling, or important. Over the whole of my schooling, the average was probably closer to fifteen minutes a week. For most children in most schools, it is much less than that. Many poor, nonwhite, or unusual kids never get any real teaching at all in their entire schooling. When teachers speak to them, it is only to command, correct, warn, threaten, or blame.

Anyway, children don't need, don't want, and *couldn't stand* six hours of teaching a day, even if parents wanted to do that much. To help them find out about the world doesn't take that much adult input. Most of what they need, parents have been giving them since they were born. As I have said, they need access. They need a chance, sometimes, for honest, serious, unhurried talk; or sometimes, for joking, play, and foolishness; or sometimes, for tenderness, sympathy, and comfort. They need, much of the time, to share your life, or at least, not to feel shut out of it, in short, to go some of the places you go, see and do some of the things that interest you, get to know some of your friends, find out what you did when you were little and before they were born. They need to have their questions answered, or at least heard and attended to—if you don't know, say "I don't know." They need to know more and more adults whose main work in life is not taking care of kids. They need *some* friends their own age, but not dozens of them; two or three, at most half a dozen, is as many real friends as any child can have at one time. Perhaps above all, they need a lot of privacy, solitude, calm, times when there's nothing to do.

Schools rarely provide any of these, and even if radically changed, never could provide most of them. But the average parent, family, circle of friends, neighborhood, and community can and do provide all of these things, perhaps not as well as they once did or might again, but well enough. People do not need a Ph.D. or some kind of certificate to help their children find their way into the world.

How are children going to learn what they need to know?

About this, a parent wrote:

> . . . During his early years, my wife and I and a couple of friends taught him all he wanted to know, and if we didn't know it, which usually was the case, it was even better for we all learned together. Example: at 7, he saw the periodic table of elements, wanted to learn atoms and chemistry and physics. I had forgotten how to balance an equation, but went out and bought a college textbook on the subject, a history of discovery of the elements, and some model atoms, and in the next month we went off into a tangent of learning in which somehow we both learned college-level science. He has never returned to the subject, but to this day *retains every bit of it because it came at a moment in development and fantasy that was meaningful to him* [Author's emphasis].

Of course, a child may not know what he may need to know in ten years (who does?), but he knows, and much better than anyone else, *what he wants and needs to know right now,* what his mind is ready and hungry for. If we help him, or just allow him, to learn that, he will remember it, use it, build on it. If we try to make him learn something else, that *we* think is more important, the chances are that he won't learn it, or will learn very little of it, that he will soon forget most of what he learned, and what is worst of all, will before long lose most of his appetite for learning anything.

Other parents have asked me similar questions and to one I wrote:

... With respect to your question, about how a parent could teach something like chemistry, there seem to be a number of possibilities, all of which people have actually done in one place or another. (1) The parent finds a textbook(s), materials, etc., and parent and child learn the stuff together. (2) The parent gets the above for the child, and the child learns it alone. (3) The parent or the child finds someone else who knows this material, perhaps a friend or neighbor, perhaps a teacher in some school or even college, and learns from them.

As for equipment, you say that your high school had a very extensive chem lab, but I'll bet that very few of the students ever used more than a small part of the materials in the lab. I have known kids who were interested in chemistry and did it in their own basements, who were able to do a great deal of work with, at today's prices, less than $200 or maybe $100 worth of equipment. The catalog of the Edmund Scientific Corp. (and many other companies) is full of such equipment. The same thing is true of physics. As for biology, except perhaps in the heart of the city, it is not difficult to find plants and animals for observation and classification, if that is what children want to do.

I won't say these are not problems, but people who want to solve them can solve them.

You ask "Would you expect a parent to purchase test tubes, chemicals, instruments, etc., that would perhaps only be used for one or two years, only to have the child become an artist or musician?" Well, why not? People purchase bicycles, sports equipment, musical instruments, without knowing that their children will ever become professional athletes, musicians, etc. None of this equipment (unless broken) loses any of its value—it could probably be sold later for at least a significant part of the purchase price. And, as time goes on, and more people are teaching their children at home, it will be easier to get these materials from other parents who have used them, or to arrange for swaps, etc.

I see no real need for "institutional" education at *any* age. There is in Michigan a man named Ovshinsky who stood solid-state physics on its ear by inventing a theory by which noncrystalline substances could be used to do things which, according to orthodox theory, only crystalline materials could do. For a number of years orthodox physicists dismissed Ovshinsky's ideas. But he was able to demonstrate them so clearly in laboratory experiments that they were finally obliged to admit that he was right. *Ovshinsky never finished high school.* There are probably more cases like this than we know, and there would be a great many more except for compulsory schooling laws. It is a kind of Catch-22 situation to say, first, that all children have to spend all that time in schools, and then to say that all kinds of things can *only* be learned in schools. How do we know? Where have we given people a chance to learn them somewhere else?

A very important function of institutions of so-called higher learning is not so much to teach people things as to *limit* access to certain kinds of learning and work. The function of law schools is much less to train lawyers than to keep down the supply of lawyers. Practically everything that is now only done by people with Ph.D.'s was, not so very long ago, done by people with no graduate training or in some cases even undergraduate training.

I hope you will not doubt your competence to help your children learn anything they want to learn, or indeed their competence to learn many things without your help.

One mother wrote me some particularly challenging questions, to which I gave these answers:

Q. My greatest concern is that I don't want to slant my children's view of life all through "mother-colored" glasses. . . .

A. If you mean, *determine* your children's view of life, you couldn't do it even if you wanted to. You are an influence on your children, and an important one, but by no means the only one, or even the only important one. How they later see the world is going to be determined by a great many things, many of them probably not to your liking, and most of them out of your control. On the other hand, it would be impossible, even if you wanted to, not to have *some* influence on your children's view of life.

Q. I also wonder if I can have the thoroughness, the follow-through demanded, the patience, and the continuing enthusiasm for a diversity of interests they will undoubtedly have.

A. Well, who in any school would have more, or even as much? I was a good student in the "best" schools, and very few adults there were even slightly concerned with my interests. Beyond that, you may expect too much of yourself. Your children's learning is not all going to come from you, but from *them,* and their interaction with the world around them, which of course includes you. You do not have to know everything they want to know, or be interested in everything they are interested in. As for patience, maybe you won't have enough at first; like many home-teaching parents, you may start by trying to do too much, know too much, control too much. But like the rest, you will learn from experience —mostly, to trust your children.

Q. Most unschoolers seem to live on farms growing their own vegetables (which I'd like) or have unique life-styles in urban areas, and heavy father participation in children's education. What about suburbanites with modern-convenienced homes and fathers who work for a company 10 to 12 hours a day away from home? What differences will this make? Will unschooling work as well?

A. Well enough. You and your children will have to find out as you go along what differences they make, and deal with them as best you can. Once, people said that the suburbs were the best of all possible worlds in which to bring up children; now it is the fashion to say they are the worst. Both views are exaggerated. In city, country, or suburb, there is more than enough to give young people an interesting world to grow up in, plenty of food for thought and action. You don't have to have every resource for your children, and if you did, they wouldn't have enough time to make use of all of them. As for the father's involvement, it can certainly be helpful, but it is not crucial. Some of the most successful unschoolers we know of are single mothers.

Q. What if the children want to go to school?
A. This is a hard question. There is more than one good answer to it, and these often conflict. Parents could argue, and some do, that since they believe that school can and probably will do their children deep and lasting harm, they have as much right to keep them out, even if they want to go, as they would to tell them they could not play on a pile of radioactive wastes. This argument seems more weighty in the case of younger children, who could not be expected to understand how school might hurt them. If

somewhat older children said determinedly and often, and for good reasons, that they really wanted to go to school, I would tend to say, let them go. How much older? What are good reasons? I don't know. A bad reason might be, "The other kids tell me that at school lunch you can have chocolate milk."

Q. I'm concerned that someone might be eager to take us to court and take away our children.

A. The schools have in a number of cases tried—shamefully— to take children away from unschooling parents. I think there are legal counters to this, strategies which would make it highly unlikely that a court would take such action. And if worse came to worst, and a court said, "Put your children back in school or we'll take them away," you can always put them back in while you plan what to do next—which might simply be to move to another state or even school or judicial district.

Q. I don't want to feel I'm sheltering my children or running away from adversity.

A. Why not? It is your right, and your proper business, as parents, to shelter your children and protect them from adversity, at least as much as you can. Many of the world's children are starved or malnourished, but you would not starve your children so that they would know what this was like. You would not let your children play in the middle of a street full of high-speed traffic. Your business is, as far as you can, to help them realize their human potential, and to that end you put as much as you can of good into their lives, and keep out as much as you can of bad. If you think—as you do—that school is bad, then it is clear what you should do.

Q. I value their learning how to handle challenges or problems. . . .

A. There will be plenty of these. Growing up was probably never easy, and it is particularly hard in a world as anxious, confused, and fear-ridden as ours. To learn to know oneself, and to find a life worth living and work worth doing, is problem and challenge enough, without having to waste time on the fake and unworthy challenges of school—pleasing the teacher, staying out of trouble, fitting in with the gang, being popular, doing what everyone else does.

Q. Will they have the opportunity to overcome or do things that they think they don't want to do?

A. I'm not sure what this question means. If it means, will unschooled children know what it is to have to do difficult and demanding things in order to reach goals they have set for themselves, I would say, yes, life is full of such requirements. But this is not at all the same thing as doing something, and in the case of school usually something stupid and boring, simply because someone else tells you you'll be punished if you don't. Whether children resist such demands or yield to them, it is bad for them. Struggling with the inherent difficulties of a chosen or inescapable task builds character; merely submitting to superior force destroys it.

3

Politics of Unschooling

In this chapter I want to look at what might be called some political objections to unschooling: (1) unschooling is something that can be done only by rich and/or otherwise privileged people; (2) people who unschool only make things harder for poor children who remain in school; (3) schools are by definition and philosophy in favor of equality, and in practice are or soon might become, or be made, very helpful to poor children; (4) people unschooling their own children ignore or don't care about the need for large-scale social and/or educational change, or are too selfish to do anything about it.

UNSCHOOLING AND SOCIAL CHANGE

When we began to advise people to take their children out of school, and began to publish *Growing Without Schooling,* we put into practice a nickel and dime theory about social change, which is that important and lasting social change always comes slowly, and only when people change their lives, not just their political beliefs or parties or forms of government. Real social change is a process that takes place over time, usually quite a long time. At a given moment in history, 99 percent of a society may think and act one way on a certain matter, and only 1 percent think and act very differently. In time, that 1 percent may become 2 percent, then 5 percent, then 10, 20, 30 percent, until finally it becomes the dominant majority, and social change has taken place. When did this social change take place? When did it begin? There is no clear answer, except perhaps that any given social change begins the first time any one person thinks of it.

We who believe that children want to learn about the world, are good at it, and can be trusted to do it with very little adult coercion or interference, are probably no more than one percent of the population, if that. And we are not likely to become the majority in my lifetime. This doesn't trouble me much anymore, as long as this minority keeps on growing. My work is to help it grow. If we think of the majority of our society (or world), with respect to children and schooling, as moving in direction X, and our small minority as moving in direction Y, what I want to do is to find ways to help those who *want* to move in direction Y to *move* that way. There's no point in shouting endlessly at the great X-bound majority, "Hey, you guys, stop, turn around, you're going the wrong way!" People don't change their ideas, much less their lives, because someone comes along with a clever argument to show that they're wrong. As a way of making real and deep changes in society, this shouting and arguing is mostly a waste of time.

It certainly has been so in education. As I said earlier, I and many others have for many years now been arguing about education with the X-bound majority, both among educators and the general public. In any large sense, this arguing has had no result whatever. Only a very few schools ever changed in the ways we proposed, few changed for long, and most are worse now than ever. What our talk does seem to have done is to help a small number of people to make truly radical changes in their work and their lives, to desert the X-bound army and strike off in directions of their own.

But are these kinds of small-scale personal changes political, that is, do they or could they help to bring about change in society as a whole? It depends. Are the things these people are doing things that many others, not rich nor powerful nor otherwise unusual, *could* do if they wanted, without undue risk or sacrifice? And are these people, as they change their lives, telling others about what they are doing and how they might also do it? Private action, however radical and satisfying, only becomes political when it is made known.

In other words, private or small-group actions are political if they have the power to *multiply*. When I used to urge people who did not like their local schools to start schools of their own, this seemed a political act, because it then looked as if almost anyone who wanted to could do the same. But we now know that if by "school" we mean a special learning place, not used for anything else, with full-time paid teachers, to run even a very small school takes far more money than most people have or can raise. As I write, one of the best small alternative schools in this area, after more than ten years of good work, has just closed its doors because it can no longer find the money to keep alive. Such schools have little power to multiply, while home schooling does. No doubt to teach one's own children also takes special qualities. But these are qualities that many more people have, or with a little help, can get.

These qualities themselves can multiply. Though many un-schoolers may not think of themselves this way, they are in the truest sense leaders. Leaders are not what many people think—people with huge crowds following them. Leaders are people who go their own way without caring, or even looking to see whether *anyone* is following them. "Leadership qualities" are not the qualities that enable people to attract followers, but those that enable them to do without them. They include, at the very least, courage, endurance, patience, humor, flexibility, resourcefulness, determination, a keen sense of reality, and the ability to keep a cool and clear head even when things are going badly.

This is the opposite of the "charisma" that we hear so much about. Charismatic leaders make us think, "Oh, if only I could do that, be like that." True leaders make us think, "If they can do that, then by golly I can too." They do not make people into followers, but into new leaders. The home-schooling movement is full of such people, "ordinary" people doing things that they never would have thought they could do—learning the law, questioning the experts, holding their ground against arrogant and threatening authorities, defending themselves and their convictions in the press, on TV, even in court. Seeing them, other ordinary people think they can do the same, and soon they do.

This is why it may be a little misleading to speak of the homeschooling "movement." Most people think of a movement as something like an army, a few generals and a great many buck privates. In the movement for home schooling, everyone is a general.

AN IRONY

The Boston *Globe,* in a story about school attendance, said, "On a typical day, about 70% of the school system's 65,000 youngsters attend classes." They say nothing about the missing 30 percent. Who are they? Why do they stay away? What do the schools do about them?

The answers are, probably, that most of them are poor; that they stay away because they hate school and can see, even if they have nothing much else to do with their time, that the school is wasting it; and that the schools do almost nothing to get them back.

There is an irony here. Compulsory school attendance laws were invented by rich people and aimed at poor kids. These rich people said in effect, "We educated people are perfectly capable of teaching our own children, but you poor people don't give a damn about your kids and don't know enough to teach them anything if you wanted to. So, unless we lock up those kids in school all day long they are just going to run around the streets, cause trouble, get in bad habits, become drunks and criminals. We've got to put them in school to make them into good, obedient, hard-working factory hands."

The irony now is that if you are in fact the kind of kid that compulsory attendance laws were first aimed at, you can skip school all year long and nobody will pay the least attention. Every day the streets are full of the kinds of kids that schools were designed to keep off the streets. But if you are one of those now rare people who really care about the growth of your children and want to take the responsibility for helping that growth, the schools are likely to begin shouting at you about courts and jails.

Thus, just the other day someone sent us a news story about a working-class father in Philadelphia who found through his own investigation that on an average day more than half the students at his son's public junior high school were truant, a rate much higher than the official figure. Feeling that in many ways this must be lowering the quality of his son's school, the father demanded that the school authorities do something to cut down this truancy. The authorities, naturally, led him a dance through all the corridors of the school bureaucracy. For a year or more he tried to get someone in the school system to go after these truants, or even to confirm his estimate about how much truancy there really was. He got absolutely nowhere. Finally in desperation he took the story to the papers. Whether he ever got satisfaction, I don't know.

My point here is that in a year of hard work this father had not been able to get the schools to do anything about the serious truancy in his son's school. But suppose he had finally said in disgust, "I'm tired of begging you to put your schools in shape; I'm going to take my kid out and teach him at home." The schools would have had the police on his doorstep in a matter of days.

WHOM DO SCHOOLS HELP?

School people believe sincerely and even passionately that schools were invented to give, and do give, poor children a better chance to rise in society. We need to understand why this is rarely so, or likely ever to be so.

When we have in a country a few rich and powerful people, and many poor and weak, the rich naturally want to make sure, or as sure as they can, that their children will not be among the poor. To be able to do this is one of the most important benefits of being rich. One way to do it is to make knowledge, and so, access to power, privilege, and possessions, scarce, expensive, and hard to get. This is part of what schools do, and they do it in every country in the world, no matter what may be their political ideas and labels.

Today, in the U.S., many people in the fast-growing field of solar energy do not have college degrees in it. Much of the work and much of the most important work, is being done by small businesses, backyard inventors, hobbyists, amateurs. Anyone can find out what is known and can join in the work. The colleges and universities are only just beginning to give degrees in solar energy. Ten years from now many (but still not all) of the people in the field will have these degrees. When there are enough of them, they, and the colleges and universities which gave them their degrees, will begin to try to get laws passed and arrangements made saying that you can't do important work in solar energy *unless* you have a degree. They will, in short, try to turn one more field of human invention and action into a "profession," a legal monopoly, which only those can do who have had a lot of expensive schooling.

This has already happened in the law, as in many other fields. Abraham Lincoln, and many others, did not learn law by going to law school, but by reading law books. Until recently people used to speak, not of "studying" law, but of *"reading* the law." (In England, studying law is still called "reading law.") It was always possible for poor boys (more rarely girls) to become lawyers by reading the law, and then working in law offices, doing lowly jobs at first, but learning more and being given more responsibility as they learned, and perhaps in the long run setting up their own law offices. No doubt even then the sons of the rich had a big advantage. But the poor at least had a way in. Not anymore. In many or most states, you can't practice law or even take the bar exams unless you have been to law school—and there are many more people trying to get into law school than there are places for them.

Beyond this, the "good" jobs in law go, almost without exception, to the graduates of "good" law schools, most of them graduates of "good," i.e., expensive colleges. (Ivy League and similar colleges now cost about $10,000 a year.) A few poor kids may make it through this obstacle race, just enough to fool people into thinking that it is a fair race. The vast majority are shut out. In fact, most poor people feel that, because they can't afford the schooling, their children are shut out of even such less prestigious careers as nursing. Yet almost everything that people now can't do without a degree, often an advanced degree, was not so long ago done by people without such degrees. How and where did they learn what they knew? They learned, like Lincoln, by reading books, by using their eyes and ears, by asking questions, by working with or for people who knew more.

Schools like to say they create and spread knowledge. It would be closer to the truth to say that they collect and hoard knowledge, corner the market on it if they can, so that they can sell it at the highest possible price. That's why they want everyone to believe that only what is learned in school is worth anything. But this idea, as much as any other, freezes the class structure of society and locks the poor into poverty.

One of the many fringe benefits of being rich and powerful, in any society, is that you are able to say that some kinds of knowledge, i.e., the kind of things *you* know, are much more important than others, and therefore, that the people who know these things, i.e., you and your friends, are much more important and deserving than people who know other things. It is easy to see why in any society the most powerful people, whether the rich or simply high government officials, should want to say that the kind of knowledge that most people pick up from everyday life and work is worth less than the kind that can only be picked up in special places, particularly when they control the access to those places.

A LIFE-TAUGHT MAN

In his book *Travels Around America* (New York: Walker and Co. 1976), Harrison Salisbury described his efforts to trace the Westward path of some of his ancestors. He describes one of them thus:

> He [Hiram Salisbury] was a man of this time [1815]. . . . I scan the journal for clues and reconstruct the post-Revolutionary American. I list his skills, one sheet of scratch paper after another. He knew every farm chore. He milked cows and attended the calves in birth. He physicked his horse. He plowed, he planted, he cultivated, hayed, picked apples, grafted fruit trees, cut wheat with a scythe, cradled oats, threshed grain with a flail on a clay floor. He chopped the corn and put down his vegetables for winter. He made cider and

built cider mills. He made cheese and fashioned cheese tongs. He butchered the hogs and sheared the sheep. He churned butter and salted it. He made soap and candles, thatched barns and built smokehouses. He butchered oxen and constructed ox sledges. He fought forest fires and marked out the land. He repaired the crane at Smith's mill and forged a crane for his own fireplace to hang the kettle on. He collected iron in the countryside and smelted it. He tapped (mended) his children's shoes and his own. He built trundle beds, oxcarts, sleighs, wagons, wagon wheels and wheel spokes. He turned logs into boards and cut locust wood for picket fences. He made house frames, beams, mortised and pegged. With six men's help he raised the frames and built the houses. He made a neat cherry stand with a drawer for a cousin, fixed clocks and went fishing. He carved his own board measures (yardsticks) and sold them for a dollar apiece. He fitted window cases, mended locks, and fixed compasses. He hewed timber, surveyed the forest, wrote deeds and shaved shingles. He inspected the town records and audited the books of the Friendship Lodge, the oldest freshwater Masonic lodge in the country (still running). He chipped plows, constructed carding machines, carved gunstocks and built looms. He set gravestones and fashioned wagon hubs. He ran a bookstore and could make a fine coffin in half a day. He was a member of the state's General Assembly, overseer of the poor, appraiser of property and fellow of the town council. He made hoops by the thousand and also pewter faucets. For many years he collected the town taxes. . . .

I have not listed all of Hiram's skills but enough. I do not think he was an unusual man. Put me in Hiram's world and I would not last long. Put Hiram down in our world, he might have a little trouble with a computer, but he'd get the hang of it faster than I could cradle a bushel of oats.

I tend to agree with Harrison Salisbury that Hiram, though perhaps not an unusual man in his time, would be a most unusual one in ours, far more knowing, skillful, intelligent, resourceful, adaptive, inventive, and competent than most people we would find today, in either city or country, and no matter how schooled.

But the real question I want to raise and answer is how Hiram learned all those skills. To be sure, he did not learn them in school, nor in workshops or any other schoollike activity. Almost certainly, he learned how to do all those kinds of work, many of them highly skilled, by being around when other people were doing them. But these people were not doing the work in order to teach Hiram something. Nobody raised a barn just so that Hiram could see how barns were raised. They raised it because they needed the barn. Nor did they say to him, "Hiram, as long as I have to raise this barn, you may as well come around and learn how it is done." They said, "Hiram, I'm raising a barn and *I need your help.*" He was there to help, not to learn—but as he helped, he learned.

Almost a century later John Dewey was to talk about "learning by doing." The way for young people to learn (for example) how pottery is made is not to read about it but to make pots. No argument about that. But making pots in school just to learn how it is done is still nowhere near as good as making pots (and learning from it) because *someone needs the pots.* The best incentive to learn how to do good work, and to do it, is to know that the work has to be done, that it is going to be of real use to someone.

In his essay, "Intellect," Emerson spoke eloquently about the worth of the knowledge of ordinary people:

> Each mind has its own method. A true man never acquires after college rules. What you have aggregated in a natural manner surprises and delights when it is produced. For we cannot oversee each other's secret. And hence the differences between men in natural endowment are insignificant in comparison with their common wealth. Do you think the porter and the cook have no anecdotes, no experiences, no wonders for you? Everybody knows as much as the savant. The walls of rude minds are scrawled all over with facts, with thoughts. They shall one day bring a lantern and read the inscriptions.

UNSCHOOLING AND THE WORKING CLASS

Dean Schneider, who taught for some time in a small alternative school in the center of Newark, wrote:

> At a workshop the other day the speaker was talking about her experiences with unschooling in Newark. She, a member of a city

poverty agency and former teacher, had a friend who actually never registered her child for school. When her child was six or seven and had not yet been to school, she started being hassled and threatened by the school authorities (I don't know how they became aware of the "offense" in the first place). Despite her repeated defense that she was effectively teaching her child at home, the powers that be turned their screws. But rather than submit, the mother took her child and moved out of state. This was around 1974 or 1975.

After the meeting, I enquired as to other cases she knew about of parents, in Newark, taking their children out of schools altogether and teaching them at home. She said she had five or six friends who are thinking seriously about it. They are single parents (the number of mother-centered households in Newark runs about 50%) who had, themselves, gone through the Newark public schools and wanted nothing of the sort for their children. They were farsighted enough to plan their work lives and finances so they could take three or more years off, or at least juggle their time, to be at home to teach their children. Whether or not they too will encounter official resistance or pressure is unknown. In 1967, home study became legal in New Jersey under *State* v. *Massa,* 95 NJ Supreme 382, 231 A 2nd 252 (1967). But this ruling, in itself, does not prevent legal or political maneuvering, as has been seen in other states where home study is supposedly legal.

I have recently heard of other instances of parents unschooling their children in Newark and New York City. My next door neighbor seriously contemplated keeping her daughter at home last year, but then decided to enter her at the alternative school right up the street.

Even when children are in schools that parents find suspect, you hear of brothers and sisters, aunts and uncles, cousins and parents chipping in at night or on weekends trying to teach at home to reverse or minimize the damage wrought by the public schools. A student at my school last year, when asked, "How are you ever going to learn this stuff if you don't listen?" replied, "My uncle teaches me at home." Another former student in our third grade had very irregular attendance and this was considered a problem. Yet I tutored her during the summer and she picked things up very quickly, and is in fact ahead in her studies compared to other third graders (who have been more regular in attending school). From what she told me, it was evident that her mother made home instruction a regular part of daily life (after school). Another student told me today that she has a tutor come to her house from time to time.

On this matter of who can unschool, a mother and teacher wrote me a very interesting letter. Here are some of her remarks, and my comments:

> The only people who can hope to get their kids out of the schools safely are upper- or middle-class whites.

This is not necessarily so, and not even so in fact. Some of the people who right now have their children out of school are not middle class at all. A number are mothers on welfare. Only a week or so ago I talked with a woman who some years ago ran a paid tutoring service in San Francisco for parents whose families were not in school. She told me that about *70 percent* of her clients had been working-class families. I don't know whether these people had taken their children out of school with the school's consent, or whether they had simply hidden their children from the schools. I remember her saying that it seemed as if every bus driver in the city had his kids out of school. I asked her why they had taken their children out. She said that in almost every case the schools were not helping these children learn and were saying that they were incapable of learning. Some families simply refused to accept this and began teaching or having their children taught at home.

> Working class, and especially black, parents who take their children out of school are likely to be hounded by the authorities to the fullest possible extent.

First, the fact is that quite a few white, middle-class and professional families have already been hounded by the authorities to the fullest possible extent. If the schools are in a hounding mood, they'll hound anybody. Indeed, they may be more worried about losing middle-class children than poor children, since they need the support of middle-class people, much more than poor, in order to get more and more money. When I talk to school people about unschooling, one of the nightmares they bring up is that they might have only poor children in their schools.

In any case, the authorities won't make trouble if they don't know the children are out of school. This seems to be easier to manage in large cities than anywhere else. As we know, in all big cities large percentages of the children are truant every day. If it is that easy for kids just to hang out in the streets, it ought to be even easier for them to be at home (or somewhere) doing something interesting and worthwhile.

I don't deny that if and when parents get into an open dispute with the authorities, poor people, especially nonwhites, will have a harder time of it than middle-class whites. No argument about that at all. But much of the time it may be possible to avoid such open disputes.

> Poor kids need a high school diploma more than middle-class kids do—they have a much harder time getting a job without it.

I don't know how much a high school diploma helps really poor kids; they have a very rough time whether they have one or not. But let's agree for the sake of argument that poor kids badly need high school diplomas. The point is that people can get high school diplomas without actually being in a high school, by taking high school correspondence courses, or by passing an equivalency exam. Also, people who stay out of schools for a number of years can always go back in if they feel they need some kind of school ticket. Experience has shown that when they go back in, they are usually well ahead of those who stayed in.

> Working-class parents have less confidence in being able to teach their own kids (because if you're so smart why ain't you rich), and therefore in fact *are* less able to teach their kids.

It may be true, but in this matter the difference between middle-class and working-class families is not very great. Parents with graduate degrees have often said to me that they didn't know enough to teach their own young children. In any social class, there will be few people who think that they are capable of teaching their children and doing a better job than the schools. We have to begin with these, whatever class they may be in, and hope that others will follow their example.

> Teaching children at home does nothing toward overthrowing the social structure.

The word "overthrow" does not describe any series of events that I can imagine happening in this country in my lifetime. As I said earlier, profound social change is most likely to come in small steps: in fact, that is the only way we can work for it.

> This movement is not building anything more than a small group of white dropouts from society.

On the contrary, true unschooling will help and is helping young people find ways to live active, responsible lives in society, and to find work worth doing.

> We should help each other teach our kids, teach each other's kids, arrange our lives so that larger numbers of people than just nuclear families share the responsibility of unschooling. I am thinking, for example, of neighborhood discussion groups about what the schools do to children and why. What experiences have people had with the schools, and what do these experiences show? Parents can give each other advice about how to fight in various situations, and help each other construct alternatives. I do not at all mean that we should water down what we say in order to be more acceptable to more people. I think we should be absolutely straightforward with as many people as we can who are oppressed by schools, and I think we will find many people who agree and have a lot of experience and ideas to offer. This kind of support would help kids and parents who are not yet ready to pull out of school to at least *see* their school experience in a psychologically healthy way. It would help them to direct their anger at the schools rather than turn it inward and blame themselves as the schools want them to.

I entirely agree. In some parts of the country parents have already formed the kind of mutual support groups you talk about, and as more and more people join a network such as the Directory we publish in our magazine we should see many more of these. As for people wrongly blaming themselves for what the schools did to them, I first wrote about this as far back as 1970, in my book *What Do I Do Monday?*

> If my husband and I make this decision, it may get us into a lot of trouble.

Avoid all such troubles if you possibly can. I see no point in confronting the authorities directly if you can dodge them.

UNSCHOOLING AND THE SINGLE PARENT

Many people who think about keeping children out of school worry about whether working mothers, especially single mothers, can do this. A woman who wrote us about her son's helping her in the lab (see Chapter 12) also wrote:

> J stayed home from school the next day—he didn't need any coaxing. He has been out of school ever since and I have felt better and better about the move as time goes on. It seemed he had been asking me forever to be able to stay home. After a few days he missed some of his friends but still didn't want to go back. We managed to see some of them on weekends, and that seemed to satisfy him.
>
> I go to work on weekdays and he is left home in the apartment. This worried me at first, but he said it was fine, and he has become quite self-reliant. A great weight has lifted from our relationship. I was no longer pushing him to school against his will, and he started to trust me again as he did in his pre-school days—I had almost forgotten. I had more time for him too, now that I no longer was spending time at the school. One day he talked of his mom "rescuing" him from school. I felt like a heroine.

A single mother wrote:

> I am writing you in response to your note in the most recent issue of the *Radcliffe Quarterly*. As a feminist single mother I cannot help but wonder what exactly the implications are supposed to be

for the real lives of my child and myself. The lives of mothers and children are not determined separately; for better or for worse, our fates are bound up together. The fact is I do not know how I would survive if my daughter were not in school.

Here is my situation: I am deeply in debt, on account of having been in law school for the past three years. I decided to go to law school, as it happens, in response to the pressures of trying to support myself and my child through do-good jobs and welfare. My daughter is now 6 years old and attending first grade in the local public school. She is unhappy there, although the school is known as a "good" one, and regularly comes home outraged at all the indignities she is subjected to, e.g., she is not allowed to go to the bathroom when she wants to, *or talk during lunch,* or draw on the reverse side of her school papers when she is forced to wait.

She also does not seem to be learning to read or do arithmetic at anything that seems to me to be a reasonable rate. And although it is clear to me that she has an extraordinarily logical and creative mind, she has begun to develop a sense that in her teacher's eyes she is actually "dumb." She begs me not to make her go to school. I am sympathetic—but the only alternative is to let her come to law school with me, and she dislikes that too (not without reason). Next year I have a job as Visiting Assistant Professor at the University of Miami Law School, which will, unfortunately, mean I am busier than ever. (Ironically one of the courses I plan to teach will be "The Rights of Parents and Children.") Money will be a problem. So I certainly doubt that I will be in a position to hire any sort of mother/teacher surrogate. We also do not know any circle of friends who might take up the slack. (Sometimes I know such arrangements do work out, but one plainly cannot count on this.) What, then, can I realistically do to provide my daughter with an acceptable environment in which to live and learn? I frankly do not know.

It seems to me that although the details of my problem are unique, its general structure is almost universal. A scarcity of time and money, a need to cope. The trouble is not that I or other concerned parents are insufficiently "radical" in outlook. I was in fact quite prepared to drop out as long as it seemed to me that that was the most authentic means of handling human existence. But my practical and human need to live in a "public" social and economic world proved inescapable. I recognized, moreover, that my daughter's need was not to have a mother dedicated to creating an immediate "ideal" world for her; she too has to ultimately live in the world I inhabit. This seems as though it would lead to a pat solution, but it doesn't; for it is never clear at what point one begins to rationalize the outrageous. Instead, I, like so many friends, find myself in a perpetual quandary.

The one thing I am certain of in thinking about my daughter now is that a "solution" to her problems will have to take mine into account too. I don't know whether I am saying all this to you in the hope that you will have anything immediately helpful to say, but since in the past you have had much to say that was useful, maybe if you recast your thinking about the lives of children as thinking about the lives of mothers-and-children, you would come up with something. I hope so, anyway.

In reply, I wrote more or less as follows:

Thanks very much for your good letter. I understand your problem, at least a little, because for most of the eight or so years I've known her a good friend of mine has been in the same spot. For a number of these years she worked to support herself and her child. Then she studied for a Master's Degree in Education, and is now in her second year at law school. During all that time it would have been very difficult for her not to have her child in school—though of course, like you, she had to make other arrangements when school was not in session.

However, I think I know her well enough to say that if at any time during those years her child had been really miserable at school, or if she had felt that school was doing the child real harm, she would have made other arrangements, however difficult that might have been. As it was, because the child's father could and did pay for private schooling, she was able to send her to a fairly relaxed elementary school, where the child was quite happy, and could learn about the world in her own way. As a result, she now reads four or five years ahead of most children her age. Her last two years of (public) school have not been very interesting, but she has at least been free of most of the anxieties that torment other children, and by now has ways of finding out about the world on her own. She is also good at sports, and liked by the other children, which helps.

I gather that your own situation is more difficult, in that you are not able to afford anything other than public school. This would seem to leave you only the choice of taking the child with you wherever you go, or leaving her in public school. May I suggest that in the very near future you may have other choices.

To take first the matter of custodial care, even if a six-year-old needs some sort of baby-sitter, I would say most emphatically that this is not true of a ten-, or even an eight-year-old. In other words, I think (because people have done it) that if you begin to train your child toward independence and self-reliance, in two years or perhaps less she would be perfectly able to spend large amounts of time at home by herself. By that time she would know who and how to call for various emergencies, how to provide for her own needs (meals, etc.), and how to occupy herself happily and constructively with many different activities.

Of course, she may not want to do this. But were she my child and I in your shoes, it is a choice I would want to offer her. I would say to her that for some time to come she was going to have to either (1) go to public school, which may be as bad as the one she is in now or (2) stay home for much of the day and maybe all day by herself. Then I would say, "If you want to take the second choice, or be ready to take it, you are going to have to learn a number of things, like how to cook and take care of food, how to look up numbers in the phone book, how to talk to strange adults over the phone, and how to find interesting things to do all by yourself for many hours at a time. Do you want to do all this? It's okay if you don't, but then the only other possibility is school."

You can give her plenty of time to think about this, talk it over, and so on. But she will have to decide. If she decides to prepare for independence and self-reliance, you can start working on that right away. If this possibility interests you, perhaps in later letters we can talk more about how to do that.

I have put the choices rather extremely, go to school or stay home all day by yourself. In reality, the choices may often not be quite that extreme. Thus, starting at whatever time of day school lets out, whether or not she is at school, you may often be able to arrange for the child to visit other children. Or there may be other places she can go, such as the children's room at the public library. After school hours, the child is no longer an outlaw and can safely be seen in public places. If you are living in a large city, and she has learned to use maps, find her way, and use public transportation, there may be a number of interesting places where she can go by herself.

Also, you may be able to find and afford people to be with the child not for the whole day but for a few hours, and perhaps in that time to take her to some places she might not be able to go by herself. Once we get past the idea that there has to be an adult with her every minute of the day, the problem may become more manageable. You may even be able to find some people to do this without pay, perhaps on some sort of barter arrangement. I'm not sure what kind of skills you have to swap, but you probably have quite a few of them.

The other question is, can you, without spending a ton of money, make your home, which will probably be a small apartment, into a place in which your daughter *could* spend many happy, interesting, and fruitful hours by herself? You not only can, but you can make it into an environment far more varied and productive than anything she is likely to find at school. And are children in fact *capable* of spending long hours happily and productively without constant adult supervision and attention? Yes, they are—not so long ago, large numbers of them used to do it all the time. You will have to respond generously to her need and requests for attention and friendship when you come home. But you will surely want to do that anyway, and she may need that comfort and consolation even more if she goes to school. And it will be helpful if, as far as she wants to and you are able to, you let her share in your daytime life—which will become easier as she grows older. My friend's daughter, at age ten, went a number of times to law school classes, and often found them quite interesting.

I hope some of these ideas may be of some use to you, and I would like very much to know, if you can find the time to tell me, how you feel about what I have suggested here.

Ann McConnell wrote back, in part:

My daughter and I have come to a solution ourselves. I agree with you entirely that she deserves to participate in any decision about whether or not she goes to school. Even at age 6 she is almost (but not quite) capable of taking care of herself, during the day at least. So the possibility of letting her stay at home by herself does not seem ridiculous to me. I already sometimes leave her for an hour or two alone. She takes messages on the phone, makes peanut butter and jelly sandwiches, and puts on phonograph records. Still, I don't think she could be happy spending the majority of her time in a solitary state, simply because she happens to be a very sociable person. That in fact is the basis of one of her primary objections to school: *the teachers there place too many barriers to interpersonal interaction.*

One idea I have had, though, about helping her to read in a nonschool setting is to hire a nine-year-old I know who is a good reader to help her. The nine-year-old is the son of a good friend of mine and he is currently in trouble at the same school my daughter goes to because he has been choosing to read *A Tale of Two Cities* under his desk instead of working on his workbook. The age difference strikes me as about right: C doesn't have to feel inferior due to the fact that A can read so much better than she, because he is obviously three years older. A seems to like the idea too. (His seriousness is being treated as a positive advantage, for a change.) I'll see how this goes, but it is occurring to me that maybe I have hit upon a large part of the solution to my problem.

Next year we will be moving to Miami. I will certainly have a lot more money than I have now. I will try to find some sort of reasonable private school for C to go to. (Though I shall certainly be discussing with her the possibility of staying home from school entirely.) There are several things that Miami offers a child that New Haven does not: a children's theater group, the chance to learn Spanish, and easy access to swimming. All of these opportunities interest C greatly. So the importance of school may not be so great there. I hope so anyway.

4

Getting Them Out

This chapter is about ways in which parents have taken, or may be able to take, their children out of school. Some have been able to get agreement and support of the local schools fairly easily; some have done so only after considerable struggle; some have enrolled their children in distant schools which have then approved and supervised a home study program; some have registered their own homes as private schools; and some have simply either evaded or defied the law.

STATING YOUR CASE

Most of these people have found that your chances of being able to teach your own children are much better if you prepare for the school a very detailed statement about why you want to do it, how you plan to go about doing it, and what the various court decisions are that uphold your right to do it. This document cannot be too long. The more you can put in about why and how you want to teach your own children, the more educational authorities you can quote, the more court decisions you can cite, the better. Your plan is a thinly disguised legal brief. In it you are speaking, not just to the school superintendent and school board, but beyond them to the courts, should the schools be unwise enough to try to take you there. It is wiser not to say anything about going to court in your plan but instead to talk as if you assumed that the schools were going to be reasonable and cooperative (as indeed some have been). But if your plan is complete enough and shows enough knowledge of the law, the school people, if tempted to oppose you, are going to wonder, "What's going to happen if we have to argue against this in front of a judge?" You want them to feel that if they push matters that far, they are going to lose.

Secondly, you should send copies of your plan to as many school people as possible, certainly to all members of the school board, to the superintendent and leading members of his administrative staff, and perhaps others as well. On every copy you send put a list of all those who will receive it. Most of them will feel that they have to read it, and then discuss it with all the others. You want them to feel, not only that you are serious, responsible, and knowing, but also that opposing you is going to cost them much time and trouble. These busy people already have to go to too many meetings, and you want their hearts to sink at the prospect of going to still more.

Thirdly, your plan should be typed, neatly and accurately, in good business form, on good 8½-×-11-inch paper, preferably a business letterhead if you have one. If you don't type well, use a friend who does, or a professional typist. This will impress the school people, and beyond them, that invisible and (you hope) avoidable judge. Appearances may not be everything, but in this world they count. Make the best paper appearance you can.

For a curriculum, try to put something down on paper that the schools will accept, without being so specific that it ties your own hands. You don't have to tell the school people everything you will be doing, far less convince them that it is right. Since practically everything in the school curriculum falls within the boundaries of ordinary daily life, you could in good conscience say that you will be studying English, mathematics, social studies, science, health, and any other subjects on the school's list. After all, in one form or another, these are everywhere around us. Avoid saying, if you can, that you will be teaching a particular subject between 9:00 and 10:00 A.M. every Thursday, or anything as specific as that. But I wouldn't hesitate at all to say that any one of these subjects will be "covered" for as many hours a week as happens in school.

For a model, in tone and content, of a letter to school authorities saying why you want to keep your children out of school, see the Hobarts' and the Kendricks' letters to their local school superintendents later in this chapter.

WHEN THE SCHOOLS COOPERATE

From Sharon Hillestad in Minnesota:

> . . . It was surprisingly easy to obtain permission to teach Matthew at home. The first step I took was to call the State Education Department. I talked to the chief, Dr. Peterson. He informed me that I would need the permission of the superintendent of our school district, to provide a qualified teacher, and arrange five hours a day of classwork.
>
> My husband and I met with the superintendent and presented him with a written proposal. Although Mr. LaCroix did not give his approval, he did grant us permission. He asked me to submit a schedule, curriculum plan, and method of evaluation. The school has been extremely cooperative. I met with Matthew's teacher at the Accelerated Christian Education School that he attended for his first and second grades. He obtained all the books and paces (workbooks) for me.
>
> We have had three days of home school. The first day was a great adjustment for me as I discovered myself being a "classroom teacher," trying to implement the schedule and "get through" the subjects. My son protested vigorously and I decided the schedule and the plans were mostly for the benefit of the administrators and could have little bearing on what Matt would eventually learn. Now we handle about four subjects a day, whatever and whenever he will learn. I think it will be a fun year. . . .

Nancy Plent writes:

> . . . Enclosed for your files is "A Digest of Laws and State Board
> of Education Regulations Regarding Private Schools in New Jer-
> sey," from the New Jersey State Department of Education, 225 W.
> State St., Trenton NJ 08625. Pages 2 and 9 have the information
> unschoolers want. As you can see by the digest, New Jersey makes
> it easy to start a private school, and they leave you alone once
> started.
>
> I have a N.J. teacher's certificate and plan to file the affidavit
> which makes me a private school. I may be able to help someone
> else with these two items.
>
> One of my first steps was to call the ACLU. They promised to
> research the laws for home education if I gave them my reasons in
> writing. They also referred me to an Education Law Center. I don't
> know whether this kind of office is unique to N.J., but it seems to
> me that other states might have similar offices tucked away some-
> where. A few phone calls might locate it.
>
> The lawyer I talked to there was very encouraging and had no
> inclination to defend public education to me. He told me about the
> *Massa* decision and that I might have to prove equivalent instruc-
> tion, the key words in N.J. He recommended having a well-organ-
> ized curriculum to show, and set hours of study. (I'll be able to
> "show" this, but I don't live well with "set" anything.) His final
> advice was to confront the local principal with my plans as a matter
> of "professional courtesy." He explained—if someone sees you out
> during school hours and reports you, the principal will feel foolish
> and annoyed that he isn't on top of things in his district and will
> come down on you harder.

The digest of New Jersey laws on education that Nancy sent
says on page 9 that people must cause children between six and
sixteen to attend school "or to receive equivalent instruction elsewhere than at school." On page 2 it says, "The State Department
of Education is not charged with approval of private elementary
schools nor private day kindergartens. Such schools which may
include all, part, or some combination of grades from kindergarten through eight, do not need a license to operate."

Albert Hobart, a teacher, found a cooperative school system in
Massachusetts:

Two years ago when our son was nearing his sixth birthday, we decided to teach him ourselves rather than send him to school. We didn't know much about the compulsory education laws then, but we did have unpleasant visions of truant officers, court appearances, and jail. Thus we asked a local lawyer, who soon discovered that parents could teach their own children [in Massachusetts] if they obtained "prior approval" from the school board or superintendent of schools.

At his suggestion we called the superintendent's office and asked how we should go about obtaining prior approval. It's my impression that no one in the office had ever heard this question before either, but soon we were referred to one of the assistant superintendents who asked us to come in for a meeting. My wife actually talked to him, and tells me that he was respectful but curious. After discovering that we were indeed serious about our intentions, he asked her to write him a letter covering the following topics:

a. Our background.

b. Why we wanted to teach our son at home.

c. Our educational goals for our son and our plan of instruction.

We worked for a week on this letter trying as best we could to explain our point of view in a straightforward, noncontroversial way. We made an effort to use words and concepts which were already familiar to school people and to show that our son was learning things in his normal everyday activities which were similar to the sort of things children learned in school.

Here are excerpts from the Hobarts' letter to the Assistant Superintendent:

Our son, Robert, turned six on August 27, and as you requested in our conversation last Tuesday, we are writing about our desire to instruct him at home during the coming school year. We apologize for getting in touch with you at such a late date, but until quite recently we were under the impression that children in Massachusetts were not legally required to attend school until they were seven. . . .

We think that children are pushed too quickly into the school environment with all of its pressures, and that many of them would be better off if they were allowed to stay home longer than they do. We realize, of course, that many people disagree with us and that there are numerous parents who are either unable or unwilling to keep their children at home. We are convinced from our experience as teachers, however, that many of the problems that children have in school would be reduced or eliminated if they had entered school when they were older and, we should add, allowed to accustom themselves more gradually to the long school day. We observed, for instance, that even some sixth grade students were unable to adjust successfully to six and a half hours of school each day, and the first graders, obviously, have a more difficult time of it.

We think children should not be pressured to learn. Instead, when they are ready, they should be provided with whatever materials seem appropriate for their needs. This is the basic approach, as we understand it, of the "open classroom" method. But in our observations of "open classrooms" both in public and private schools, we see that the teachers still find it difficult to resist the temptation to pressure. We can hardly blame them, considering the numbers of children they have to deal with and the ambitious expectations of the parents and school administration.

Lest we be misunderstood when we speak of protecting our child from this kind of pressure, let us emphasize that we are not referring to "permissiveness"—that is, a laxity regarding standards of behavior. As far as Robert can understand the difference between right and wrong, we hold him strictly accountable.

You have asked us for a plan of instruction, especially for Language Arts and Math. As you can see from what we've just related, our approach is to wait until the appropriate time to help Robert learn a particular skill or bit of information, so it would be difficult to give you the plans and goals one might find in a teacher's manual. Naturally we want him to be able to express himself articulately both in speech and in writing, and to have a good practical and theoretical grasp of mathematics. . . .

You mentioned a problem that might occur if Robert entered the second grade in Lexington—would he have covered the same work? That's a fair question, but the chances are that we would send him to a private school. If he should enter a Lexington second grade, however, we would certainly give him adequate preparation. For instance, we would be in touch with his school to find out what would be expected of him and perhaps go through the various workbooks to give him a proper foundation.

Finally, you asked us whether Robert might suffer because he will have less opportunity than other children to get to know people his own age. Robert does have a number of friends his age already, and he spends time with them on a fairly regular basis. He also has friends who are other ages. What he is doing now seems to be working because people often compliment him on his social development and the parents of his friends appreciate having him as a playmate for their children. Incidentally, we think the school environment tends to overemphasize peer group relationships and that many children would be better off if they had more opportunity to be with people of all ages. We also think that parents tend to depend too much on schools as the basis of their children's social relationships and, we might add, their moral values.

Thank you again for our meeting. If you have any further questions regarding our plans for Robert's education during the coming year, please let us know.

Albert Hobart told of later developments in his letter to *GWS:*

Soon we received a reply from the assistant superintendent stating that the superintendent "looked with favor" on our request and that we'd be allowed to withhold our son from school for one year and teach him ourselves. But he added that if we wanted to continue teaching him ourselves the following year, we'd have to ask again. Thus the next year when our son would have been entering the second grade, we wrote a short note to the same assistant superintendent (the superintendent, himself, had retired) saying how well things had been going for our son and asking permission to teach him at home for another year. No one bothered to answer this letter, and we haven't heard anything more about it.

Perhaps our local newspaper, which has considerable influence in our community, was helpful to us. Although it's usually traditional in its outlook and quite conservative politically, it printed a long, sympathetic article about the way we're teaching our son at home. This article was instrumental, we think, in giving us legitimacy in the eyes of our school-oriented community and in persuading the school officials to maintain their approving point of view.

My wife is a certified teacher, but she didn't receive her certification until after we had permission from the superintendent to teach our son at home. Massachusetts law has no specific requirements about the qualifications of parents who want to teach their own children, but our teaching experience may have been a factor in the superintendent's decision.

Actually there's nothing we do with our son at home that in any way resembles what we used to do as teachers. The only real advantage we've gained from teaching is that it's given us the opportunity to see for ourselves that there's nothing special or even necessary about schools and that more children would probably be better off if they weren't forced to go.

By the way, only five of the thirty-two states which allow home instruction require that one of the parents be certified (Alabama, Alaska, California, Colorado, Iowa) and none of the parents we know who are teaching their own children have ever had classroom experience.

Art Harris, father of two sons in Vermont, describes a different but equally effective approach:

Seven years ago, my wife and I came to the conclusion that the public schools our two boys were attending were damaging, rather than enhancing, the learning process for them, and we decided to do something about it. Our older son, a voracious reader then in the sixth grade, was bored in the classroom because almost everything that was taught he had already discovered on his own. For him school was a long review and an authoritarian prison which sapped his strength.

Our attorney discovered a provision in the education laws of our state (then N.Y.) that provided for in-home schooling. True, the statute was undoubtedly drafted for the infirm, and perhaps, for child actors as well, but if we could provide an "alternate" but "equivalent" educational experience, we could conceivably comply with the law.

The Board of Education decided not to fight us, perhaps to avoid the possibility of our pointing out publicly the deficiencies of the schools. We were assigned an advisor from the school system who, after a nervous six months, left us alone. . . .

The very best thing I did was put aside a weekend and write a long (nine-or ten-page, single-spaced) explanation of what we intended to do, where we got our ideas (Holt, Illich, Leonard, Kozol, Dennison, et al.), how we felt about education, what our qualifications were, etc. Made a dozen copies or so for school people— anyone who'd take one—truant officer, superintendent, head of grade schools, school psychologist—even had copies for the school's lawyer. I believe this was the turning point—to put it in writing. It showed we were serious, gave people a chance to appraise us calmly by what we said. Half the time people don't listen —they resist and are thinking of how they'll reply. But when you catch them quietly by giving them some reading material, it often reaches them. I feel that weekend was well spent—they realized too how serious we were, and the books we'd read. I quoted from some of these books, your own included, JH.

Vermont apparently has some cooperative school authorities. Catherine Lowther, parent of two, wrote *GWS:*

> I am sorry to hear that so many people are having such a hard time taking their kids out of school. I thought you might like to balance the scales a little with a positive story.
>
> I never sent my kids to school. They are nine and seven and I have always taught them at home. I have been approved by the state every year, the local authorities have been friendly, supportive, and even enthusiastic. The local school board has bought all our books and materials, to be returned to them when we are finished with them.
>
> I noticed in *GWS* #4 you said that the burden to prove that a program is not equivalent to public school should rest with the state. In Vermont it does [state supreme court decision].
>
> I also know three other families in Vermont who have taken their kids out of school without harassment.

Along with the letter, Catherine Lowther sent a copy of Vermont state law. Subject to this law, the state board of education approved a process for looking over and approving alternatives to public schooling. Within the state department of education there is a Committee on Equivalent Education which reviews private schools and also home instruction plans. The state says that home instruction plans shall be built around the Calvert Home Study Plan for the elementary years, and approved correspondence courses for secondary.

I asked her whether the state watched her very closely to be sure she was using the Calvert materials. She replied:

. . . The state prefers to have people use the Calvert course because it is, of course, tidier for them, but they cannot enforce this. . . . In our case, we chose to use Calvert for the first two years after our daughter turned seven (legal school age here). We didn't feel qualified to take on teaching her without experience or guidance. However, we found it becoming very limiting by third grade. It was like inviting public school standards into one's home. Greta was memorizing names and dates to pass tests and get grades and was getting more and more miserable under the absurdity of it.

So for last year, fourth grade for her, first for our son, I devised my own curriculums which I submitted to the state on their application form and they approved it. I arranged that the local elementary school would review the children's work quarterly during the school year to comply with the state's request for a "reliable means of showing evidence of learning." The Town funded us $200 (my estimate of our costs) for materials. Public money for this is contingent upon state approval and will not be given for anything connected with religious purposes.

For the coming year, I have again written my own plan. Based on our record of having accomplished more than public school classes (according to the principal who reviewed our work), I am asking to report directly to someone in the state and that we show our papers only once at the end of the year. It is unnecessary and inconvenient both for me and the teachers who have to look over our work to spend any more time on it than that.

No officials have ever been to our home. I have voluntarily gone to the state twice and to the local superintendent often for information, and a variety of other reasons. I like to be out front and get along and feel that the people in authority may also be benefitted by an open, cooperative attitude. Example lays the groundwork for trust. Everyone I have met has been friendly and respectful of our rights.

Shawn and David Kendrick, of Rehoboth, Massachusetts, wrote a long letter to their local superintendent of schools saying why they wanted to teach their children at home. It is a model of what such letters should be, and it did in fact persuade the local schools to allow the Kendricks to teach their own children.

We have always felt and continue to feel that, as the people closest to our children, with the greatest opportunity to know and observe them, and with the most compelling motivations of love and concern for their mental health and emotional well-being, we have the ultimate duty and responsibility to provide them with the best possible environment in which they are free to learn and live as God and nature intended them to. We firmly believe that that environment is a loving home in which the natural authority of the parents does not exclude the child's rights as a person. Through close, meaningful interaction we are able to observe and know our children well, and to supply them with the emotional support necessary to the development of a positive self-image. In such a setting we can best present our own spiritual and moral beliefs while simultaneously satisfying the State's interest in an educated citizenry.

An additional advantage of the home environment is the small child-to-adult ratio which allows the individual differences and needs of our children to be recognized and provided for with greater proficiency. Our study plan is based on each child's interests and abilities because we feel that true learning, the kind which lasts a lifetime, is self-discovered and cannot be communicated directly to another. Such learning is frequently inhibited by the fear of failure, by ridicule and humiliation, by overstimulation, by the tension which accompanies competition, and by pressures to achieve beyond one's present ability. In order to encourage true learning, therefore, we have provided a calm, positive atmosphere, learning materials, and access to friends, mentors and community resources. We have chosen to avoid the above-mentioned pressures which often prevent learning or make it a negative experience.

As a result, we have modified our use of the Calvert School correspondence course. Although we will continue to include the Calvert instruction in our plan, we will no longer adhere rigidly to the time-frame of the lessons. We have found from last year's experience that such adherence interferes with an individualized program which allows the child "saturation learning," i.e., to study a subject thoroughly before going on to another area of interest. Our daughter Anna, for example, will often complete several days' reading or math assignments in one sitting because we allow her enthusiasm for the subject to take precedence over notions that one must study only what is allotted for in that period. Similarly, because of a high interest, she read the first grade health book over the past summer and is now reading the second grade book. The idea that one learns more over the nine-month school year than at any other time is foreign to our children, since their school year is year-round. Not having been encouraged to believe that one must go for certain months of the year to a place called school in order to learn things, they view the world around them and every day of their lives as the place and time in which they are free to learn. To respond to their broad interests, we have arranged for our children to meet regularly with Mr. Jack Friedel, a certified teacher and natural scientist, and are including other subjects, such as photography, film animation, and zoology, in our study plan. Whereas our daily activities will not follow a set pattern, over a period of days or weeks all of the various subjects will be studied and discussed.

We have found that our children learn most readily and with retention when they have a need to know something and an opportunity to assimilate in experience what they have learned through their own initiative. One example was our daughter Celia's difficulty learning to write cursively. Despite daily attempts, little progress was made. We discontinued the writing lessons for a period of time until Celia asked us to help her learn cursive writing again. This time, with her own initiative as the key factor, her progress was rapid. As another example, Celia did not seem to recall the various ways of telling time when working in her arithmetic workbook. Her interest in the exercises was minimal. On her birthday, however, she received a watch as a present, and the next day was able to recite the time accurately and with no difficulty at all. Similarly, a page of arithmetic problems holds little appeal to Celia, yet when working out a purchase, budgeting her allowance, keeping track of a game score, or measuring an object to construct, her interest is high. Celia especially looks forward to selling berries next summer that she is helping to grow in our garden and handling the cash flow herself. The practical application of arithmetic in her life stimulates her toward achievement.

It is the close and continuing relationship we have with our children which enables us to observe their growth in skills and comprehension without the use of standardized, routine testing. ... Although quantitative testing may be the most practical method of charting students' progress in school where a high teacher-student ratio exists, it is not necessary in our own situation.

A tremendous amount of confusion shadows the issues of competency and accountability, all pointing to the difficulties of measuring a child's needs and development in a system of mass education. New standardized tests are being devised to determine at a late stage in a child's school years what his classroom teachers would be able to ascertain at every grade level if more individualized attention were possible. Testing itself is not necessarily an accurate indicator of a person's knowledge or capabilities. The tensions and pressure of the testing process itself are enough to obscure facts from memory. The language of tests is often ambiguous, so that more than one answer would seem logical to someone who has not acquired "test consciousness" or does not have the cultural bias which would point out the best answer. Tests are designed to cover a certain area of knowledge, but one is not given credit for knowledge outside of that area. Even the state of one's health and mental outlook on the days of testing can make test scores vary widely.

It is the objectives of testing, however, with which we primarily disagree. Because of the administrative difficulties of mass education and its underlying assumption that children must be taught something in order to learn it, it is deemed necessary that by a certain age a certain body of knowledge must have been accumulated. This premise denies the individual differences between people, the fact that many children are not ready to learn certain things by a certain age, and that children have the capacity to learn independently. The fact that a child does not know a particular math skill or history date by age 7 or 8 does not mean that he or she will never know it. Conversely, that a child does know that skill or date at age 7 or 8 does not mean that he or she will retain that knowledge into adulthood. Indeed, when a child is especially motivated to learn something, the material that would normally take years to cover repetitiously in public or private schools can be assimilated in a matter of days or hours.

A natural approach to children's learning does not force facts and skills on them before they are ready, but allows their own interests and talents to lead them into areas of knowledge and provides them with assistance and resources when they are asked for. Having been read to frequently, our daughter Celia began to recognize words when she was three years old. I decided to enlarge this ability and sat down with her intending to teach her how to recognize other similar words. This first and only "reading lesson" lasted five minutes; Celia closed the book and said that was enough. She simply was not ready to be taught, and yet, before she was five, she learned to read on her own. The first book she read unassisted at age four was *Curious George* by H. A. Rey, a book on the first or second grade level. At that young age she was able to read as fluently as most adults. Still there are words to figure out and questions to ask which we are more than willing to answer. We provided her with reading materials, the time to read aloud to us, verbal language games, and the answers to her questions. Because we did not compel her to read, but rather supplied the opportunity to do so, her ability grew at a tremendous rate. Given this approach to learning and instruction, we feel that the only legitimate form of evaluation is qualitative and descriptive rather than quantitative.

. . . We have not felt right about sending our children out of our home to be influenced in their formative years by people whom we do not know personally and whose morals, values, and political and religious beliefs may differ from ours. Once a child starts school, the home becomes school-centered, not family-centered. The hour before school getting ready, the six hours of school, the hour or two of unwinding afterward and the hour or more of homework later in the evening leave little time for parents and children to communicate and involve themselves jointly in activities not directly related to school. We do not feel that this amount of routine and regulation is essential to education *per se,* but rather is the outcome of attempting to teach large numbers of people with few teachers. The necessity for control and discipline outweighs the energy devoted to discovering and meeting each child's needs.

We began to read material relating to our situation and have found reassurance in both federal and state court rulings that our decision to educate our children at home is a constitutionally-protected right and that our actions are within the law. In a 1923 decision the United States Supreme Court stated:

"Corresponding to the right of control, it is the natural duty of the parent to give his children education suitable to their station in life. . . ."

In 1925, the Supreme Court held:

". . . The fundamental theory of liberty upon which all governments in this Union repose excludes any general power of the State to standardize its children by forcing them to accept instruction from public teachers only. The child is not the creature of the State; those that nurture him and direct his destiny, have the right, coupled with the high duty, to recognize and prepare him for added obligations."

In 1944, the Supreme Court said:

"It is cardinal with us that the custody, care and nurture of the child reside first in the parents. . . ."

This decision also recognized ". . . the private realm of family life which the state cannot enter." In 1965, the Supreme Court stated that ". . . the right to educate one's children as one chooses is made applicable to the States by the First and Fourteenth Amendments."

In 1972, the Supreme Court noted:

". . . The history and culture of Western civilization reflect a strong tradition of parental concern for the nurture and upbringing of their children. This primary role of the parents in the upbringing of their children is now established beyond debate as an enduring American tradition."

A U.S. Supreme Court decision of 1972 reads:

". . . a State's interest in universal education, however highly we rank it, is not totally free from a balancing process when it impinges on fundamental rights and interests. . . ."

This decision also says:

". . . however strong the State's interest in universal compulsory education, it is by no means absolute to the exclusion or subordination of all other interests."

The situation as the courts see it, then, is that both parents and the State have an interest in the education of children, that the State must be cautious in its use of the police power, and that it is the goal of education more than the means of obtaining it which is crucial. It is not only our own rights as parents, but also those of our children which we feel obligated to uphold. . . .

In this matter, you as the Superintendent of Schools, the School Committee, and we as the parents of our children all have the same goal in mind, that is, that our children be educated. We hope that we have made it clear to you in this letter that our children are being educated, that the manner in which they are being educated is of their own choice, as well as ours, that the Massachusetts Supreme Court respects that children need not be educated "in any particular way," and that the U.S. Supreme Court recognizes that parents have "the right to educate one's children as one chooses."

We have made a detailed presentation of the facts and our beliefs to assure you that our actions are sincere and within the law, and that in cooperating with our plans to educate our children, you are satisfying the State's objectives and interests. We do not wish to go to court; the courts are overburdened already. Yet we do believe that our position would be upheld.

. . . We thank you for your concern and again assure you that our deepest commitment is to our children's welfare.

This news item from Wisconsin shows that sometimes state authorities (as in Vermont) will approve home schooling:

PARENTS GET PERMISSION TO TUTOR
THEIR OWN CHILD

The New Lisbon School Board, at their meeting Monday night, were informed by a letter from State Superintendent of Schools Barbara Thompson, that permission had been given to a rural New Lisbon couple, Mr. and Mrs. Tom Spicer, to educate their son, 8-year-old Jacob Spicer, in a home tutorial program, rather than to send him to school.

The letter from the State Superintendent told the Board that any family who prefers to educate their own child, may be given permission under the provisions of Wisconsin Statute 118.15(4), providing the curriculum drawn up by the parents is approved by the Department of Public Instruction. Such permission is given for a one-year period. . . .

A mother from New Jersey describes the persistence that may be necessary before schools will cooperate:

. . . I chose, before my oldest child was old enough to go to kindergarten (she is nearly 8, so that was spring 1976), to ask school authorities what the law was in regard to kindergarten and to tell them that I did not expect to send my child. (I had made the decision about no school before she was born.) Since the compulsory attendance law in N.J. starts at 6, there was little they could do anyway. I also went to the library . . . and studied the law myself.

. . . Since "they" obviously knew about us, I contacted the school in early 1977 to tell them what we were considering. They responded by suggesting that I come to the local elementary school (just down the street) and let the principal talk with me and show me the wonderful school they had to offer.

I took this opportunity to be quite frank about my concerns, also stressing how difficult it must be for schools to meet the needs of every child every day and expressing my concern for my own children's development myself. I also implied that I would be willing to go to court to gain the right to raise my own children, mentioning I knew people all over the country who would be very interested in a case like this. This was mostly bluff at the time (I now have a lawyer and could fight it), but the schools were afraid of the publicity. Many of my objections were "conservative," but my knowledge of what schools are doing and my willingness to speak out about it did make them uncomfortable. I object to schools acting as agents of social change and I let them know this. I should add that I was very nice about all this. I made it clear that if they left me alone, I'd do likewise to them.

Promptly after that meeting, I let them know that my mind had not changed. Up to this point, except for this meeting and a thank you to the principal for his time, our contact had been on the phone.

I then called and asked what if anything I had to do in order to comply with the law. I should mention that I do not think I would have called again had the law not been kind to us as unschoolers. I also have my teaching degree. I think I would have gone pretty far, however, to secure the right to do this.

. . . The local officials . . . asked for our program. To that point we had only enrolled the children (I have another girl a year younger, as well as a 3-year-old boy) in the Calvert School, for "enrichment." We decided to continue with Calvert for a while, and I planned an elaborate program which I thought would be necessary to fulfill their expectations. Although the program looks detailed, we do not follow it all that closely. I am more structured than many unschoolers and place a high value on learning, but I refuse to regiment our lives needlessly. We try to explore all the subjects we are supposed to cover, especially if the children decide to pursue something further. And I do feel there are some things the children should be learning as they grow and I help them do this.

I avoid what is obviously too unpleasant or needless, however, as it is as unpleasant for me to make the children suffer as it is for them to suffer.

However, back to the point. The program was submitted in March and by July after numerous phone calls and questions on my part, they gave me their official OK. There has been very little contact with the authorities since, other than to let them know each year that we are continuing. They have come to our home, at my invitation. We happen to have a room in our basement we use as a "schoolroom." In it are three desks, purchased from the school system for two dollars each—rejects which are perfectly good for lots of things besides schoolwork. We have pictures, mostly by the children, on the walls, maps, a globe, lots of art materials, books, magazines, and other "school" objects collected there. When the school people come, the children are there doing their work. . . . It is very effective.

We have found that this room, as it is the kids' and has most of our art supplies, is used a lot for their crafts and fun—activities which they direct themselves. I appreciate having all the mess in one place. The desks make good tables and are very useful for storage. This might be unique in our town,but the school system sells old desks and chairs, many in very good condition, to get rid of them. I simply called the school number and asked if they did this. They told me who to call, and we are quite happy about it. Of course, since my children never went to school, these desks don't represent school to them; they represent very useful pieces of furniture.

At the moment, the relationship with school officials for us is very good. . . . I have always been courteous to school officials and given them as much credit for what they are doing as possible— even though I hate what they do in most ways.

I do know that while the local board of education actually does not care that much about what we are doing and they approve it formally, the school personnel hate it. However, no one has ever allowed this antagonism to surface—they are in fact very friendly to us. A neighbor happened once to run into one of them at a dinner, however, and was astounded at the expressions used to describe us. Especially since he knows that our children are very happy and well adjusted and are doing fine.

From the *Cape Cod Times,* June 22, 1979:

An aquarium sits on the kitchen counter and colored squares of construction paper line the refrigerator door. A bowl of turtles is on a coffee table in the living room, and a quail cage sits on the fireplace. This is the Mahoney home in Centerville—and it is also the schoolhouse for Elaine Mahoney's daughters, Kendra, 11, and Kimberlee, 9, who are being taught by their mother at home instead of attending school.

The experiment was initiated by Mrs. Mahoney, 31, last September after months of research and study.

"I think, so far, that this is the best way for my children," Mrs. Mahoney says. "There are so many different ways of learning, and it doesn't have to be confined to the four walls of a school, five days a week for nine months. Education is not something that should be done to you, but something that you do."

Mrs. Mahoney's . . . criticisms of the Barnstable schools, however, are not an attack on the administration or teaching staff. Instead, she is more concerned with the structure of public education itself.

"The Barnstable system is the closest to the kind of schools I'd like my children to attend," she says. "The school committee and staff have been very receptive to my children's needs and to my ideas. But, I'm looking for a special way of educating my children, by assuring their independence, fulfilling their individual needs, teaching them through experience and pacing their work accordingly. The school tries to match learning and individual development but this is impossible in a classroom of 20 students who all make demands on one teacher. . . ."

Consequently Mrs. Mahoney, who is divorced, approached William Geick, Assistant Superintendent of the Barnstable Schools last spring with her proposal.

"Mrs. Mahoney came to me not as a parent angry at the school system, but as a parent with a different philosophical approach, based not only on her opinion but on sound recommendation," Geick says. To his knowledge, Mrs. Mahoney is the only parent on the Cape who has suggested and carried through with a plan for home education. . . .

"The duty of the school is to act in the best interest of the child," Geick says. "In that respect, Mrs. Mahoney's program seemed sound, and her criticisms of her children's previous educational experience were valid ones."

Although the children were never individually consulted by school officials, before approval of the plan Geick said that they felt confident that Mrs. Mahoney knew her children's needs better than anyone.

"All we can do is guide their education, and act on good faith. In Mrs. Mahoney's case, this has had a very positive result."

Geick and Mrs. Mahoney then presented her proposal to the five-member school committee, whose reactions were mixed in the beginning.

"I wasn't very receptive to the plan until I met Elaine," said the head of the committee. "She impressed me as a serious, conscientious woman who was able to give this time to her children. It's quite a responsibility and we felt she could handle it."

A major concern of the committee was not only the quality of education the children would be receiving at home, but also the social disadvantage of their not attending school with their peers.

"Children must learn to live in large groups and interact. In that sense, we didn't want to see the children hurt by a home education plan," [the chairperson] said.

However, through a written contract between the Barnstable schools and Mrs. Mahoney, a flexible plan for home education was agreed upon and is reviewed annually for renewal. For academic guidelines, Mrs. Mahoney is required to rely on a certified teacher. . . . Mrs. Mahoney is also relying upon the Calvert School instruction booklets, a prescribed home teaching program, as a backbone for teaching the basics. She says the children are drilled at least three hours a day in reading, writing, and arithmetic.

"Since I only have a high school education, I'm learning with my daughters," she says. "If I feel inadequate in a subject matter, I go to outside resources, particularly in the community." When her daughters expressed an interest in electronics, Mrs. Mahoney took them to a sound studio.

The school committee has made it possible for the Mahoney children to attend special programs offered in Cape schools in order to round out their education and provide opportunities for them to socialize with their peers. In the past year Kendra and Kim have attended school workshops in solar energy, wood carving, beekeeping, jazz, and arts and crafts. Both are members of the 4H Club and the YWCA and Kim is currently the only girl on a Little League baseball team.

"I think the girls are interacting as much as ever with kids their own ages," their mother says. "In fact, even more, because they have met many new people, from classmates to community members who have opened their doors to us."

"Elaine has sought out more resources to teach her daughters in nine months than most teachers do in four years," [a special education teacher] says. "I'm amazed at the number of things she's thought of. When the children express an interest in an area, she picks right up on it, whether it be marine life at a beach, or physical fitness. They go, and do, and see, something that public schools just can't do when on a strict class schedule." . . .

When the school committee reviewed the Mahoney's progress this past month, they were unanimously pleased with their achievements. They were particularly impressed with a scrapbook the girls had made illustrating a year of activities. Although the girls were not graded, they will be required to take the Iowa Basic Skills Tests.

"Learning goes on every hour of the day," Mrs. Mahoney says, "so how can you grade or test that accumulated knowledge?"

She indicates the reactions of parents in the community were mixed. "Some were very supportive and others angry or fearful because my way of educating is threatening an established institution."

Kim notes that her friends called her "a lucky duck" when they learned she's been staying home all year to learn.

"When they find out the things we do and places we go, they want to go too."

And the future? Mrs. Mahoney plans to continue teaching again next year. In fact, the girls will still be "in school" this summer on a lighter schedule so they don't have to review in the fall.

"I'd like to go on doing this for as long as we can." But after next year, Kendra will be of junior high age, so an entirely different set of circumstances may enter into their decision.

"I might want to go back to school then," Kendra says, although she adds she sees her friends all the time. "It'll be my choice." . . .

So far, no other parent in the Barnstable school system has approached the administration with an alternative education plan. "We regard it as a valid premise, although what follows is no snap decision," Geick says. "But, we are pleased with the Mahoney family."

Mrs. Mahoney only has words of praise for the school committee. "I respect them because they care. Because of that, anything is possible. I'd like to see more parents and children attempt this system and I encourage other parents to come to me for suggestions."

REGISTERING AS A PRIVATE SCHOOL

Sometimes a single family can register as a private school without much difficulty. Karen Demmin wrote from Illinois:

Last September many of us in our area pioneered keeping our children home from public school. Our family (children 7 and 4) registered as a private school. The form was very simple—didn't ask about "staff" credentials at all. I am the "teacher" without a credential. In December the State Board of Education came for a visit. They asked questions like "How many hours do you spend in formal academic lessons?" The superintendent of this region told another family that a child getting one-on-one instruction didn't need 5½ hours a day and couldn't be compared with one instructor in a room of 30 children (one-on-thirty). We spend about an hour or so "practicing" reading or arithmetic most mornings, and they suggested we schedule more time. Another question: "What texts are you using?" One we use is Dr. Seuss's early readers—they thought they were fine.

They did ask why we didn't want to send the kids to public school and I answered "Too many children, and restrictive environment." I used basic ideas from *Instead of Education* including the idea of a "club" for exploring and learning unpressured. I was never more diplomatic in my life!

. . . They seemed happy with a journal where I jot down what projects or learning goes on—especially the spur of the moment question/answer, "Mommy, how do you make clothes?"

It's been a month now and I haven't heard from them pro or con. But another family took the route of advising the superintendent that they were keeping their three children home (ages 9, 12 & 14) and asked for the school board to okay their curriculum outline. These folks talked to the superintendent in person and his words were ". . . Well, I believe in public education or I wouldn't be in it, but you do have a legal right to teach your children at home." Those words brought a sigh of relief from a lot of people around here.

This same family also had a visit from the state board with much the same questions and results. Neither of us have been contacted since. . . .

A mother and former teacher from the Midwest had useful help from a local teachers college.

. . . Last summer after profuse study, *GWS* included, we made the decision to educate our three children at home (7th grade boy, 5th grade boy, 3rd grade girl). My husband and I are ex-teachers, four years each in the early 1960s. (We hesitate to add that fact as we don't feel being a teacher is necessary. In this state it helps.)

We approached the administration with our plan—Calvert Home Study. According to the state's definition, Calvert isn't a school. Administration suggested we become a school by becoming recertified teachers. Then as we travel about (which we do a lot) our school could go with us.

Thankful to have the chance to educate our own children without legal hassle, we decided one of us would take classes (6 hours) for recertification.

Desiring to be consistent in our philosophy of education, we wanted to be able to have some choices in what we studied. We feel you can educate yourself better than any institution but I (not my husband) would have been willing to be led back into the herd to avoid hassles and just take standard courses.

I was told to take "800's" courses as these would qualify for recertification. Among these classes we found Independent Study Courses. I was excited. I could decide what I really wanted to learn, get a faculty member to guide me and allow me to pick his or her brain, and become legal, all at once!

It all worked out beautifully except for a slight problem. When I went to register, I found Independent Study Classes wouldn't be acceptable for recertification.

At the onset of our inquiries we had already spoken with the Dean of the Teachers College and he supported our ideas by sending us to like-minded faculty members. (Note: we have often found the people at the top to be very open and understanding. Don't overlook them if you have a problem with an institution or the like.) A phone call to the Dean at this time resulted in settling the problem of having Independent Study accepted for recertification.

I am now registered to take six hours of Ind. Study with two professors. My areas are adolescent development with a reading course set up to develop as we go along. My second area is computer use in education. My goals at this time are to become computer-literate and determine the strengths and weaknesses of computers for educating our three children at home.

Right now, I truly feel "This is the first day of the *best* of our lives."

A success story from Arkansas:

> . . . With the start of the new year we took our three children out
> of public school. We followed the procedure suggested by Hal
> Bennett in *No More Public School* (Berkeley, Calif: The Book-
> works), sending a letter to both principal and homeroom teachers,
> explaining that the children would no longer attend that school and
> had been enrolled in a private school. Everything went very
> smoothly, with which we are very pleased. This is a small commu-
> nity, pop. 5,000, and the news about our kids out of school spread
> from people just being curious to people wanting to do the same
> thing. Some people wondered which private school they were at-
> tending as there are only two small parochial schools in the area.
> We explained to them that we had enrolled them in the Calvert
> School which is a correspondence school that offers a home study
> program, and that teaching my own children was something I had
> been wanting to do for many years and felt the time was right for
> us to take this step.
>
> The law on school attendance in Arkansas says that children
> need to be enrolled in a public, private or parochial school. On
> further checking with the State Department of Education, I found
> out that a private school need not be state approved and there are
> no rules governing unapproved private schools, except that it would
> be expected that the private school work toward state approval.
>
> . . . There are several other unschoolers in the area. One family
> who took their child out of a neighboring school several years ago
> had a lot of trouble including having to go to court. Eventually the
> case was dropped. This year two other families took their children
> out without any resistance. We are very pleased to see this coopera-
> tive attitude. . . .

A friend, whose large family has had a number of unschooling
experiences, explored the same route in Pennsylvania:

> Our fifth child was five when we moved to the commune. He had
> had a few months of kindergarten—which he loved—but we could
> already see the effects of acculturation on him—e.g., increasing
> possessiveness, preoccupation with money and spending, giggling
> attitude towards sex and nudity, sassy, silly, rebellious patterns he
> was picking up from the other children. We were eager to get him
> out of school and keep him out.

We investigated the laws in Pennsylvania, where our commune is located, and found that one could not qualify for home instruction unless there were evidence of physical, emotional, or mental disability—and if one so qualified, the system would send instructors into the home (which we wanted no more than we wanted him to go to school). So we applied for a license as a private school with one student. We had plenty of people with credentials on the farm, plenty of educational materials, and we were amused and confident as we filled out the elaborate forms asking whether the boys and girls had separate bathroom facilities (we have a two-holer, one marked *men* and the other *women*), and so on. . . . We complied with the most absurd inquiries.

. . . Nothing happened. For nearly six years now, nothing has happened. Our application, with its $25 fee, apparently is sitting in the back of the file of the Head Honcho of Private Schools in Harrisburg. . . . Each fall—at least for the first three years or so— the local superintendent would send us a letter demanding that we report where our school-age children were enrolled, and we would reply that he was enrolled in our private school, and tell the superintendent that if he had any questions he should consult the State Department of Private Schools. . . . Recently he has stopped asking.

Richard and Joyce Kinmont of Utah sent me a copy of their book, *American Home Academy* (privately published, see Appendix), about how and why they unschooled their children and began teaching them at home. Many unschoolers, above all in Utah, will find it very encouraging and helpful. It is partly philosophy; partly a day-to-day account of what they did with their children, the most detailed and useful I have seen; and partly an account, again very detailed, complete with copies of letters from both sides, of their dealings with the school authorities. The Kinmonts also called their home a private school:

If you decide not to enroll your children in the public school system, your local district may feel faced with a problem. At best they may be honestly concerned that your children are being well taught. At worst, they may feel threatened by your automatic no-confidence vote and the money their district will lose by not having your children enrolled. In either case, they will probably feel that they hold a stewardship over you. Do they? Should they?

Certainly they shouldn't. If the public schools held stewardship over private education, there really wouldn't be any private education. Who, then, should hold stewardship? Who will check to see that the students are being well taught? The answer is, the private schools should answer to the same people who are now checking on the public schools to see that they are teaching the children well —*the parents*. If the parents don't take the responsibility, no one else can. Both public and private education must answer to the parents!

. . . If your school board feels obligated by the compulsory attendance law to know that you are in fact teaching your children, and if they are well motivated, it should be easy to satisfy them. If they are really interested in stopping you and in possessing all power, you will have a more difficult—but not an impossible—time. . . .

Here is Mr. Kinmont's first letter to school authorities, in this case the state board of education:

This letter is to inform you that we have established a private school, known as ———, located at the above address.

Our school is in operation at least 180 days per year, at least 5½ hours per day. Our curriculum includes reading, writing, math, social studies, music, art, physical education, science, health, crafts, industrial arts, fine arts, free enterprise, and the Constitution. The student body consists solely of the members of our own family.

To the best of our knowledge, this letter completes our legal obligation. If there are any further requirements *established by law* [Author's note: Mr. Kinmont emphasizes this point in all his letters to school people], please let us know and we will promptly comply.

Later in the book, Mrs. Kinmont makes this important point:

A few weeks after this visit [from school officials] I received from a friend . . . a message from an attorney that I should under no circumstances allow any school administrators into my home. I now see that this is very good advice. It would be nice to believe that these men are really only trying to help, as they say they are and as they should be, but we must be prepared for the possibility that they are really looking for ways to intimidate. In every case I know of where they have been allowed in, it has worked out badly for the family involved. Since this advice was unsolicited, and from a good man, we will heed it.

The following letters from Mr. Kinmont to the Director of Pupil Personnel of the local school system seem to me a model of what such letters should be:

Thank you for your letter of. . . . We believe it would be most beneficial to be able to insure that our program is giving the equivalent of instruction required in public schools. In order to do this, we will need the following:

1. A copy of that part of the Utah Code which identifies the instruction required in public schools.

2. A copy of the public school curriculum by grades.

3. The minimum learning requirements in each subject.

4. The final examinations which determine that the minimum information has been learned.

5. A description of the action taken when a student does not meet the minimum learning requirements in any subject.

To further insure that we will be in compliance with any possible future court decisions, we would also appreciate receiving the following:

1. The full text of the Attorney General's opinion.

2. The qualifications you would require of a private school teacher if that responsibility were ever legally granted to the District.

3. Copies of the laws you mention relating to health of children, construction of buildings, course of study, etc. . . .

We appreciate the kind tone of your letter. As my wife informed you on the telephone, however, we no longer feel a personal visit to our home would be necessary or appropriate.

We would be happy to inform you about our courses of study. We cover a great many subjects; and you are, of course, only concerned with those courses which are required by law. So if you will please provide us with a copy of the law which identifies the required courses, we will be happy to provide you with the information you requested.

To insure that we have met the minimum standards of the public schools, we do want to set up some minimum learning requirements and testing procedures for those courses prescribed by law. Again, we are awaiting information from you as to what these classes and the minimum standards are. . . .

Some final remarks by Mrs. Kinmont:

If we should ever be required by a court of law to enroll our children in the public schools, we would do so. But I would continue to teach them during non-school hours, *and I would spend a great deal of time in their school classrooms* [Author's emphasis].

This little book is not meant to be a tirade against the public school system. No matter how great their schools were, we would still want to teach our own children. Ours is much less a step away from the public schools and much more a step toward family education. . . .

I do strongly recommend this book. Joyce Kinmont said to me in a letter that if she were starting all over again, knowing what she does now, she would do much less teaching, less planning of the children's learning. But that is all right. Parents who start to do this have to do it in a way that makes them feel comfortable, otherwise their worries will worry the children and the whole thing won't work. If it gives parents a little needed security at first to say that we will have reading at 9:00 A.M. and arithmetic at 10:00, that's okay.

After I appeared on the Phil Donahue show in 1979, I received through their office another booklet on home schooling, along with a letter from the author, Mary Bergman, who is now editing the *Home Educators Newsletter*. The booklet is called "Legal Papers and Letters Used for Establishing Pioneer Trails Academy". It is from this book that Richard Kinmont got the text of the letter that he first wrote to the state board of education; I gather that the Bergmans have been schooling their children at home for longer than the Kinmonts. Mary Bergman says, ". . . We use these books with seminars for setting up families into schools. *This summer we established over three hundred home schools.*"

ENROLLING AT ALTERNATIVE SCHOOLS

One of the ways in which people get their children out of school is by enrolling them in a private school, which may be in another town or even state, which then approves and in varying degrees helps to plan and supervise a home study program. The school that has been doing this longest is the Santa Fe Community School (see Appendix). I asked Ed Nagel, who teaches there, how many people have used the school in this way. He replied:

> Re home-study students enrolled at Santa Fe Community School, since 1974–75 we have enrolled about 100 students, from different states, of whom only three that I know of were ever challenged. One was Eric Sessions (still enrolled). Another was the child of a lady from Pa., on whose behalf William Ball [Author's note: probably the most informed and experienced of all attorneys favorable to private and/or home schooling—he was the lawyer for the Kentucky schools in a very important case described in the later chapter of this book] wrote a letter, obtaining a substantial delay of any action against her. Later she returned her child to school. Actually the child was never formally enrolled at SFCS during this period. The third parent was fairly mobile; when her child's "attendance" was challenged in Pa., SFCS wrote a letter verifying her employment with the school as a supervisor of off-campus travel-study. This satisfied the local superintendent and ended any further queries.
>
> There are others, occasionally, who attempt to obtain a legal "guarantee" from the local public school officials—asking the "boss" in effect if they can undermine his operation—and who, failing in this, become intimidated and soon retreat from their position. Or, they may *move,* literally, to another area or state where they may then proceed less conspicuously to provide an educational alternative, in some cases, at least, through SFCS.
>
> As I write, it occurs to me that there may have been another challenge, but NONE of the parents whose children enrolled at SFCS have ever had to go to jail, or paid a fine (the unenrolled child's parent from Pa. paid a fine, as I recall, *prior* to Ball's intervention), or lost a challenge throughout this five-year period.

Currently, there are between forty and fifty students enrolled in home-study programs through SFCS, several within our own state. Of these, I would estimate about ⅓ have been enrolled for more than two years now. Of the many alternative schools doing this in other states which have been made known to me—roughly thirty —only three have given me permission to put searching parents in touch with them and then only under certain conditions. No one wants to go to court; not the parents, not the schools, not the public officials who can manage to keep the news and noise down about the few "unusual" arrangements they allow within their district. . . .

In this connection, quite a number of parents have told me that they had had their children out of school, often for some years, and that their local schools, even though they had not formally approved this, almost certainly knew about it and had been willing to let it go on, *as long as nobody complained.* But as soon as some nosy neighbor reported to the schools that some children were not in school, the school officials became very nervous. They seem to fear that someone will say publicly, "How come you let those people get away with not sending their children to school?", and that if they can't answer they will get in some kind of trouble. Quite recently one superintendent told a mother, when she said that she wanted to teach her children at home, "I'm not going to jail for you." This seems to be their extraordinary notion of the law: If you try to teach your kids at home, you go to jail, and if I let you teach your kids at home, *I* go to jail.

What we need is not just an answer that we can give the nosy neighbors, but one the schools can give as well. Perhaps if the schools could say, "We know about those children, they are enrolled in a private school and we have nothing to say about them," it would solve their problem, and so, our problem.

The mother from California who in Chapter 1 reports that she never saw anyone using the resource centers in the "open classroom" later wrote us:

> I told the teachers and principal that we would soon be moving and that L would be enrolled at [a private school in the area]. Transfer papers were rapidly issued and we walked out—free!

L went through a few days of sadness about leaving "her" school, but soon began doing math games, drawing great pictures, reading a biography of Thomas Jefferson and a book on astronomy (she's 6!).

[A few months later] I got in touch with a free, open school I had heard good reports about. They agreed to take my daughter on their enrollment as a "correspondence, home-study student." . . . We lie low in the morning and then if she's asked why she's not in school, she says she's "connected" to the X school. Soon we'll drive there (about 1 hr.) and meet the teachers and set up whatever needs doing to keep the authorities off us.

If I'm accepted at the university, we'll be moving there and I'll neglect to enroll her anywhere, continuing her X school thing. Another option possible is to make my home a "field school" of the X school and me their "delegated teacher."

I feel great about the decision and L seems so much less tense and hyped up. The secret, I think, is to not ask anyone for permission—then no one has to say no.

Guess what? *She's not writing any numbers or letters backwards anymore!* [Author's emphasis.]

You were right—The Calif. State law is *very* lenient regarding private schools and very vague about what constitutes one.

WHEN THE SCHOOLS DO NOT COOPERATE

More from the Indiana mother of Chapter 1:

We contacted a young, interested, and sympathetic lawyer who after some research found out that Indiana requires school attendance except in cases where the child is so physically or mentally handicapped that he/she cannot attend. Then, the child must be taught in English by a certified teacher and receive an education equivalent to what he/she would be getting in the public schools. Our attorney also discovered that "equivalency" has not yet been established in Indiana.

On his advice we had P tested by a child psychologist to assure "the authorities" that he had no emotional or mental disorders. Next we secured a first grade curriculum from a correspondence school and had it evaluated by the Dept. of Education at a local university.

Four weeks after we began our campaign, we flew with our lawyer to Indianapolis to meet with the superintendent of Indiana public schools. He was stone-faced and unsympathetic and told us that if we took our son out of school we would be prosecuted. Later on during the interview he *did* tell us of a couple of Indiana families who had removed their children from schools for religious reasons and, after a court hearing and some investigation into their home schooling, had been permitted to teach them at home. My husband told them that we had hired an attorney and had gone to great lengths and considerable expense to remove our son from school as discreetly as possible. He felt that if this whole thing hit the newspapers the school district would be the ones to suffer, not us. I guess that the superintendent must have agreed, inwardly, for he directed us to the State Attendance Officer. She was sympathetic but not hopeful. She suggested that we meet with the local attendance officer and tell him of our plans, hoping that he would wait a couple of weeks before handing us a citation.

Two weeks later we had interviews with the attendance officer and the superintendent of the elementary schools. We found out later from our lawyer that the officials in Indianapolis had called the local officials advising them to let us take P out of school. An emergency meeting was called and it was decided to let us go ahead with our plans without prosecuting. This did not mean that they were happy about it! The school superintendent was alternately distraught and angry. He wound up, however, begging me to let P try any school in the city—they would forego the usual zoning restrictions for him. But it was too late for that. P hated any mention of school. The fact that neither my husband or I are teachers and have never even taken an education course was never mentioned. (We do both have master's degrees.) So, we were free to take him out of school provided I sent a monthly attendance report to the local officer. . . .

To show how different things may be from one part of a state to another, here is a letter from a mother in Illinois, a state in which a number of families have been able to unschool their children without great trouble:

The first meeting with the principal and N's teacher was not good. The principal refused to transfer N because Santa Fe Community

School was not on the list of approved schools in Illinois. I was lectured on the inadvisability of home study, including all the classic statements such as, "We have certified teachers to do that, what makes you think you can teach him? What are your qualifications? Do you know how much money we've lost due to N's absences already?" (They knew down to the penny.)

Asked what I would do about teaching N reading I replied that he already reads and now needs the space to do so on his own. I was nearly laughed out of the room and told that I obviously didn't know the fundamentals of reading and could not teach it to N. N's teacher told me with great concern that there is no way that N could pass a test to get into third grade if he did not remain in school (her school, of course) for the last few months of the year. (Strangely, there is no such test for children passing from one grade to the next.) I won't carry on about this meeting further except to say that I did expect to meet with resistance but was still amazed to be treated with total lack of respect.

My next meeting was with the Assistant County Superintendent. He was more calculated in his response. He informed me right away that it was impossible to teach N at home, that it was against the law, and that we were violating the truancy law by his absences and would be prosecuted for it. He quoted that statute which says, "Whoever has custody or control of any child between the ages of seven and sixteen years shall cause such child to attend some public school in the district wherein the child resides." I informed him that the statute goes on to exempt "any child attending a private or parochial school where children are taught the branches of education taught to children of corresponding age and grade in the public schools." He then immediately contended that we were not providing N with an equivalent education.

The issue shifted quickly here. I was prepared to explain our program for N but he was not interested in hearing about it. Instead he simply declared that our program was not equivalent because we did not use the textbooks N was using in public school. I said that I had tried to get the names of the textbooks from the school but they had not cooperated. He said, "The school doesn't have to cooperate." He then told me that I would be subjected to an (oral) master's degree level exam before he would be convinced that I was qualified to teach N. He referred to all these mystical things that only teachers know, about the components of learning and how the branches interrelate. He stated that the school would have to meet the provisions in the School Board Document #1. Later we found this is totally untrue, that it is a completely different and more lenient set of rules than Document #1, which is for public schools. The proper document is "Policies and Guidelines for Registration and Recognition of Non-public Elementary and Secondary Schools."

In a later phone conversation my husband was told that a "bank of six lawyers" in Springfield (the capital) had told the A.C.S. that home schooling was clearly illegal.

Meanwhile my husband had stopped at the public school to get N's workbooks, which the teacher had refused to give me, saying, "Why should I give you his workbooks; I consider N to be truant." We also requested to see N's records and to make a copy of them. We were refused. My husband then requested that a record of this refusal be put into N's record at this time. The principal refused to make this a matter of record. My husband wrote out a note himself and asked the principal to include it in N's file. The principal refused. My husband said he would leave it on the principal's desk. The principal replied that he had never seen the note and that it did not exist. My husband then went to the front desk and asked the person there to be aware that the note was left in the principal's office. The principal ran out of his office to say that this person could not come into his office and that the note did not exist.

Fortunately, with your good advice, and the help of a friend who is an ex-teacher, now chicken farmer, still certified in Illinois as a second and third grade teacher, we put together a convincing package to present to the officials. It helped that our attorney had paved the way with some blunt statements to them. By this time *someone* had given them the word to change their attitude and approach and they did their best to cooperate. Dr. H. told us as we were leaving that he was sure N would get an excellent education from us, but he had trouble getting this out audibly. When my husband did not quite hear all of it and asked him what he had said, he almost died and simply could not repeat it.

We found your advice to keep a telephone log of conversations and to ask many questions and get it clear what each person's interest is to be very valuable and in keeping with my husband's approach from the legal angle. It is exactly the way we proceeded, after bungling the beginnings, that is.

This painful experience certainly confirms what a number of people have said. Once it becomes clear that your schools are not going to cooperate, all your dealings with them should be in writing. If you can't avoid a personal or telephone conversation, then try to tape record it. If you can't do that, take detailed notes as you go along, saying if need be, "Wait just a second while I write that down," and going to some pains to get the words straight—"Did I understand you to say . . . ?" Then as soon as possible after these conversations you should write a confirming letter, saying more or less, "This is my understanding of our conversation of today (give date). If it does not agree with your understanding, please let me know in writing as soon as possible how it differs. Unless I hear from you, I will assume that your understanding of this conversation is substantially the same as my own." This puts the ball in their court; if they say nothing, your version goes down on the record as the official one. If they want to change your version of the record, they have to put their own version in its place. Either way, they are committed to something.

There are more suggestions about dealing with uncooperative school systems in Chapters 13 and 14.

OTHER TACTICS

Readers of *GWS* have tried many different approaches to keeping their children out of school. One mother wrote:

> After being turned in last winter (we got out of that one because the oldest wasn't yet at the compulsory age in this state) we decided to do a little smokescreening, so enrolled them at a private school, and they started school in September like everyone else, as visibly and audibly as we could manage—new clothes, lunchboxes, much talking about it with neighbors, etc. Then we quietly pulled them out. We don't do anything foolish, like let them wander all over the neighborhood or go to town in the middle of the day, and so far, so good.
>
> I think the private school tactic was good, not only for the obvious reason, but because it offers us a broader margin of safety

with the neighbors' suspicions. Holidays, "early dismissals," even "special programs" are all unknown to the neighborhood—much more is "legitimate" before it becomes reason for suspicion—like being seen not in school at an odd time.

Deborah Jones in Nevada tried still another tactic:

> We went for the medical exemption in the compulsory education law. Our doctor agreed to help us and sent a letter stating that our children were hyperactive and that he recommended I keep them home to take care of this problem. This threw me for a little loop. If there had been more time, I probably would have sent the letter back and asked for a different diagnosis, and under any other circumstances I would have fought that diagnosis tooth and nail. But under the circumstances, since I very much agreed with his recommendation, we decided to send the letter. We sent an accompanying letter stating that we would keep in contact with our doctor, that we didn't feel it would be necessary for the school board to meet with our children, and that we felt we had fulfilled the requirement of the law.
>
> We have not heard from them since. At first we were in suspense, expecting a letter, caller, or subpoena any day. But eventually we decided that they must have been satisfied. We have taught our children at home these past months and have found it rewarding and worthwhile. I still need to learn a lot about it but feel that even if I don't do anything, the children would be better off just being home than in school. Thank you again for your help. . . .

A mother in Arkansas writes of a rather different tactic:

> . . . Gena was six years old and still not in school, because Arkansas law says children must begin compulsory school attendance on their 7th birthday. I researched state law and local school policies to find out how I could MINIMIZE SCHOOL ATTENDANCE.
>
> I did several things before Gena's 7th birthday:
>
> 1. I taught her study methods that would enable her to work in workbooks without much instruction or supervision. Examples: circling important clue words in instructions; crossing off answers already used when all answers are provided in mixed-up fashion; doing what she KNOWS first so she can find right answers to what she doesn't know through a simple process of elimination, etc.

2. I went to the school and discussed the whole situation with the person I thought would be most helpful and understanding; in this case, the instructional supervisor, who is still the person who makes it all possible for me.

3. I had the instructional supervisor inventory Gena's reading ability, and I saved the inventory results for future documentation.

4. I decided which teacher would be right and saw to it that Gena got that teacher. Schools will generally [Author's note: well, sometimes] let the parent choose if they do so before school actually starts.

Gena started out in an advanced reading group, but before long I asked that she be allowed to work independently in reading because, since I taught her to read by Kottmeyer encoding methods, the decoding methods taught in the reading series couldn't help her learn what she already knew, and could only confuse, at best.

Permission was granted to work independently; good-bye reading groups—hopefully forever. She just does the workbooks with my assistance and the instructional supervisor tests her out of that level when I say she's ready. I asked for a copy of the reader, but she is not required to read from it or answer any "comprehension" questions. She reads what she wants to read, in or out of school, and we usually discuss her current book.

As I mentioned earlier, I researched state attendance laws and local attendance policy. Any school district should have a book of school board policies: parents should know this! State law allows 25 days' absences, and local policy says a student who leaves school after 10:30 will be counted ½ day absent, so theoretically that's 50 days she's allowed to leave at 10:30, although I didn't use that many.

State law only considered two types of absences: parentally caused absence and truancy, which is when the parent thinks the child is in school and he is not. State law gives the parent complete control over deciding whether the child is truant or not, inasmuch as they require a written statement from the parent saying that the absence is the fault of the child before they will prosecute for truancy. This is important to know because the local school district has lots of policy concerning "acceptable reasons for being absent" and "counseling for more judicious use of absences" and giving the impression that the school can declare the child truant, but it is all a lot of baloney for psychological effect. When I write a note to the school, I just say "Gena was absent on (date)," which shows it is a parentally-caused absence and not a truancy.

Once Gena had established that she was working above grade level in all subjects, I started taking her out every day at 1:30, because students who leave after 1:30 aren't counted absent at all. Even if she ever became in violation of the 150 days compulsory attendance requirement, and was referred to the prosecuting attorney's office (truants—so declared by the parents—would be prosecuted in juvenile court and parents causing more than 25 days' absences would be prosecuted in probate court), there is some question in my mind as to whether or not the prosecuting attorney would *choose* to prosecute under the circumstances. Prosecuting attorneys like to win cases, and the fact that I can so well *document* the fact that Gena is working above level, and she is, after all, enrolled in the school and continuing to attend, *might* make the case seem a little pointless and ridiculous.

Anyway, now it was time for Gena to start second grade. My conversation with the instructional supervisor went like this.

Me: Could you test Gena out of the third grade level workbook in reading during the first couple of weeks, and ask the teacher not to put her in any reading, spelling, or math groups? Also Gena wants to learn cursive now, so I will be teaching her that for the next couple months. She won't start working in *her* third grade spelling workbook until she has learned cursive, because she wants to do it in cursive.

Her: Fine!

Me: I think she is ready to test out of the second grade math book, but she has gotten to the point where she will not do all the problems and assignments, because once she knows how to do the work, she rebels against having to do tedious and repetitious work, and I want her to stay interested and not get turned off!

Her: Yes. Once she knows it, it's just busywork. I'll talk to the teacher. Will you be sending things for Gena to do to school each day?

Me: Yes, but she'll be doing music, science, and social studies with the class.

Her: Okay. I'll talk to you about testing next week.

This is NOT a liberal school district; the superintendent has extremely tight control. This school district has one of the toughest attendance policies in the state. So we are getting by in spite of a very tough attendance policy here. I go to school board meetings so I can get a *real* education regarding what I would be up against if it ever comes to a confrontation.

I'm afraid I've given the impression that Gena spends most of her time drudging in workbooks. Actually, she does a week's worth of work in the time the teacher allots for a day's worth, so many days she doesn't work in the workbooks at all. She might read a book, or just play, or be absent. She really likes and needs the spelling and penmanship workbooks that *I have provided* and that she takes to school (they will provide *consistent* lessons through the eighth grade, whereas the school may adopt a different series in a few years). She completed one reading workbook in a week this summer. We don't take the reading workbook skills seriously—just "do the page." In reading and math, she is just doing enough to learn the skills taught in the book, to be tested, so she will spend a lot less time doing assignments than most kids.

The important thing to the school is that her progress is tested and documented, and the important thing to me is that she still wants to learn.

So that is our story. It is not an unschooling story. But I wonder what would happen if the schools had to deal with a lot of students who were "working independently above grade level and had very poor attendance records"?

A UPI release from Providence, Rhode Island, tells an unusual "unschooling" story:

A 14-year-old boy who skipped high school and has been pulling straight A's at Rhode Island Junior College [has been] allowed to stay in school while authorities test him to see if he is smart enough for college.

Jonathan Dellinger graduated from Cranston Junior High in June. The state said an education law prohibits the boy from leaving high school until he is 16.

But the boy enrolled in the college's continuing education program this fall and was getting A's in Spanish, introductory chemistry, algebra, and fundamentals of writing when the college forced him to withdraw Oct. 8.

Jonathan and his mother sued the college, contending his constitutional rights were violated when he was expelled because of his age.

Under the agreement announced in Superior Court Thursday by the State Education Department and the boy's lawyer, Jonathan will be allowed to take courses at the college for one semester.

In the meantime, he will undergo tests at the University of Rhode Island and lawyers for both sides will file written arguments within two weeks on whether the case [Author's note: I assume this means his mother's suit] should be dismissed.

"I can't wait to get back to classes," the youth said after the court settlement. "All my friends are there. It's the first school I've gone to where I felt I really belonged."

An amazing story. The schools have some test which they say is a "good predictor of college success." That means, most of the people who score well on the test later on get good grades in college. So now, with perfectly straight faces, they are going to give this test to this boy, *who is already getting straight A's in college,* to find out whether he is smart enough to go to college!

But this does suggest another way in which children who are good at school (know how to play the school game) might get out of one or more years of high school. Indeed, one reader of *GWS* told me that during her high school years she was able to get out of going to high school by taking extension courses at the state university. It seems to me very likely that most courts would agree that a child who was taking college courses and getting good marks was getting an education "equivalent" to that provided by the local high school, and therefore need not attend that high school.

5

Home Schoolers at Work

In the following letters some parents give answers to the question, "What do people *do* once they get their kids out of school?"

FOLLOWING A CHILD'S INTERESTS

Art Harris wrote of his two sons' unstructured learning:

> . . . We did not draw up a curriculum, a study plan, or an outline of courses. Such moves are the first step in *formalizing* the learning process, whereas we feel the best learning takes place informally. The narrow structuring of the school courses has always appalled us. Who are these schools to decide that architecture, archaeology, anthropology, astrology, or astronomy (to take only the A's) don't belong in the elementary grades? We believe that all subjects fuse and interlock and the mere definition of a subject is the first step in taking away some of its mystique. For the joy of learning (remember that?) is in discovering—even in discovering subjects—and in satisfying one's curiosity.
>
> More for appearances than anything else, we borrowed some of those dull textbooks and readers from our school-assigned advisor, stashed them away, and proceeded on our own—or rather, I should

say, our two boys proceeded pretty much on their own, for all too often an adult gets between a learner and the material.

Perhaps I sound vague about this. There's a reason. We simply left our oldest boy alone. He read, sometimes eight to ten hours a day. He watched some TV, went to a fair number of movies. With no adults around to order him, to test him or spoon-feed him, he delved in metallurgy (his interest in cycling got him into this), nutrition (on his own he became a vegetarian), architecture. In fact, you name it, chances are he was into it—geology, Zen, meteorology, etc.

Yes, we bought a few books, but mostly he used the library. Nobody taught him the Dewey Decimal System; he learned it because he needed to find books. Sometimes a radio or TV host would discuss a book with an author on tour. More often than not the host had not read the book, but (to the surprise of those who feel TV kills reading) our son often went to get it from the library, even if that meant paying 25 cents for a reservation.

Shortly after he turned 17, our oldest son took his high-school equivalency test and scored well in all areas. He promptly got his high school diploma. The very first college he applied to, Bard College in New York State, accepted him and gave him a full scholarship. I had always said an admissions director would be enchanted with the idea of accepting a self-educated child. He began college this fall.

. . . Our other boy developed in a way that gratified us. It took almost a year of not doing very much at all for him to shed the school-instilled idea that he was dumb. I think our six-month trip to Mexico did much to dispel that notion, for of the four of us he learned the most Spanish. Nobody "taught" him a word of the language—he just picked it up along with a lot of confidence in himself.

We put absolutely no pressure on him to read. True, we bought a few books on dyslexia and by using their suggestions helped to introduce him to simple printed words. And when others his age got interested in comic books, he really wanted to read. Only then did we make a big effort to help him. He still reads below what the schools call "grade level," but that doesn't bother us. . . .

A few years ago, when his son was about seven, Albert Hobart, whose experience unschooling his child was mentioned earlier, wrote the schools, telling how he and his wife worked with the boy:

Language Arts

Robert expresses himself quite well verbally and, considering his age, he has a broad vocabulary. We're not sure how much of this is a result of our efforts, but we make it a point to always speak to him as clearly as possible and to explain any word or phrase he asks about. He has not shown a direct interest yet in learning to read, though he knows all the letters and the sounds they make and can figure out most simple words. He regularly takes books home from the library, and he's enthusiastic about having us read them to him. Sharks, dolphins, planes, and rockets are his favorite subjects. He also asks us to read the captions under an interesting photograph in the newspaper. He often makes his own books by drawing or cutting out and pasting pictures, and he asks us to write down the story as he dictates it to us. He can identify and print all the letters of the alphabet quite legibly and sometimes prefers to write the words in his books himself if we tell him how they are spelled. He has an old typewriter he uses to write the alphabet or to invent new words, which he asks us to pronounce. Over all we think Robert is building a strong foundation for reading and that when the proper time comes he will find it a relatively easy task.

Math

Robert knows the value of numbers and can write the numerals. He can do simple addition and subtraction, and he can count to 100 with a little help. Although we occasionally ask him to add or subtract, our main approach at this point is to play games together which involve numbers, such as Sorry, Dominoes, Battleship and simple card games. He's also interested in the sort of number games one finds in the comics of the Sunday papers or in children's "activity" books. From time to time we use a pocket calculator together, and he's developing a familiarity with spacial concepts by observing and helping us with a number of activities which involve measuring, such as carpentry and concrete work. He also has a collection of blocks, Tinkertoys, Legos, and an Erector set, all of which he uses regularly.

Art

Robert is very interested in drawing. He was particularly inspired by Patriot's Day and the history it commemorates, and he's made numerous drawings and a diorama of the Battle of Lexington. He's also developed competence with other materials we have provided for him—colored pens, paints, scissors, paper, cardboard, glue, clay, etc. He has his own toolbox and can build simple projects, such as a boat he made recently.

Science

Robert is interested in the outdoor work we have done around the house. He is particularly involved in our vegetable garden. He knows the names of all the plants and often observes them more closely than we do and reports to us on their condition. He saved his own seeds from last year's fruit, planted them this spring, and has actually grown a tasty watermelon. He has seen us spraying our apple trees and helps us pick the apples, blueberries, raspberries, and blackberries around our property. He helps us prune trees and build our compost pile. He learns a lot from television. Among his favorite programs are "Crockett's Victory Garden," "Wild Kingdom," and Jacques Cousteau's expeditions. We also make visits to the Aquarium, the Museum of Science, and the Museum of Fine Arts. Robert is learning something of animals firsthand since we have a dog and two cats. Also he's interested in the animals that live around our house, especially the birds and toads.

Social Studies

Robert has enjoyed watching and talking to different workmen who have come to help us renovate our house. They've often been very helpful in explaining what they were doing, and thus he's learned quite a bit about various occupations. We make an effort to take him with us on any errands where he might have a chance to learn something. Recently he's developed an interest in maps and he often puts together a map puzzle of the United States.

From a later letter to the schools:

So far as our teaching is concerned, we do very little in the way of formal instruction, first, because he seems to learn quite effectively without it, and second, because his academic progress seems like such a minor aspect of his overall development. What we do instead is simple and relatively effortless.

First, we provide him with the materials he needs to learn with. These include such things as paper, pencils, pens, art materials, books, magazines, good toys—the sort of things many parents get their children anyway.

Second, when he has a question or needs help with something, we try to assist him, but no more than necessary.

Third, we're patient. We don't expect him to learn anything he's not ready for.

That's all there is to it. We probably don't spend more than twenty minutes a day helping him with the traditional school subjects, and the help we give him is the same kind of help most parents give their children even if they are going to school. If he asks us, for example, we might read him a story, or tell him the meaning of a new word, or answer a question about numbers, or listen while he talks about a new project he's involved in or reads us a story.

Actually the way we handle our son's education now is the same way we've handled it right from the beginning. We haven't changed anything just because he's reached "school age." From our own experience we've become convinced that most parents who have done well with their children up to the time they would normally be entering school could continue teaching them afterward with little difficulty.

Incidentally, we're aware that our approach may not sound much like teaching to some people, but we think it's best to let children take the initiative so far as possible in their own education. If we make a mistake with our son, it's usually because we've been tempted to give him more help than he really needs, not less, and to try to interest him in activities he's not ready for yet. Fortunately he's not bashful about complaining when we overdo it.

Our biggest problem as far as his instruction is concerned is that we've sometimes lacked the courage of our convictions. When he was old enough to be a first grader, for instance, he had no interest at all in learning to read. We were well aware that every child has his or her own timetable for learning such skills, but we were also aware that many children his age in school were well into their first year of reading, and we were concerned that the school authorities might check up on his progress and discover he was "behind" his grade level. Fortunately our common sense prevailed, and we didn't pressure him in any way to learn to read. The following summer he suddenly became interested in reading, and now with seemingly little effort he has learned to read as well as most children two or three years older than himself.

UNSCHOOLED DAYS

Judy McCahill wrote about her first home teaching experiences:

We are using the Calvert Home Instruction courses—because we said we would. But we are not using them the way they were intended to be used. For one thing, they are highly structured, so well organized that any dummy who can read could use them with his child. If they were followed faithfully, there would be no time left for teaching, that is, being there when a child needs help in learning something. I've been in a quandary several times and I've tried to teach a child something he either already knew or wasn't ready for. All in the name of following the curriculum and staying on schedule. And my heart really isn't in it. I think, for instance, that doing a scheduled lesson on the Industrial Revolution, which right now is utterly boring, when you've spent hours over the last few weeks watching and discussing the Rome of "I, Claudius," is stupid. You scribble some hasty answers to questions about the Industrial Revolution and you forget all about it.

But I am getting smart and here is basically what we do about "education." At the beginning of each month the children each make and decorate a folder out of 12-×-18-inch sheets of construction paper. We fill the folders with paperwork, including the tests which Calvert provides; we never send these in to Calvert since we are not using the Advisory Teaching Service. This "proves" that we are keeping up in (almost) every subject. There is not nearly so much paperwork done as Calvert demands, but every paper is perfect. When the children make mistakes, they erase and correct them immediately. I make no traditional teacher's marks on their papers such as X's, checks, happy faces, etc.; but I dispense National Wildlife Stickers freely. (I hope I am teaching them that mistakes, in work and in life, are not irrevocable; and though I don't know if it means anything, I like the idea of keeping reminders of myself off their work.)

Many of the drawings that they all do spontaneously at the

dining room table are put into the folder in case anyone wonders if we are having "art." If on a school day we go somewhere "educational," we paste a souvenir of the trip on a piece of colored paper and include it. The two older children each keep a list of pages done in separate workbooks and include these in their folders. So we actually look pretty good, even if we aren't. And the filed folders at month's end, which we ritually arrange and staple, seem to give the children a sense of accomplishment.

What I would really like to do is put all the Calvert courses out in the rain. (The children keep them in their original cartons.) For one thing I am really too busy for all that nonsense, between housework, normal family activities, and a couple of my own interests, and for another I think it is an empty ritual.

From time to time I keep some notes on academically related activities which the children do spontaneously. Here are the notes for one day:

Colleen (then 12) taught Michael (then 9) and me to play "Go Fish" and "Concentration." She asked if "Concentration" helped in life.

C and I played gin rummy.

Sean (then 7) worked on crossword puzzles.

S read *Put Me In The Zoo* silently twice, then aloud to Kevin (then 5).

When asked, C, M, and S each helped with chores.

C tested her memory of names of states (45/50) and their capitals (35/50); invented charades to describe three countries.

M showed S placement of U.S. and England on map (which hangs on wall).

C read *Rocky* and we discussed possible jealousy of Stallone's wife.

I played "War" with K and used phrases "greater than" and "less than."

S read aloud phrases on back of Ivory Snow box.

S went out to play in his knight's costume (homemade: result of reading about knights).

I read *Little Toot* to M and K; M asked questions about vocabulary.

S and I discussed bees (when the queen flies out of the hive; how bees aid in pollination) after he got stung by one.

M counted his money.

Also from that week:

M cut open avocado seed and we discussed seed coat, embryo, seed leaves and true leaves.

K built aircraft carrier with blocks.

S made reconstituted juice, reading label to determine amount of water to add.

C suggested own math project, figuring cost to carpet upstairs rooms.

I took C to Self-Sufficiency seminar at community college.

S and K read *The Question and Answer Book of the Human Body.*

C took her and S's temperature.

S used tape measure to measure several objects around house. He reported lengths and widths in both centimeters and inches.

C read *The Metric Book of Amusing Things to Do,* and did an exercise with curves and straight lines.

C continued with her project to average a book a day for a month for the Mental Health Read-a-thon. The most serious books included *David Copperfield* and *Treasure Island.*

We went to the library.

We toured the replica of the Santa Maria in the harbor.

What is important to remember about these activities is that because they were self-initiated they were meaningful; that is, because they fit in with an on-going and/or current interest, what was learned is not likely to be forgotten. This deepened my curiosity about what the children would teach themselves if they were freed from imposed schoolwork entirely. Hopefully, next year (if we are stationed abroad) I can move toward satisfying this curiosity.

More learning comes out of just plain talk that can be imagined. I hung M. C. Esher's "Verbum" (a black and white print of a repeated design in which frogs gradually turn into fish) on the dining room wall and several conversations that started with "How did he draw that?" occurred, and careened wildly through design, artist's materials, optical illusion, evolution, and the Gospel of St. John. With Colleen, I can see the encrusted layers of school-rigidity falling away; several times a lesson with her has dissolved into a conversation about her real worth as a loving, responsible human being versus the graded, classified, surely stupid person she sometimes felt herself to be in school.

In *Blackberry Winter,* Margaret Mead (who did not attend school regularly until she was eleven) said that children used to be brought up by means of stories. I thought I'd like to try that with my own children but didn't know how to start until Sean began to ask me questions last summer about the origins of man and the universe. He would ask me, "How did God make Adam and Eve?" or "How did God make the earth?" Knowing nothing, I knew everything, and I began to enjoy answering his questions, which I did with stories. One evening as his father was tucking him into bed he said, "You know, Daddy, every day I ask Mommy how you make things—and she always knows the answer!" Sure enough, the next morning as soon as he awoke he sat up and asked me, "How do you make stones?" My knowledge of geology is scant, but I managed to bring the earth from big hunks of rock through earthquakes, thundering ocean waves, etc., to little stones, which by the way are made of minerals like gold, copper, and calcium. He nodded his head, satisfied, and lay back on his pillow.

When Kevin asked me where he came from, I followed the advice of A. C. Harwood (who was writing on Rudolf Steiner's philosophy of education) to tell the child a truly spiritual story of his origin and not to get bogged down in biological details. He loved hearing what went through God's mind as He decided where to send a little blond baby. I included some biological details, too, but we had already discussed them several times (on his level, of course). He was delighted.

Nancy Wallace writes:

... A few words about our school. Every morning we practice our French, play the piano, and do some writing—letter writing, journal, poetry, etc. Every evening we read aloud to Vita and Ishmael for about 1½ hours. And in between? Ishmael takes two drama classes, a French class and a piano lesson for 1-hour periods once a week, we go to the library, explore the woods, observe nature and read (Ishmael reads for about three hours a day).

... We never ask our kids to do things that we don't do ourselves, and consequently we inspire each other. We *all* read a lot, we *all* write a lot, we *all* speak very broken French, we *all* practice the piano, etc. People are often amazed at how "selfless" I am. They think they could *never* spend so much time with their kids, do all the necessary preparation it must take to "teach" all those subjects, etc. Actually, I have never been so self-indulgent. I always wanted to learn French and take piano lessons and when Ishmael asked to do these things, I knew that here was my chance! As for math, I can barely balance our checkbook, so I enjoy learning along with Ishmael. And he teaches me spelling and history (don't tell!), so I am feeling very alive and full. And I can't even begin to tell how much Vita benefits. She's only 4, but she keeps right up with French and piano and is beginning to read and loves numbers. . . .

A reader in Alberta writes:

. . . A competitive game S (8) enjoys is chess. We both learned at the same time last year using a child's chess set with the moves marked on the pieces. When we play we both play to win but I allow him to change his move if he realizes it was a mistake after removing his fingers. I nearly always win but he makes me think very hard in order to do so. He does not get upset about losing because he is not made to feel inferior because of it—I tell him he played a good game and that I enjoyed it.

Another competitive game S likes is Pick Up Sticks; this game we play on our honor, i.e., the player decides if he has moved a stick, not the opponent. However, if a person is cheating a great deal, the other player may refuse to play anymore.

A card game he has enjoyed since the age of 4 is Slap Jack. Although all these games have a winner and a loser, we enjoy them because there isn't a great deal of emphasis placed on whether or not you won—the main thing is playing the game.

A cooperative game we play is what we call tennis, only we don't use a net or court, just a paved area. The object of the game is to see how long we can hit the ball back and forth without missing.

S enjoys mazes and designs his own. I have also taught him how to play Solitaire. A good game book is "Deal Me In" by Margie Golick (Jeffrey Norton Publishers, N.Y.).

A father writes:

I have found your newsletter increasingly interesting and valuable. As I wrote to you about a year ago, I will not be sending my children to school (the oldest, now five, would normally be entering Kindergarten this September). He has been reading now for about a year. I would not have believed anyone who told me a child could make the kind of progress D has made. He is interested in space travel and astronomy and we have made available to him all literature on the subject we could find. He gobbles it up at an incredible speed and begs for more. He reads books about the planets and can discuss intelligently the effects of gravity on the various planets and moons (e.g., that the moon has no air because it has insufficient gravity to hold the air, and that on Jupiter he would be squashed flat).

A mother, in what she describes as "a born again Christian family," writes:

> Finally, we settled in on a one-day, one-child routine. One day I would teach John all his subjects, while Jim was to read and match all his spelling words. He could do the reading and spelling at any time of the day or evening as long as he did something; the rest of the time he could play and do what he wanted. The next day I would work with Jim, and John would be free. They really liked this, and since they enjoy reading and spelling, this was no burden to them.
>
> Many people who knew we were doing this asked if we set up "School." No! We started our day around 9 A.M., since that was when we all were finally up and finished breakfast. It would take us about three hours to do the day's work, and the rest of the day the boys were free. Some days we took off completely to go places of interest to *them*: playing in the local park, going to a peanut butter factory nearby, and visiting McDonald's for a tour and some goodies. Since we considered life-learning and learning-life, school was always in and always out. It was great!
>
> We did not work at a table or desk; we bought each of them a notebook and we sat on the sofa together and held our books on our laps. (It is wonderful to be able to sit next to your own child and touch arms and hug if you want or wrestle and still get work done.) We could yell and cry and laugh, we could read with the most ridiculous expressions whenever we wanted and no one cared.

EXPLORING TOGETHER

A mother writes from Ontario:

> About helping children make books—I really enjoy getting together with a young friend or friends, folding several pieces of paper

into the size and number of pages that we want, cutting edges where necessary. Next we either staple or sew a binding. If we want to we add a cover (not always needed). Covers are easily made from pieces of wallpaper books. (Wallpaper books are a great free source of beautiful paper for all kinds of projects!) Or a cover can be a piece of cardboard folded and covered with cloth—glued, stapled, or sewed together with the pages.

So now we have a book or books. We work on them together or individually—whatever we feel like at the time. Often the children draw pictures in their books that go with a story they are making in their minds. After they have drawn the pictures they tell me what words they want written on each page, and I write the words. Some children of course can write their own words. Some of the children like me to write out the words on a separate paper for them to copy. Some books just have drawings. Some even remain empty. Sometimes several of us work on one together. Anyway, they're usually a lot of fun to make and read or look at.

One of C's books had a beautiful white satin cover. He made himself a quill pen from a chicken feather. This book had to be drawn and written with a quill as it's a story set in the Middle Ages, about two mice princes who are cousins and have adventures with a blimp, a rat, and a lovely kangaroo. I've decided to make marionettes of the characters in this story which I'm in the process of doing. C has helped with some of the sewing and shaping and drilling of the wooden controls for one of the mice. B plans to help make the kangaroo.

A friend recalls her own freedom to explore books, thanks to a childhood illness:

I was a bouncing child until I had measles at four. . . . After that, my temperature was erratic. At that time normal temperature was supposed to be 98.6°, with no recognition of a normal range of variation. Any deviation had to mean something bad. Mine would go up to 99.2° in the afternoon.

Sometimes they would be told to keep me in bed until my temperature had been normal for three days. If that had ever actually been done I'd be there yet. The longest I was ever in bed was three months. After a while they'd try letting me up for half an hour a day, and gradually I'd work back to normal activity, except for not going to school, until someone would take my temperature and put me back to bed.

I always took a pile of books and *National Geographic* magazines to bed with me, and of course writing materials. I kept my poems and stories hidden until I got into college. I still like to curl up in bed with a book or a clipboard.

Aside from the few compulsory books and a little while with Mother or Father on arithmetic a few times a week, I was free to explore the world of ideas. The little Carnegie library in town was my oyster, and I had the freedom of my parents' bookshelves. Later I learned the resources of the college library. Whenever I was in school I was amazed at the inane level of the reading done by my classmates.

I suspect that my mother was glad to keep one child out of the school's clutches. She used to say that vacations were just long enough to get the kids civilized, and then they'd go back to school and be savages again.

She encouraged the memorizing and "spouting" of poems or dramatic scenes that we liked. No one was allowed to ridicule this. She also encouraged all kinds of things to develop physical coordination, bouncing, juggling, balancing, etc. . . . . I kept notebooks in which I meticulously copied poems and quotations that I liked before returning books to the library. I didn't realize until much later that my mother had initiated this idea in the belief that mastery of the language came from familiarity with it, rather than from the study of grammar and composition. Copying fine literature, comma for comma, gave me a grasp of sentence structure and punctuation such that I never needed to learn English grammar— a monstrosity invented by Latin scholars who tried in vain to force the language into the classical mould. . . .

I should mention my effort to learn to read. I don't know how old I was, but since I was reading books at four it must have been fairly early. I decided that it was time to learn to read, so I asked my mother to read me *Beauty and the Beast* every night. I thought that by watching the first and last words that she said on each page I would learn a lot of words. It didn't work. When she asked me why I had to have that story every night I told her what I was doing. She said it hadn't worked because she turned the page several words before her voice got to the end. Being thus alerted that I was ready for reading, she began to cooperate with me, and helped me in various ways so that I soon learned.

One of the finest features of not going to school was being able to get absorbed in a subject or project for a day or a week without having to keep skipping to something else every time the bell rang. I could spend uninterrupted hours memorizing a poem or building a birdhouse or taming squirrels.

I did have to read the school books, but they could be finished within a few weeks. I'd put them in a basket with a long rope, climb a tree, pull the books up, and sit reading in the branches. Even geography went pretty fast that way, though the book was deadly dull compared to my National Geographic magazines.

In my second year with my French tutor, when I could read any textbook in French fluently but was still stymied by French literature, I was consigned to bed for a while. I asked my father to bring me *The Three Musketeers* in French from the library. I had read it in English, and the story was lively enough to carry me over any tough spots. I just read along, ignoring things that weren't clear, until the rhythms and patterns of the language became my own, and from then on I could read anything.

As long as I worked at home my standard was perfection. I didn't think I had done anything until it was done right [Author's emphasis.]. When I was admitted to college, and for the first time had to cope with academic work of some substance, I soon found that if I hadn't done an assignment no one knew the difference, and the class went right ahead. Being human, I soon became a shrewd bluffer and goofer-offer, spending my time reading, writing, hiking and philosophizing with friends rather than working on my courses. In most courses if I listened well in class there was no need to read the book at all. . . .

Jud Jerome writes about using textbooks:

. . . I wanted something to work on algebra with Topher. . . . We are finding that, in general, though they are in themselves pretty terrible, college texts are about at the level that "elementary" students find the material interesting. There is enough in the content to engage them so that they can concentrate on the processes. This is true even of literature: Sandy read and discussed a Hawthorne story recently with two 7-year-olds and an 11-year-old and found they had the important ideas even though they didn't know all the vocabulary. I could give many examples of how this works at various ages with various subjects, but, anyway, I tried this two-volume programmed text on algebra. Topher started and got bored working alone, and by working with him I could easily see why, as the text is endlessly repetitive, going over the same thing again and again with slightly different wording, apparently in the effort to drum it into heads of young people being cattle-prodded through junior colleges. It wasn't appropriate for Topher, who still takes adults and learning seriously. So by working with him I showed him how to skip ahead ten or twenty pages at a time, read a question, see if it was still obvious, and if it wasn't, go back a few questions to see where the necessary information was included. In a couple of hours we were able to cover a hundred pages this way. . . .

UNCERTAIN BEGINNINGS

A mother writes about difficulties when home schooling begins:

The first couple of months of home schooling were rocky. P, relieved to be out of the formal school situation, went along with a fairly rigid home schedule for two weeks. Then it was nothing but rebellion. I think the only thing that made him go along with any reading, math, science, etc., was the fear that he might have to return to school. I overorganized his days and weekends with activities including children his own age, so afraid was I that he would end up some sort of weird recluse.

Along about mid-Feb. I re-read *Summerhill* (A.S. Neill. New York: Hart Publishing Company, 1960), and *The Children Played* (Jondry. Plattsburg, N.Y.: Tundra Books, 1975), and your book *How Children Learn.* I re-read some of the *GWS* issues and gradually have come to my senses. Some mornings we have "school," some mornings we don't. We visit museums, libraries, farms, and parks. We go to the movies. We meet my husband for lunch and go horseback riding. At home P builds villages with his Lincoln Logs, plays in his treehouse, skateboards, rides his bike, plays with his dogs, jumps on the trampoline, paints pictures and (sometimes) practices his violin. Last winter we sledded every day. Late in the afternoon our backyard is the gathering place for youngsters of all ages. During a recent trip to Florida, P was as much at ease with adults as with the vacationing youngsters in the hotel. So, I let up on the forced sociability along with the unreasonable academic demands. The books are there when he wants to look at them and now that I am no longer pressuring him, he wants to learn.

From a later letter:

Many people have asked me if I used a curriculum with P and I did—this past year, from the Home Study Institute in Washington, D.C. . . . I was not planning to use a definite curriculum this year but I have changed my mind, simply because I think it is a good idea to have some textbooks around in case the school authorities start snooping!

I wanted to tell you of our experience with P and a compass. A few weeks ago he bought a small camper's compass with money he had earned doing chores. We took a walk around the neighborhood with the compass noting how our direction changed although the needle always pointed north. But this was not enough. P wanted me to explain the numbers along the edges of the compass and wanted to know exactly how they were used. I referred him to his father and they spent hours working out hypothetical "problems" on paper. During this time P asked me to read to him from our encyclopedia about compasses. There *we* learned that the first compass (1000 A.D.) was merely a magnetic piece of iron stuck into a cork floating in water. P proceeded to unearth two nails from our basement, both of which had some magnetic qualities. He stuck one of them in a cork so that it was evenly balanced, filled a bowl with water and—lo and behold!—a homemade compass that actually works!

Later my husband drew an intricate compass course which P followed with very little help, at the end of which he found a dollar bill "prize" in our mailbox. My husband tells me that he didn't know that much about reading a compass until he was in the army. (He never was a Boy Scout.) . . . I am hoping that eventually we will have several unschoolers in our area. It will then be easier to exchange ideas and, perhaps, to organize a day each week when the children can be together. . . .

The following excerpts are from letters written by one *GWS* reader to another. They describe very well the uncertainties that some parents feel in the early stages of home schooling:

May 23 . . . There are still several issues to settle. The biggest is whether I want to take care of my own children full-time; whether it will be mutually beneficial. I would like to think yes, but there are times when a week of vacation seems too long. Perhaps that's because we aren't used to always being together. My preferred course of action would be to send Phoebe, my eldest, who is in first grade, for the music-art part of the day and keep her home the rest of the time. A half-day away would be fine: she still would have the energy when home to direct her own activities.

. . . We have two other children. Jennie is 3½ and so has one year before she would enroll in kindergarten. Nathaniel is 8 months, and it was because he was born that I was glad to send Phoebe off last fall. He is older now, my perspective seems different. . . . I am slowly thinking of withdrawing Phoebe next year and trying a year at home. If it doesn't work out, I'll let her go back the next year when she and Jennie would go off together. With no alternative school close, this is a very hard decision for me to make.

. . . I should add that I took Phoebe out of public kindergarten last year in Pennsylvania when the teacher wouldn't let her read, and put her into an alternative that was *very* exciting growth for mother and daughter. I guess I hesitate now because I have no such "school" to offer.

. . . School vs. no school seems to come down to the issue of having faith in the inherent nature of growing. . . . My faith grows; our family nurtures and helps strong people start.

July 11 . . . We went to the principal and second grade teacher and asked to be able to do home study with Phoebe in the morning and have her attend school in the afternoon when they do a lot of nonacademic stuff—gym and art and music. Today the principal finally returned our call and said that we could do this. We will be meeting with the superintendent of schools, etc., setting up a Calvert program and having a certified teacher check her every two weeks or so and review what she's doing. We're free! I am really hopeful that this will meet our needs—to be more in touch with her growth, make sure she is getting the emotional as well as the academic, and free her to read to her interests and do piano and bake with me (this is how we work on fractions). And half a day is something I can easily live with. . . .

Sept. 14 . . . We have begun our fall schedule of keeping Phoebe at home half the day. I am very happy to have her here but I struggle with recordkeeping to help us justify what we're doing, and confrontations with the principal over testing and so forth. I am somewhat timid by nature and all of this is difficult for me. We are operating on guidelines from the state office of education which allow home study with a correspondence course with "progress" monitored by a certified teacher each month, with written reports to a superintendent each quarter. Our superintendent is most cooperative; Phoebe's principal is still trying to control what is no longer hers to control. . . . She wants to test Phoebe three times a year for reading level and has said she expects to see "more than a year's growth" from Phoebe because she is bright. . . . We have been told that we are a test case in Maine in that we want half-and-half split time, and hence are being "watched closely." What a nuisance!

The time we have Phoebe now is great—she has time to read and breathe and do her own things. I find I struggle with allowing her mistakes in her work—I know that to deal with her long-term I must relax—but I still wonder if she will learn to spell without spelling tests, although she does most other things well. How lovely it is to have her again, even though school has started.

. . . I feel our adventure is well begun. Phoebe is happy and relaxed. And learning. All else is superfluous. . . .

Oct. 16 . . . The reason we sought half-time was because I felt Phoebe was expending too much energy in school and needed more freedom each day; I missed her presence five days a week; and she wasn't being challenged or stimulated enough academically. But, I felt there was some benefit to her being there. I needed a break from all three kids all day, and I think there are many benefits from regular contact with the kids and feeling part of the group. As we get into this plan I have misgivings about trying to mix home and school, and wonder whether we will end up pulling her completely out. . . .

Since September I have had both happiness and sadness over this whole thing. The sadness reflects my uncertainty over what to do (the correspondence course is woefully inadequate) and difficulty standing up to the principal. The happiness is that the routine of Phoebe working with me is getting established and she plods through a little piece of language arts daily and has lots of free time which she occupies very productively. I love watching her creative juices flow. I didn't see enough of that last year: I got only a crab home in the afternoon from school and to bed early in preparation for the next day. (I was amazed that the whole summer passed this year and Phoebe never said she was bored, or asked me what she could do.)

I feel that what we are doing is right. Whether it wouldn't be much better to have her completely free, I can't tell yet. I will hopefully let that be her choice by next year. As it is, she hates school right now. Sheds a few tears some mornings before she goes in. I feel that this may reflect her picking up things from me that she may have overheard in a phone conversation or some such. I used to be very discreet, and not speak of my philosophical differences in front of her at all. At any rate, I am going to bat for the teacher a little, and selling Phoebe on it. I encourage her to talk to her teacher about what goes wrong for her and I think the teacher listens. I'll need more time about that to be sure. Ultimately, if Phoebe still wants out, OK.

Doing half-time in school is almost untenable in a lot of ways. Who would believe in freedom and only half-carry it out? I feel guilty making Phoebe go. (If she resists too much longer I'll have to opt for total home study.) . . .

. . . In ways I don't really want to unschool at all, I just wish there was a freer school available to us. I would like to participate and be respected for my abilities there and have Phoebe and the other kids pace *themselves.* A community. Growth for kids and parents both.

So. A complex picture. Phoebe does "reading" and language arts and art with me and goes to school at 10:45 to join in lunch and recess before the afternoon classes begin. Afternoons feature math, gym, music, and odds and ends. Phoebe is telling the teacher the math is boring and the teacher promises more stuff.

. . . I am just beginning to be comfortable in a formal teaching relationship—though the same rules apply as in the informal one we've been doing for years—I try to quit when I meet resistance. Often it is me, not Phoebe, who flies off the handle. I am learning to expect less. This little 7-year-old body doesn't know punctuation because she's never been told about it or given it much thought. Much, much joy in dealing with her. Jennie, who is 4, *demands a place at the study table* [Author's emphasis] and struggles to read. How nice it is to see the girls together learning. . . .

UNSCHOOLING A CHILD WITH
DOWN'S SYNDROME

A mother who has unschooled her teen-aged daughter born with Down's syndrome writes about this experience:

> . . . As for unschooling L, I had long wanted to do this with my older children, but the time was not right—in the world or in me. . . . Only when it was as obviously desperate as it clearly was to save L from their awful effects was I able to do what I knew was the only way to proceed.
>
> L only once had any special ed. involvement, at a nursery school run by the local association for retarded children, and it was bad to useless. From there on she went to regular schools—private nursery school, private kindergarten, a public school which was running an experimental open primary, and a Catholic private academy. I wanted to keep her out of special ed. situations, which I feel *increase* the degree of handicap by providing handicapped models of behavior. . . .
>
> From the beginning, L and I have planned what she'd do. I collected clippings from all over for a year, then sorted out the ones I could afford, and presented those to her for her consideration. Choices like cooking, horseback, trips to New York and elsewhere, tutoring. We did have to keep changing things when, for instance, a teacher who was going to give her cooking lessons (an overnight deal) got divorced and went to work in New York.
>
> But we kept consulting and revising, and ended up with the present schedule of swimming, ballet, drawing and painting, and needlepoint. There were other considerations besides the learning ones involved too. I felt it was not safe for her not to swim well, and her ear operations had made her fearful of going whole hog on her own. So she has private lessons in that. And I read about a ballet dancer who had taken ballet initially to overcome flat feet, so we began this mainly for that reason. Too, the more I went into it, the more I decided that what L needed was a reprieve from the morass of schoolwork that, in spite of the good-as-possible situations I'd been able to find, was not at all as helpful or satisfying as I felt might

be possible—somewhere, somehow. So I decided not to do anything at all academic for a while. Just say the heck with it.

So we went to the beach in the lovely October and even November weather that had been denied us as prisoners of school, played kickball in the back field, and proceeded with the courses.

On one trip to the shore, paying tolls, it was again clear that L still didn't know one coin from another, so that became the first academic venture. And it provided one of my first principles: though the general ideas are the same for L as with regular kids out of school, certain things have to be done differently. While other kids probably need only a bit of assistance and guidance in following what they learn and are interested in, L really has to have regular exposure. Not lengthy but regular—daily, if possible, including weekends.

Every day I put prices on four things and she worked them out with a plastic measuring cup full of change—a permanent collection of coins. I remember trying to get the school people to have her use real money but they seemed to think that was quaint. They just loved their big cardboard coins. Within a month she had it cold. I switched to numbers on paper, and she could do it that way too. [Author's note: And in the schools we have all those "normal" children who after years of school arithmetic still supposedly can't make change.]

However, a second principle of unschooling with L is this: Like free-lance writing, unschooling is subject to cancellation at any time, whenever somebody comes to visit, or the neighbor's car breaks down and she calls you to go pick her up, etc. Now this is probably one of the advantages of unschooling with other kids— that you can live your regular life and still keep learning. But with L, Christmas, and long visits from my mother, who had not been well, meant a far-less-than-hoped-for routine. I had a hard time concentrating on what I was working on, and L would get tense. Early in our unschooling one of the first things I saw was an increased sense of success—a euphoric "I can do it" feeling, in contrast to the tight lips, lowered head, long hair hiding eyes that had been typical of the earlier work with school stuff. Yet when life got hectic that same posture quickly returned.

I worried about the possibility that it was only the one-to-one situation that was doing the job—and then answered myself that this was what all kids could use. Yet it did seem somewhat unrealistic to try to manage it when life was so uncooperative. I still haven't solved this problem. I suspect it's a problem with others to some degree too, but it's more difficult when the youngster has some learning barriers.

In fact, it seems to me that this question of scheduling is central. I suspect that it's only the school requirements that keep some families at it at all, and that in doing so, they *undo* some of the benefits of trying unschooling in the first place. That is, feeling under pressure to produce for the satisfactions of the schools and their requirements, they may lay a lot of pressure and guilt on the kids.

. . . I feel I have done nowhere near enough in this letter to indicate how enthusiastic I am about the whole unschooling enterprise, in spite of the difficulties I've indicated. L's typing goes well, her needlepoint is terrific (and her instructor is out of her mind with joy and amazement), in ballet she is just barely less competent than the older girls in the class (20–40), and in art, according to her teacher, she is really gifted.

. . . For the past year she's been taking a variety of vitamins, thyroid, etc. She has lost 15 pounds. Weight is often a problem with children with mongolism. She has also grown ⅝", her general appearance has improved greatly, and her intellectual functioning is enhanced. Her art teacher says of her, "This is not the same child I met last fall."

6

Living with Children

CHILDREN, THEIR NATURE AND NEEDS

Many people who quite like and enjoy children still seem to be in the grip of the old idea that in civilizing them we have to give up or destroy some important part of them. To me that idea seems mistaken and harmful. It simply is not true that every virtue is some kind of suppressed vice, or that civilized human beings are nothing but cowed savages. As Abraham Maslow used to say, this explains human virtues only by "explaining them away." Such explanations do not fit everyday experience. A famous child psychiatrist has long been quoted as saying that the infant is a psychopath. I take the side of a mother I know well, who after raising seven babies said, "Babies are nice people."

Paul Goodman once wrote of "the wild babytribe," an affectionate and accurate expression. Children do often seem to me like talented barbarians, who would really like to become civilized. Many free schools, and some kindly and well-meaning parents, have suffered from the notion that there was something wild and precious in children that had to be preserved against the attacks of the world for as long as possible. Once we get free of this idea we will find our lives with children much easier and the children themselves much happier. As I write this, I have spent much time recently with young babies, and my overwhelming impression is that basically they want to fit in, take part, and do right—that is, do as we do. If they can't always do it, it is because they lack experience, and because their emotions sweep them away.

Oddly enough, the reactionary view and the romantic liberal view of children are like opposite sides of the same coin. The hard-nosed types say that to fit children for the world we have to beat the badness out of them. The romantic child-worshippers say that in fitting children for the world we destroy most of the goodness in them. One group claims that children are undersized and defective adults; the other, that adults are oversized and defective children. Neither is true. There really are ways to help children, as they grow, to keep and build on all their best qualities. How we may do this is the subject of this chapter.

We can learn much from *The Continuum Concept* (New York: Knopf, 1975), by Jean Liedloff, as important a book as any I have ever read. Liedloff (along with a number of others—Leboyer, Montagu, Bowlby, etc.) says and *shows* that babies grow best in health, happiness, intelligence, independence, self-reliance, courage, and cooperativeness when they are born and reared in the "continuum" of the human biological experience, i.e., as "primitive" mothers bear and rear their babies, and probably always have through all the millions of years of human existence. What babies have always enjoyed, needed, and thrived on, for the first year or so of their lives, until they reach the crawling and exploring stage, is constant *physical* contact with their mothers (or someone equally well known and trusted).

Babies have always had this, at least up until the last thousand years or so, and each newborn baby, knowing nothing of history but everything of his own animal nature, expects it, wants it, needs it, and suffers terribly if he does not get it.

Here, in only one of many passages of extraordinary vividness and sensitivity, is Liedloff's description of the early life of a baby among the Yequana Indians of the Amazon basin, with whom she lived for some time:

From birth, continuum infants are taken everywhere. Before the umbilicus comes off, the infant's life is already full of action. He is asleep most of the time, but even as he sleeps he is becoming accustomed to the voices of his people, to the sounds of their activities, to the bumpings, jostlings, and moves without warning, to stops without warning, to lifts and pressures on various parts of his body as his caretaker shifts him about to accommodate her work or her comfort, and to the rhythms of day and night, the changes of texture and temperature on his skin, and the safe, right feel of being held next to a living body.

The result of this kind of treatment is not, as most modern people might expect, a timid, clinging, whiny, dependent infant, but the exact opposite. Liedloff writes:

> When all the shelter and stimulus of his experience in arms have been given in full measure, the baby can look forward, outward, to the world beyond his mother. . . . The need for constant contact tapers off quickly when its experience quota has been filled, and a baby, tot, or child will require reinforcement of the strength it gave him only in moments of stress with which his current powers cannot cope. These moments become increasingly rare and self-reliance grows with a speed, depth, and breadth that would seem prodigious to anyone who has known only civilized children deprived of the complete in-arms experience.

As Liedloff shows, children so reared very quickly notice what people are doing around them, and want to join in and take part as soon and as far as their powers permit. No one has to *do* anything in order to "socialize" the children, or *make* them take part in the life of the group. They are born social, it is their nature. One of the most peculiar destructive ideas that "civilized" people have ever invented is that children are born bad and must be threatened and punished into doing what everyone around them does. No continuum culture expects children to be bad as a matter of course, to misbehave, to make trouble, to refuse to help, to destroy things and cause pain to others, and in cultures with long traditions of child-rearing these common (to us) forms of child behavior are virtually unknown.

Some years ago a group of American child experts went to China to study Chinese children, child-rearing, and schools. To their Chinese counterparts they eagerly asked what *they* did when their children had tantrums, fought, teased, whined, broke things, hurt people, etc. The Chinese looked at them with baffled faces. The Americans might as well have asked, "What do you do when your children jump three hundred feet straight up in the air?" The Chinese could only say over and over, "Children don't do those things." The American visitors went away equally baffled. It never occurred to them to suppose that one reason Chinese children are not bad in the way so many of ours seem to be is that nobody expects them to be. Being small, ignorant, inexperienced, and passionate, they may now and then stray off the path of good behavior. But correcting them is only a matter of patiently pointing out that they *have* strayed, that here we don't do things like that. No one assumes that their deep intent is to do wrong, and that only a long hard struggle will break them of that intent and force them to do right.

In short, the problem children of the affluent Western world are as much a product of our culture as our automobiles. What we call psychology, our supposed knowledge of "human nature," is and can only be the study of the peculiar ways of severely deprived people, so far from the norms of long-term human biological experience that it would not be stretching matters to call them (us) freaks. Liedloff's description of "modern," "medical," "scientific" childbirth, and the ensuing days and months as a baby must experience them, is enough to make one weep, or have nightmares, or both. It's a wonder we're no worse off than we are.

But I wish that Ms. Liedloff had said early in the book what she finally says at the end, that some or many of the most harmful effects of severe early deprivation (of closeness and contact) can be largely made up for or cured if a human being is richly supplied with these necessities, in ways she suggests, later in life. This is important. Many sensitive and loving mothers and fathers who bore and raised children in the modern "civilized" way, upon reading this book and realizing what they had unknowingly denied their children, might be almost overwhelmed by guilt and grief. With enough kindness, tenderness, patience, and courtesy, one can make up for much of this early loss.

It is impossible for me to say how important I think this book is. For most of the past twenty-five years it has become clearer to me all the time that our worldwide scientific and industrial civilization, for all its apparent wealth and power, was in fact moving every day closer to its total destruction. What is wrong? What can we do? Many people have pointed toward some useful answers. But only in the last year or two has it become clear to me that one of the most deep-rooted of the causes of our problems is the way we treat children, and above all babies. I am equally convinced that no program of social and political change that does not include and begin with changes in the ways in which we bear and rear children has any chance of making things better.

I hope that many people will read *The Continuum Concept,* the more the better, and above all mothers and fathers of young children and babies, parents-to-be, people who have no children but think someday they might, young marrieds or marrieds-to-be, teen-agers, baby-sitters, older brothers and sisters of babies, and also doctors, nurses, psychologists, etc. In short, anyone who may have any contact with, or anything to do with, babies or little children. The human race, after all, changes with every new generation, and only a generation or two of healthy and happy babies might be enough to turn us around.

BORN KIND

From a letter to an old friend of mine, an elementary school teacher:

> Loved being with your kindergarten class. I don't remember when I have ever struck up so strong a friendship with a child so quickly as I did with Molly. Our conversation was very serious, the kind of talk you might expect to have with someone much older. Above all, I was so touched with her concern about me. At one point— I didn't tell you this—I was squatting down beside a table at which some of the children were working. After a long time I stood up, and as is always the case, I was a little stiff, and took a few seconds

to get the kinks in my knees and back straightened out. Molly and a couple of the others asked me what I was doing, and I explained that when people my age squat down for a long time they tend to get a little stiff. It must have been at least an hour later, when I was again squatting down beside some children, that Molly said to me, "Don't squat down too long." Surprised, I said, "Why not?" She said, "You'll get stiff." I had forgotten all about the earlier time. Then, as I said to you, when she saw where I had bumped and scratched the top of my head a week or so earlier in Maine, she was very concerned, wanted to know how I had done it, and did it hurt. This is much more empathy than I would have expected from such a little person, much as I like them.

The June 1979 issue of the magazine *Psychology Today* had a most touching, revealing, and encouraging article by Maya Pines called "Good Samaritans At Age Two?" The point of the article is that extensive research has shown that many children, even as young as one year old, when they see other people distressed or suffering, are upset and want to help. The article says, in part:

A two-year-old hits a small girl's head accidentally. He looks aghast. "I hurt your hair," he tells the little girl. "Please don't cry."

Another child, a girl only 18 months old, sees her grandmother lying down for a rest. She toddles over to her crib, grabs her own blanket, and covers her grandmother with it.

These children are normal Americans, neither angelic nor exceptional, says Marian Radke Yarrow, chief of the Laboratory of Developmental Psychology at the National Institute of Mental Health. After a detailed study of children between the ages of 10 months and two-and-a-half years, she *expects* infants to show empathy for the feelings of others. Babies have amazingly generous impulses, she says, and many children perform acts of altruism at a surprisingly early age.

Such findings challenge traditional theories of child development, which hold that young children are totally self-centered and selfish creatures, quite unable to act altruistically before the age of five or six. Yet Yarrow and psychologist Carolyn Zahn Waxler are very sure of their evidence. Their data show clearly that children have a capacity for compassion and for various kinds of pro-social behavior from at least the age of one, though it may co-exist with the capacity for aggression and rage that psychologists have emphasized ever since Freud.

One of the study's most surprising findings was that as early as the age of one, some babies actually try to comfort people who are crying or in pain. They snuggle up to them, pat them, or hug them. Sometimes they even attempt to help them. When one of the mothers went to a doctor with a sore throat, she had her throat swabbed and made a strangling noise. At once, her small son, only 50 weeks old, tried to knock the swab out of the nurse's hand to defend her.

Another mother told of her 13-month-old son who was hungrily eating his cereal when his father came home, obviously tired, and sat down, resting his head in his hand, next to the boy. The child immediately pulled the father's hand away and tried to feed him some cereal. ("A noble gesture," his mother noted, "because he wanted cereal himself.") . . .

At approximately 18 months it becomes very common to imitate other people's laughter, crying, or grimaces. One woman who had accidentally bit her cheek and winced reported that her daughter's face was an "exact mirror of the pain." Another child saw a newborn cry; she watched for a minute as tears welled up in her eyes and she began to cry, too.

The children who are on the path to altruism develop many different ways of helping others. . . . When Laura was 14 months old, her mother reported, she never did anything for children who happened to cry in their house. Once, when a three-year-old boy cried loudly, she seemed upset and puckered up her face, raising her arms to show her mother that she wanted to be picked up and comforted; but she was concerned only for herself. Her mother hugged her and stroked her hair.

About a month later, Laura heard another child cry. She started to cry, too, in full-blown imitation. At 17 months, she made her first move toward a child who was crying. She approached tentatively, pulled back, then approached again and offered the child a Kleenex.

By the time she was 18 months old, she had become a very inventive altruist. When a six-month-old baby began to cry after throwing his cookie from his high chair, Laura picked up the cookie and gave it back to him, looking concerned (she usually tried to eat everything she could lay her hands on, her mother noted). But the baby went on crying—he missed his own mother. So Laura patted him on the head. When that didn't work, she tried speaking to him: "Baby, baby." He went on crying. Laura then started to whimper and insisted that her mother come over. She even put her mother's hand on the baby's head. The baby calmed down a little, but Laura still looked worried. She continued to bring him toys and stroked his hair (as her mother had done for her) until he was completely pacified.

Such findings give strong support to a theory of altruistic motivation developed in 1975 by psychologist Martin Hoffman. Hoffman argues that there are no grounds for the widespread Western assumption that all altruism can ultimately be explained in terms of egoistic, self-centered motives. He believes that altruism derives from a primitive involuntary feeling of distress in the presence of others' distress—an "empathic distress" response—which can be seen even in infants and appears to be inborn. Two-day-old infants in hospital nurseries often become agitated and cry loudly at the sound of another infant's cry, much more so than at other loud sounds, he notes. Empathic distress is so unpleasant that children are driven to help others in order to relieve it. . . .

ON SAYING "NO"

Since few of us raise children in continuum ways, most of us still have the task of teaching them to live by our rules. We tend to make this task much more difficult than it needs to be, not least of all by the way in which we use the word "No."

Not long ago I visited a friend who had a beautiful, lively, affectionate year-old Husky pup. He had only one fault. He loved to be petted, and if you had been petting him, and stopped, or if he had just come up to you, he would put his paw up on your leg, let it fall, put it up again, and so over and over until you did *something.* This dirtied clothes, scratched skin, and hurt. His owner had tried now and then to break him of this habit, by scolding him, pushing him away, or whatever, but it hadn't done much good. He was too busy with his work to spend much time on it. One day I thought that as long as I was visiting, had some time, and loved the pup, I would see if I could break him of this habit.

So every time he came up to me I would pat him for a while and then stop and wait, my hand poised to block his paw when it came up. When he raised it, I would catch it a few inches off the floor and lower it gently to the ground, saying at the same time just as gently, "No, no, keep the paw on the floor." Then I would pat him, say what a nice dog he was, and after a while stop again. Soon the paw would come up once more, and I would catch it and go over the whole thing once again. Sometimes I would do this with him sitting, sometimes with him standing. After a few repeats I would back away from him; then, as he came toward me, I would say in a gentle but warning voice, "Now, keep those paws down," or "Now remember, four on the floor." I would have my hand ready to catch the paw when it rose, which at first it always did. But before long he began to get the idea, and quite often the tone of my voice, the sound of my words, and perhaps the position of my body and hand, would be enough to remind him, and he would keep the paw down. I was only there for a few days, and can't claim that I broke him of the habit altogether. But he was certainly much better about it, and usually only one warning and paw-catch would be enough to remind him.

The point is that even a young dog is smart enough to know that "No" does not have to be just a *signal,* an explosion of angry noise. It can be a word, conveying an idea. It does not have to say, "You're a bad dog, but we're going to beat the badness out of you." It can say instead, "You're a good dog, but this thing that you're doing isn't what we do around here, so please don't do it anymore." Even a young dog can understand that, and act on it.

And if a dog, why not a child? Except in rare times of great stress or danger, there is no reason why we cannot say "No" to children in just as kind and gentle a tone as we say "Yes." Both are *words.* Both convey ideas which even tiny children are smart enough to grasp. One says, "We don't do it that way," the other says, "That's the way we do it." Most of the time, that is what children want to find out. Except when overcome by fatigue, or curiosity, or excitement, or passion, they want to do right, do as we do, fit in, take part.

Soon after my visit with friend and dog, I visited two other friends, and their delightful fifteen-month-old boy. Around dinner time, in the little kitchen-dining room, I took out my cello and began to play. The baby was fascinated, as I hoped he would be. He stopped what he was doing and came crawling across the floor toward the cello at top speed. His parents looked a bit nervous, but I said, "Don't worry, I'll defend the cello, I won't let him hurt it." He came to the cello, pulled himself up to a standing position, and began to touch and pluck at the strings, below the bridge. At the same time, keeping the bow (which he might have been able to damage) out of his reach, I plucked the cello strings above the bridge, which made nice sounds. Now and then I could see that he was being overcome with a wave of excitement, and that he wanted to bang on the cello, as little babies like to bang on things. But when his hands began to make these impulsive gestures, I would catch them, like the paw of the pup, and slow them down, saying softly, "Gently, gently, easy, easy, be nice to the cello." When his motions grew smaller and calmer I would take my hands away. For a while he would caress the wood and pluck at the strings. Then he would begin to get excited again. But as soon as he did I would catch and slow down his hands again, saying as before, "Gently, gently, nice and easy." After a while he would crawl away, while I talked with his parents. Then I would play some more, and he would come crawling over for more looking and touching. I might have to say, "Gently, gently," once or twice, but hardly more than that. Most of the time this tiny boy, still just a baby, was as gentle and careful with the cello as I was. And all this in only one evening, the first time he had ever seen such a strange and fascinating object.

Louise Andrieshyn, a parent in Manitoba, says about this:

> You've made an excellent point about the difference between "No" the angry signal and "No" the meaningful word. . . . There is a third kind of "No," perhaps the most common of all, neither an angry explosion nor a meaningful word—the no, no, no that goes on all day with some parents. This constant hassling is simply a running, ineffective banter. The parents don't even *mean* it; there's no anger or even much reprimand in their voices . . . our cultural expectation is that kids are bad, always getting into trouble, and parents must be dictators controlling their kids (in the name of "protection").
>
> How to cope with these 3 kinds of "No" is much more difficult, though, than you make it sound.
>
> You're saying, if we can become aware of how we use "No" we can change our use of it. And I agree with you in two cases. First,

as parents, we can simply SHUT UP! if we can sit back and listen to ourselves, we can hear how much negative harassment we throw at our kids. If a parent would seriously and objectively listen to what he says (through his child's ears), he would be appalled and could probably with some effort change that kind of "No."

I think here of Lisey (then 3) who was pouring herself a glass of milk yesterday. She had gotten it from the fridge, opened it, poured from a fat 2-qt. carton a very small juice-glass of milk, had drunk it, then had gotten a paper towel and was wiping up the milk spilt on the table. There was more milk spilt than the towel could absorb so as she wiped now, the milk was being pushed off the table onto the floor.

I walked in at this point and started with the running "No, No" commentary in a whiny voice: "Ooooh no, Lisey, you should have asked someone to pour you a glass of milk—no, don't wipe it up, it's going on the floor, now stop, don't do it, I'll do it, it's bad enough on the table—look, now you've got it on the floor—you're making more work for me."

Happily at this point I was struck by a rare beam of sanity and it said to me, "Oh, quit being such a bitch, Lisey has just poured her first glass of milk all by herself and you're ruining the whole thing for her."

And suddenly I looked and saw a very little girl trying very hard to grow up—trying to wipe up herself the mess she had made getting herself a drink of milk. And I said, "Lisey, I think Sparkle (dog) would like this extra milk."

Lisey stopped and looked at me. I had finally said something of meaning. All the negative harassment up till then she had been trying to ignore.

I said, "If you get Sparkle's dish we can put the milk in it."

She got it and we did.

AND immediately she began an animated chatter about how Sparkle would like this milk and how she had poured them both a drink of milk, etc. Until then, she had barely said one word. In fact, if I had pushed her far enough—"OK, Lisey, get out of the kitchen while I clean up your mess"—she would have probably ended up crying (over spilt milk!).

But the happy ending here did not require too much effort on my part because I wasn't very emotionally involved. My mind could still be objective about the situation to the extent of being able to control and change it.

TESTING ADULTS

In his very good book, *Growing With Your Children* (Boston: Little, Brown, 1978), Herbert Kohl—like just about everyone who writes about children—says that they have to keep testing adults in order to find limits. I absolutely disagree. They do it all the time, no question about that. But I don't think they *have* to do it, or do it primarily for that reason, and I don't think we ought to let them do it. If they want to find out, as they do, the rules of family life and human society, there are other and better ways to do it.

One year, when I was teaching fifth grade, I had a boy in my class who had been kicked out of his local public schools—no small feat. He was a perfectly ordinary-looking, middle-sized, middle-class white kid, didn't pull knives or throw furniture, no *Blackboard Jungle* stuff. It took me a while to understand *why* the public schools had shown him the door. In a word, he was an agitator, always stirring things up. One day, when everyone was trying to do something, I forget what, and he was trying to prevent them, or get them to do something else, I turned on him and shouted in exasperation, "Are you *trying* to make me sore at you?" To my great surprise, and his (judging from his voice), he said, "Yes." It took me a while to understand, or at least to guess, that he had learned from experience that the only way he could be sure of getting the undivided attention of other people, children or adults, was to make them sore at him.

As the year went on, he improved, became only difficult instead of impossible. But he was still a long way from being at peace with himself—the roots of his problem were deeper than I or my class could reach in a year. Our school only went through sixth grade; what became of him later I don't know. Meanwhile, he had taught me something valuable.

At about that time I was beginning to know the interesting but angry and difficult child of a friend. One day I was at their house, talking with his mother about something important to both of us. The boy kept interrupting, more even than usual. I knew by then that children hate to be shut out of adult talk, and tried from time to time to let this boy have a chance to speak. But on this day it was clear that he was trying to keep us from talking at all. Finally, looking right at him, I said, not angrily but just curiously, "Are you trying to annoy me?" Startled into honesty, like the other boy, by a question he had perhaps never really asked himself, he smiled sheepishly and said, "Yes." I said, still pleasantly, "Well, that's okay. Tell you what let's do. Let's play a game. You do everything you can think of to annoy me, and I'll do everything I can think of to annoy you, and we'll see who wins. Okay?" He looked at me for a while—he knew me well enough by this time to know that I would play this "game" in earnest. He considered for a while how it might go. A look at his mother showed that, for the time being at least, he could not expect much help from her if the game went against him. Finally he said, "No, I don't want to play." "Fine," I said. "Then let us have our conversation, and you and I can talk later." Which is what happened.

That was many years ago. From many encounters I have since had with many children, I have come to believe very strongly that children as young as five and perhaps even three are well able to understand the idea of "testing"—doing something to someone else or in front of someone else, knowing they don't like it, *just to see what that other person will do,* and to understand that this is not good. If I thought a child was doing this to me, I would say, "Are you testing me, just doing that to see what I will do?" If the child said "Yes" I would say, "Well, I don't like that, it's not nice and I don't want you to do it. I don't do bad things to *you* just to see what *you* will do. Then it's not fair for you to do that to me."

I think children are perfectly able to understand these ideas, to see that they are fair, and to act upon them. When they do, it will make our lives together much easier.

"OKAY?"

When adults want children to do something—put on coats, take a nap, etc.—they often say, "Let's put on our coats, okay?" or "It's time to take our naps now, okay?" That "Okay?" is a bad thing to say. Our lives with children would go better if we could learn to give up this way of talking.

The trouble with this "Okay?" is that it suggests to the children that we are giving them a choice when we really are not. Whatever people may think about how many choices we should give children, children should at least be able to know at any moment whether they have a choice or not. If we too often seem to be offering choices when we really aren't, children may soon feel that they never have any. They will resent this, and resent even more our not saying clearly what we mean. By giving what we intend as a command and then saying "Okay?" we invite resistance and rebellion. In fact, the only way children *can* find out whether or not we are offering a real choice is to refuse to do what we ask. It is their way of saying, "Do you really mean it?"

Many adults feel that in saying "Okay?" they are only being courteous. But this is a misunderstanding of courtesy. It is perfectly possible to be firm and courteous while making clear to someone that you are not offering a choice but telling them what you want to happen or is going to happen. When I visit friends, I expect to fit myself into their life and routines, and count on them to tell me what they are. So they say, "We get up at seven o'clock," or "We are going to have dinner at six-thirty," or "This afternoon we're going to this place to do such and such." They are not asking me whether I approve of these plans, just letting me know that they *are* the plans. But they are perfectly polite about this.

Some friends of mine have a No Smoking rule in their house. They are in earnest about this. Inside their front door is a sign saying "Thank You For Not Smoking." But every now and then a guest misses the sign, or takes it as a plea and not a command, and starts to light up. My friends gently but firmly inform their friend and guest that if he or she wants to smoke, the porch is the place to do it, but not in the house. No one argues, no one is offended.

Few adults seem to be able to talk to children in this way. In the Public Garden, or airports, or other places where adults and children gather, I hear hundreds of people telling their children to do things. Most of them begin with "Okay?", pleading and cajoling. If this doesn't work, they soon begin to threaten and shout. They can't seem to give a firm request without getting angry first. Then the child is genuinely confused and resentful, doesn't understand why the adults are angry, or what he has done to deserve the shouts and threats.

If a child really resists doing what you want, it may help to say, "I know you don't want to do what I am telling you to do, and I'm sorry that you don't, and sorry that you're angry, but I really mean for you to do it." It doesn't by any means solve all problems, and it may not even stop the child from being angry. But at least it makes clear where things stand. And of course, at such times we must not get angry at the children for being angry with us. We may have a right (as well as the power) to make children obey, but not to demand that they pretend to like it.

TANTRUMS

People who write about tantrums seldom give any strong sense that the anger of two-year-olds is *about* anything. One might easily get the impression that these little children are swept by gusts of irrational "aggression" and rage as the coasts of Florida are from time to time swept by hurricanes. Instead, I would insist that much of the seemingly irrational and excessive anger of little children—"tantrums"—is in fact not only *caused* by things that happen to them or that are said and done to them, but that these things would make *us* angry if they happened or were said and done to us. Even in the kindest and most loving families two-year-olds must be reminded a hundred times a day, perhaps by the words and acts of their parents, perhaps by events, by Nature herself, that they are small, weak, ignorant, clumsy, foolish, ignorant, untrustworthy, troublesome, destructive, dirty, smelly, even disgusting. *They don't like it!* Neither would I. Neither would you.

On this subject, the mother of J, the little boy whom I described playing with my cello, wrote about his tantrums and how they were both learning how to avoid them.

> J is great. No naps now which means he is super go-power all day with a huge collapse about 7:30. He has his room all to himself now, and he really likes to hang out in there alone for an hour and a half

most days, driving trucks around mostly. I've never seen a kid more into organizing things. He plays with dominoes and calls them either adobes, for building houses, or bales of hay, and has them stacked, lined up, or otherwise arranged in some perfect order; same with the trucks; he'll scream and yell, as per your theory of two-year-old behavior, if you snatch him up from a group of trucks and carry him off to lunch. But if you give him a couple of minutes to park them all in a straight line then he'll come willingly. Your theory (treat them like big people) works out over and over again; brush past him, leave him behind in the snow when you're hustling up to feed the goats and you get a black and blue screaming pass out tantrum. Treat them "Big" and things roll along. Only hangup is the occasional times you have to take advantage of your superior size and pull a power play. The trick is to learn to avoid the situations that once in a while make that a necessity, like not getting in a rush, and not letting them get so tired they break down completely—like letting dinner be late.

One thing he gets mad about is being left behind by anybody. However, we just went on a trip. . . . I was quite nervous about leaving him with friends as he had been doing his falling down pass out tantrums for our benefit all week whenever anyone went to town without him (in spite of having the other parent on hand). But he just waved Bye Bye and went in the house and had a really good four days. As his father said, obviously he would only bother to pull the tantrum bit for us. He was very calm and very full of new games and words when we got him back, and I know he made progress on all fronts as a result of being away from us and with other interesting people.

. . . Later we were to go on a long trip down the river so we left him with some friends, but decided at the last minute our boats weren't sufficient to carry us and our gear on that rugged and remote a trip, so we picked up J and just went camping on the river, taking our boat and going on short hops along stretches of the river where the road was. Again he was super and loved being with grownups who ate with their fingers and mushed all their food up in one cup just like him. His father wanted him to go in the boat so he put him in a life jacket then tied a rope between them. J hated that and had all kinds of misgivings as water sloshed into the boat and he got wet and cold, but he didn't complain. Amazingly he just sat there and looked pissed off for about two hours. I think he was so glad to be included that he bore with the misery.

Susan Fitch applies this same sensible and respectful attitude to the often difficult issue of bedtime:

> My husband and I have always been concerned with having "our" time so our son, Jesse's (4) bedtime was very important to us. Although he was very cooperative, Jesse did not enjoy the limited time he had with his father between his arrival and bedtime. This left everyone frustrated and unhappy.
>
> One evening while I was reading *GWS* it occurred to me that he was perfectly capable of going to bed when he was tired. The next day we talked about being tired, how much sleep he needed, when to go to bed in order to wake up in time for playgroup, and about our need to talk with one another and have quiet times. The tension evaporated with his father, and he immediately assumed responsibility for getting undressed and brushing his teeth. Because of just this one letting go, our time alone and together follows a natural pattern that seems to satisfy everyone. . . .

I can't help noting that no cultures in the world that I have ever heard of make such a fuss about children's bedtimes, and no cultures have so many adults who find it so hard either to go to sleep or wake up. Could these social facts be connected? I strongly suspect they are.

COOKING AT TWO

Children are so much more capable than most adults realize. Susan Price of Vero Beach, Florida astonished and delighted me with this letter about her children:

> I am making lists with the kids. We each have a list of what we do during the day and cross off as we do them. In the grocery store we each have a list of the stuff we need to get, each person having certain things to get. I got my typewriter fixed and the kids take turns typing on it. If they both want to do it, we use a timer so each person can do it a certain number of minutes. . . . Matt (6) is making the sauce for lasagna and Faith (4) is waiting for the water to boil to put in the noodles.
>
> Matt has learned his letters since he was one or two but hasn't

learned words because, I can see now, I was trying to sound them out. We found a box of cardboard letters at the thrift shop. He spelled out a sentence in a book that he got from the library, and we picked out the letters from the pile and made the words on the rug. That was fun.

When Matt was less than two, one of his favorite snack foods was peas. Faith was going to sleep in my arms and I didn't want to get up and make him any, so he got a pan out, put water in it, got a chair and got a package of peas out of the freezer, opened it, put them in the pan, and turned the fire on. From the time they were about one-and-a-half or two they have used knives (which had not been sharpened for a while) to cut vegetables and stood on chairs by the stove to cook them. They know how to cook french fries themselves. A couple of weeks ago they climbed up the ladder and helped David (their father) paint our mobile home roof white. (I'm too scared to climb up the ladder!) The thing is, any child could do the same if their parents let them. . . . I don't think the risk is much greater, if at all, than the risk we'll get hurt doing the same things. Kids don't want to get hurt any more than we do. They welcome suggestions that will prevent them from getting hurt (such as putting french fries in with a slotted spoon instead of dropping them in with their fingers).

I suspect that children get hurt most often when doing things they are not supposed to do, in a spirit of defiance and excitement, rather than when doing something sensible and natural that they do often and like to do right.

The head of a big adventure playground in London once told me that as long as parents could come right into the playground, the children often hurt themselves, doing things to impress, scare, or defy their parents, but that once the parents were told that they had to wait for the children outside the playground (in a spot with chairs, benches, etc.) the accidents stopped.

Later I asked Susan how Matt learned to cook so young. She replied:

The stove. What could have become my first battle with Matt. He learned to turn the burners on. I said no, dangerous. Effect, naturally: *fun, interesting, do it all the time.* So I slapped his hand, slightly, grabbed him up, me in tears, was he, I don't even remember, holding him on the couch, what to do, what to do. Slowly it dawned on me. There wasn't a damned thing dangerous about him turning them on. I was always with him, could keep the stove cleared, his hand was way below the flames. What was I afraid of? *If people knew,* of course. So I let him turn them on, watched, kept my mouth shut. He turned them all on, went over to the table, stood on a chair and looked at them (he was so far below the flame he couldn't see them standing by the stove). How old was he? Less than sixteen months. Did this for a while, then a couple of times the next day, and *that was all,* never "played" with them again except to turn one on when he saw me getting a pan out to cook something in. Or after Faith was born to turn them on for himself, when he wanted to cook something. No, one other time when he was much older and his friend was over he thought it was funny to turn them on and see how afraid his friend became.

Why did he not respond to my "No, dangerous!"? Because there was no real fear in my voice. Children *will* respond to you when you say something's dangerous if you really are afraid they are going to get hurt *at that minute.* I read somewhere that you have to teach children to do what you say because if you don't they could be out in the street and a car coming and they wouldn't get out of the road when you yelled at them to. That's not the point at all. They're responding mostly to the fear in your voice in that situation, not to the fact that you're telling them to do something.

People are always worrying too much about the future, extrapolating out of the present, with children. They think, if I let them turn the burners on now, they'll always want to turn them on. . . .

My guess is that the main reason Matt no longer needs or wants to play with the stove is that *he can cook on it.* It isn't a toy any more, but a serious tool, that he and the grownups use every day. Before they know how to drive, and can drive, little children love to sit at the wheel of a parked car turning the steering wheel this way and that. But who ever saw a child doing that, *who could actually drive?* It would be baby stuff. And it would be baby stuff for Matt to play with the stove on which he and his younger sister regularly cook food that the whole family eats.

I suspect, too, that one reason that Matt responds so quickly to strong fear or other negative emotion in his mother's voice is that he doesn't often hear this kind of emotion. Children who constantly hear in the voices of adults the tones of fear, disgust, anger, threat, etc., soon take that tone of voice to be normal, routine, and turn it off altogether. They think, "Oh, that's just the way they always talk." Then, when we try to make them pay attention to some real danger, they no longer hear us at all.

INSTEAD OF GOLD STARS

Unless warped by cruelty or neglect, children are *by nature* not only loving and kind but serious and purposeful. Whenever I hear school people say, "The students aren't motivated, how do I motivate them?" I think of the story about Margaret Mead and the Balinese.

This took place in the 1920s, when very few Westerners had ever been to Bali. Margaret Mead was talking to some Balinese, trying to learn about this strange and very different culture. At some point she asked about their art. The Balinese were puzzled by this question. They did not know what she meant by art. So she talked for a while about art and artists in Western cultures. The Balinese considered this for a while. Then one of them spoke. "Here in Bali we have no art," he said. "We do everything as well as we can."

Very little children are like the Balinese. Just about everything they do, they do as well as they can. Except when tired or hungry, or in the grip of passion, pain, or fear, they are moved to act almost entirely by curiosity, desire for mastery and competence, and pride in work well done. But the schools, and many adults outside of school, hardly ever recognize or honor such motives, can hardly even imagine that they exist. In their place they put Greed and Fear.

But what about people who have taken out of school children who have been numbed and crippled in spirit by years of "reinforcement," petty rewards and penalties, gold stars, M & M's, grades, Dean's Lists? How can unschoolers revive in their children those earlier, deeper, richer sources of human action? It is not easy. Perhaps the only thing to do is to be patient and wait. After all, if we do not constantly re-injure our bodies, in time they usually heal themselves. We must act on the faith that the same is true of the human spirit. In short, if we give children enough time, as free as possible from destructive outside pressures, the chances are good that they will once again find *within themselves* their reasons for doing worthwhile things. And so, in time, may we all.

7

Learning in the World

ACCESS TO THE WORLD

Even in supposedly "free" or "alternative" schools, too many people still do what conventional schools have always done. They take children out of and away from the great richness and variety of the world, and in its place give them school subjects, the curriculum. They may jazz it up with chicken bones, Cuisenaire rods, and all sorts of other goodies. But the fact remains that instead of letting children have contact with more and more people, places, tools, and experiences, the schools are busily cutting the world up into little bits and giving it to the children according to some expert's theory about what they need or can stand.

What children need is not new and better curricula but *access* to more and more of the real world; plenty of time and space to think over their experiences, and to use fantasy and play to make meaning out of them; and advice, road maps, guidebooks, to make it easier for them to get where they want to go (not where we think they ought to go), and to find out what they want to find out. Finding ways to do all this is not easy. The modern world is dangerous, confusing, not meant for children, not generally kind or welcoming to them. We have much to learn about how to make the world more accessible to them, and how to give them more freedom and competence in exploring it. But this is a very different thing from designing nice little curricula.

Here is how a family in Washington, D.C., opened up the city to their child:

> We are a family of three: mother, father, and daughter Susan, age 8 years this May, who have been home tutoring each other for two years. After we had watched our beautiful daughter's life, liberty, and creativity systematically destroyed by kindergarten teachers, Susan decided she wanted to stay at home the next year. The last chapter of *Instead of Education* gave us strength, especially the last paragraph. For us, schools are foreign lands that are difficult to imagine. Our life is free and our work and learning are directed at goals that we hold dear to our own needs, not the goals of society. We have taken control over our lives, we have attained power to run our own affairs. Susan takes care and responsibility for herself, she stands on her own two strong legs, she speaks clearly, thinks clearly and answers only to her conscience. She is happy, talkative, interesting and interested and can choose for her life any damn thing she pleases.
>
> We live in Washington, D.C., on Capitol Hill about two miles from the museums of the Smithsonian Institution. Susan and her mother walk there almost every day, observing, playing, meeting people, going to movies, listening to music, and riding the merry-go-round. They see a fantastic variety of nature movies. . . . They know art and history museums exhibit by exhibit. Susan can drag you through the history of the universe, through natural history, on up to the latest Mars landing. They eat lunch near the water fountain, see the latest sculpture, take pictures of their favorite spots, marvel at the beautiful spring and fall days. They attend mime shows, tape record jazz concerts, ride the double-decker bus to their favorite "explore gallery" where things can be played and jumped in. Tuition is very cheap, we all have fun, and we all learn a great deal.
>
> Susan lives in a world of marvelous *abundance;* her resources are unlimited. She has not been "socialized" by school to think that education is a supply of scarce knowledge to be competed for by hungry, controlled children. She doesn't play dumb "Schlemiel."

. . . Our home and neighborhood are like a garden full of fresh fruit to be picked at arm's length by all who want to.

She likes to paint, draw, color, cut out and paste. She compares her work to that in the museum. We give our comments and ideas when requested.

We have hobbies in astronomy and camping. Her father is a pediatrician who enjoys working with her in constructing electronic gear. She has excellent soldering techniques and has soldered many connections in our home brew electric computer now used in his office.

It is not just "educated" and middle-class families who can use the city as a resource. In the chapter "The New Truants" in his book *Acting Out* (Boston: Little, Brown), Roland Betts writes:

Today's truants are [New York City's] most misunderstood children. They are also perhaps the most enlightened, aware that neither the schools nor the streets have anything to offer them. They fear both worlds. They sense the futility of the jobs that are available even for those who do finish high school. . . . Most of them are intelligent, sensitive children, far more accomplished in the arts of reading and mathematics than their peers who either attend the schools or lurk outside of them. These truants rarely brush with the law. Their trademark is their solitude.

Randolph Tracey is one of them. He is now (1978) sixteen but he has not been to school since the last day of fourth grade. He is poor and black. . . . [He] is a quiet and meek child, honest in his admission to his mother that he has not been to school in years. He was always a good student, but although he was able to read at a level several years above his grade, he had no tolerance for the continuous noise and confusion that characterized his school. Randolph is never with other children, or with other adults for that matter. He has spent the better part of the past four years in the Metropolitan Museum of Art. Although he has patronized all of the city's museums, he prefers the Met, and humbly claims that he is very familiar with each piece in the museum's standing collection. He recalls being cornered there one afternoon by a class of children he had grown up with from the school he should have attended, a class that might have been his own. He hid motionless behind a Minoan vase for twenty minutes until the danger had passed. Randolph draws and paints on his own, but derives far more pleasure from seeing and studying art in the museums.

Danny Hartman is another dropout. His life is consumed by drawing and tracing figures from comic books and art books, which he borrows from the public library. He can mimic perfectly the drawings of Leonardo and Michelangelo and the most intricate of Rembrandt's etchings. He stayed in school, reluctantly, until the spring of his eighth-grade year [where] he was discovered by an art teacher who encouraged him to apply for admission to the High School of Music and Art. For three years she saw to it that he attended daily classes in English and math, and she allowed him to work in her room while cutting gym, science, typing, and social studies. . . . He was lauded for his talents by his fellow students and was in the eyes of his art teacher a "clear genius." His work was extraordinary. The portfolio he had amassed by Christmas of his eighth-grade year was breathtaking. . . .

But the High School of Music and Art did not admit Danny. His accomplishments on standardized reading and math tests were unconvincing and his cumulative grade-point average was distorted by his many class cuts and subsequent failures. . . . The day that Danny received word that he had been denied admission to Music and Art was the last day he ever spent in school. . . .

What Mr. Betts means when he says that Danny's record was distorted by class cuts and subsequent failures is very probably that Danny's school, like most schools, gave him failing grades for cutting classes, regardless of whether or not he knew that material or could do the work. If this was so, it means that to punish him for cutting classes *the school lied about his academic work*—an outrageous and I would think, if tested in court, probably illegal practice which is common in schools all over the country.

Another of the truants Mr. Betts describes is a voluminous and expert reader; another, an expert on the geography, flora, and fauna of Central Park; another, an expert on television shows and movies; another, a raiser and trainer of pigeons; another, an expert on New York City's enormous transportation system. All of them have learned how to learn from the city what they want to learn. None has ever had any help or encouragement from any adult, or any way to use or get credit for any part of what they know. How easy it would be, and how much less expensive than running giant schools, and jails for those who won't go to them, to find ways to help and encourage the interests and talents of these children, and many others like them. As far as learning goes, they clearly don't need much help; the best help society could give them would simply be to stop treating them like criminals, so that they could do their exploring boldly and freely instead of furtively. They do need, and would probably welcome, help in finding ways to *use* what they learn—which is, after all, one of the things the schools are supposedly for.

Meanwhile their experience shows very clearly that for all its hugeness and harshness, the modern city is rich in resources, and that children don't necessarily have to have an adult holding them by the hand every second in order to make use of them.

Judy McCahill writes from England about a small child's very active way of using the resources of his world:

> Last Saturday for something to do, because D was out of the country, I said to the boys, "Let's go to the art exhibit." S and K thought it was a wonderful idea and began discussing what sort of art they would do there and what pictures (of their own) they might bring from home. Startled, I tried to explain to them what an art exhibit was all about and they were genuinely puzzled at my trying to tell them they were just going there to look at somebody else's pictures. Puzzled, but not deterred, S gathered his supplies, two sets of paints, a brush, some paper, and a jar full of water which he handed me to carry; and K made us all wait while he finished a full-color marker pen painting of an army tank.
>
> When we got there, we strolled along the sidewalks near the craft shop that was hosting the exhibit, dutifully examining the works and passing several fully-grown and wise-looking artists sitting in portable lawn chairs, all the while S at my heels urging me to find out how he was supposed to enter the show and me ahead of S, stalling.
>
> Finally an old man who works in the shop, who once told me a long story about his difficulties getting home to Cobham one night during the war when London was being bombed, greeted me. I introduced S to him and asked *him* to explain what an art exhibit was. He started to, but then he and his daughter, who also works

in the shop, saw that S was ready to do some work and after a good laugh with a couple of customers over it, gave him a couple of nice big pieces of "card" to paint on. He sat on the doorstep of a small office building nearby and painted, while the rest of us strolled through the exhibit again, window-shopped, and ate ice cream cones.

When he had finished, it was a beautiful picture of a black dog, fur flying, running up a hill on a windy day, a glorious sun in the sky. It seemed to reflect his mood of magic. He took the picture into the shop, where the man said he would put it on sale for 50 pence (and confusedly explained about how the artists had to pay rent to the exhibit), and we went home.

A few days later, still full of the experience, S told a friend of mine about it. She promptly went out to buy the picture, and it was gone! When I suggested to S that he go and check to see if his painting had been sold, he replied that he already had, the next day (which of course was Sunday), and the shop was closed.

And that was that. He was too busy doing something else to give it another thought.

LIFESCHOOL

A young teen-age reader writes eloquently about how much she learns from that part of her life that is *hers:*

I started going to public school right into the second grade and in every grade up to the sixth I was a straight A student. All the teachers were nice to me and I was praised and praised again for my work and I got good grades for it too and that's what kept me going.

When I left school at the end of sixth grade to be out for two years, I learned a new realization. Grades are not what make you a good person. I have a pretty good memory so I remembered all the things I had to, to pass the tests that gave me A's. But I've learned from experience that when I'm not interested in what I am supposed to be learning, I forget everything. Unfortunately, I wasn't interested in anything that I was doing, so my second through sixth grade years of public schooling are pretty much blank.

In the two years without any school contact I learned how to live without grades and not to need someone to tell me "It's good" every time I did something. It got so that grades didn't mean anything anymore. Basically, I learned that grades prove nothing. I also learned a lot of different things that I wouldn't have, if I had been in public schools. Public schools can't offer experience. I learned how to deal with and relate to adults better because I was around them so much—all the kids were in school! I learned many practical skills that I never would have learned in public school.

At first I wasn't so sure about the idea of not being in school but I soon adjusted and found it very fun. When I look at kids my age, it makes me glad that we did what we did. I am capable of doing so many more things it amazes me. And it's all because I had the time to learn, and enjoy while I was learning. So things stuck in my mind and they are still there because I am still doing new things, while these kids are doing things just to "get out" and then forgetting them in the meantime *plus* not enjoying much of it anyhow. Whew!

At L [the alternative school she attends now] the thing is that the kids don't think they are learning as much as the kids in public schools because they don't seem to do as much. I think that's rather silly and I proved it to myself, by seeing that after being out of school for two years, I'm not any dumber than any other (supposed) ninth grader.

Now that I'm involved in L, I am running into the same old thing. When I first went there I was so happy that I had finally found a school place where they didn't believe in grades, etc. This was fairly true until the new high school began. They have this thing now about credits. All of the other students are there (at the high school) to get the diploma and get out. I am there to have fun learning and learn about the things that interest me. One of the main reasons I am there is for the social life. But in order to be there for that reason, I feel that I must do some of the things they want me to do.

I am already getting overdosed with "their stuff" and then my teacher says to me, "Your lifeschool is becoming too important to you." My lifeschool *should* be more important to me; my lifeschool is my home and family and if they shouldn't be the most important then what should?

I have such a neat home and lifeschool! I consider myself to be very lucky to be who I am and to have the parents I have for believing in nonschooling!

Jud Jerome writes about the experiences of two of his children in "lifeschool"

> One daughter was twelve when we moved to the farm. She finished that year of school on "independent study," living at the farm, turning in work to teachers back at the city. But when fall came she did not want to enroll. To avoid the law we enrolled her in a "free" school in Spokane, Wash., run by a friend, who carried her on the rolls, though she has not yet, to date, seen that city or that school. She spent most of the first year here at the farm, pitching in as an adult, learning from experience as we were all learning. While she was still thirteen we went to help another commune, in northern Vermont, with sugaring, and she loved that place—which was very primitive and used horse-drawn equipment—so asked to stay. This was an agreeable arrangement on all sides—and she has lived there now for over five years, except for one, when she was sixteen. That year she and a young man ten years her senior went to Iceland for the winter, working in a fish cannery. The next spring they traveled, camping, to Scandinavia, hiked the Alps, then flew home—coming back with $3000 more than they left with, after a year abroad.
>
> Last year she wanted to apply for a government vocational program, for which she needed a high school diploma, so went to an adult education class for a few months, and took the test, passing in the top percentile (and being offered scholarships to various colleges). She "graduated" earlier than her classmates who stayed in school. I think her case illustrates especially dramatically the waste of time in schools. She is by no means a studious type, would never think of herself as an intellectual, has always been more interested in milking cows and hoeing vegetables and driving teams of horses than in books, and in her years between thirteen and eighteen moved comfortably into womanhood and acquired a vast number of skills, had a vaste range of experiences in the adult world, yet managed to qualify exceptionally by academic standards. By comparison, her classmates who stayed in school are in many case stunted in mind, emotionally disturbed, without significant goals or directions or sound values in their lives.
>
> In the six years we have lived here we have not had other school-age children than Topher living at the farm. At times he grew very lonely, and at times visiting relatives and friends would strongly imply to us that we should do something about his schooling. We

explained that he had "lessons," but we were very lackadaisical about them. That is, we had a wide variety of books and educational materials available, and when he asked for us to work with him, we did so, and occasionally we would take the initiative in encouraging him to work on reading, mathematics, or some other academic study.

Mostly, though, he learned simply by following adults around, helping, asking questions, becoming involved. By age eight he was baking bread and cakes, repairing machines, wiring lamps and rooms, and had considerable knowledge of automobiles, calculators, tape recorders and videotape equipment, and usual farm tasks such as gardening, animal care, forest and wildlife, rocks (he has always had a strong interest in geology and electronics), weather, and machines of all kinds. He helped us at many tasks in our small factory, manufacturing planters from oak logs.

Children can learn a great deal from many of the "unhappy" experiences from which we try so hard to protect them. The mother who wrote about studying with her children on the sofa (where she could hug them whenever she felt like it) also wrote:

We had one long experience that gave us a different kind of "social" activity. Right after we were approved to home-school, my father was taken seriously ill with a stroke, so when he had recuperated enough, he was put in a convalescent home for therapy. Because the boys and I were free, we would go in each day to visit him. (They would not have been excused from school for this.) But my father was very depressed and the therapist at the hospital had on his record "uncooperative." This didn't give us much confidence, so we went in each day to make sure they didn't give up on him. It was a good experience for the boys as well as me, for whenever the grandchildren would come my father would get undepressed. He would laugh at their antics and then sink back into depression when they left.

So we agreed that we would take our books (it was now September) to the home and stay most of the day with their Pop-Pop. It worked out well, for the boys had a large place to do their work and they could go outside to play whenever they got tired of being in. They would go to the vending machines and get us things, and several times when the home was short-handed because of the "flu" season, we would sort some laundry and the boys would help take it to the rooms. We made it a game and the patients loved having the boys come in to their rooms and talk to them.

At therapy we kept assuring my father that when he could walk well, we'd take him home, so he really worked hard, and the boys and I would cheer him on, and the other patients, with "You can do it, Pop-Pop. Hurray!" "Great, Pop-Pop!" The other patients enjoyed us cheering them on and when the therapist saw the positive results from this, he was glad we were there. We saw many patients recover in weeks when the therapist had thought it would take months. We don't hope to have this kind of experience again this year, but it showed us that we *could* take a "sad" situation and turn it into one of rejoicing.

CONTROLLING ONE'S TIME

A mother from Washington state writes about freedom from schedules:

We entered the year with no preconceptions or plan of action. I just figured life would go on, and so it has. We go to bed each night and wake up each morning, the day passes and the necessary work gets done. I know that I live in a healthy environment and that I continue to grow as a person, and I trust that is so for my children, as well, though I haven't been "monitoring" their "progress," nor can I point to any tangible proof of "achievement."

About ten days a month I go to the city to work in a printshop. It is my habit, generally, to wake up early and spend an hour or two quietly planning my day according to what needs doing and what I feel like. But on my "work" days I find it very difficult to "get into" that kind of contemplation. Such a large chunk of the day is already planned for me. If I go to work several consecutive days, by the fourth or fifth day I feel very removed from the core of myself, and find it much easier to contemplate doing what at other times would seem irresponsible to me. I seem to have less energy for recycling, conserving fuel, paying good attention to my husband and children, etc. *When I abdicate the responsibility for structuring my own time, a certain moral strength seems to be lost as well* [Author's emphasis]. Who can guess at the degree of personal alienation we as a society cause our children by structuring so much of their time for them? I am beginning to think the greatest

harm is not in the "what" or the "how" of this structuring, but in
the very fact that five days out of seven, nine months out of twelve,
six hours out of the center of those days, we remove from children
the responsibility for their time. Perhaps it is not even the length
of the time that is crucial, but simply the fact of the interruption.
I know from my own experience that even a small interruption—
a dental appointment, say, or a meeting or lecture I have to give
—can halt the flow of my own creative energies for a length of time
much greater than the interruption itself. Once I change from active
to passive participant in structuring my time, a certain numbing
takes place so that it is much easier to stay passive, "killing time"
until the next prescribed activity, like fixing dinner or whatever.

I have noticed that the only periods of real "boredom," when the
children complain of having nothing to do, are on days when a
chunk of time has been planned *for* them. There is certainly nothing
wrong with planning things to do together, but I have grown wary
of too much planning *for,* and of removing it from its natural niche
in the unique pattern of a particular day to an artifical projection
into the future of anonymous days: "Every Tuesday we will . . ."

I have never known how to "stimulate" the children. I know that
as a parent I should be raising my children in a "stimulating"
environment, so that they will not be "dulled" or "bored," but what
is more stimulating: a roomful of toys and tools and gadgets, bright
colors and shiny enameled fixtures, or a sparsely furnished hand-
hewn cabin deep in the woods, with a few toys carefully chosen or
crafted, rich with meaning, time, and care, and intimate with the
elements of the earth? The only world I can show them, with any
integrity, is my world.

Perhaps that is why field trips were such a disappointment for us.
We started off in the fall doing "something special," i.e., "educational field trip," once a week. After about a month we all forgot
about taking these trips. They were fun, certainly interesting, but
I think we were all sickened by the phoniness. Everyone knew the
only reason we all trooped into the city to the aquarium was because Mom thought it would be a "good experience." Of much
more continuing interest and, probably, greater educational significance in the truest sense, are the weekly trips into town to do the
errands—to the bank (where we all have accounts and are free to
deposit and withdraw as we please), the post office, grocery store,
Laundromat, recycling center (source of income for kids outside of
parents), drugstore and the comic book racks—and the evenings at

the library and swimming pool. Those things are real, things I would do even if no one joined me, that just happen to be important activities for all of us.

When I am trying to "stimulate their interest" in something, the very artificiality of the endeavor (and rudeness, really—I have no business even trying) builds a barrier between us. But when I am sharing something I really love with them because I also really love them, all barriers are down, and we are communicating intimately. When they also love what I love—a song, a poem, the salmon returning to the creek to spawn—the joy is exquisite; we share a truth. But our differences are also a truth. Common thread and fiber we share, but not the whole piece.

And so I do my work each day, work which is full of meaning for me, and offer to teach it to them: cooking, sewing, splitting wood, hauling water, keeping house, writing, reading, singing, sailing on the lake, digging in the garden. Sometimes they are interested, sometimes not. But if I were to try to "stimulate" them, sugar-coating various tasks, making games of various skills, preaching, teaching *me* to them, they would not have the time—great, empty spaces of time—in which to search deep within themselves for what is most true about them.

And neither, then, would I.

Who can explain the chemistry of creativity? I can sit at a desk in a well-lit room, with paper and typewriter in front of me, a subject clear in my head, yet the results of my efforts are merely mediocre. But when I am in a spot of my own choosing, a spot in which strands of fantasy, imagery, memory, and emotion, and perhaps some other deeper, indefinable essence converge, I am able to produce an immensely satisfying piece of work. Sometimes when I am writing I appear to be wandering aimlessly through the woods, or sitting idly on the bridge, dangling feet and tossing pebbles into the slowly moving water. But all the while my mind is working, trembling with the tension of an unarticulated thought, until I find the linear expression for that formless entity. Knowing these things about myself, how can I presume to interfere, to lock my children into sterile rooms, to lure them away from "idle" moments?

Many parents have written to us about the feelings of liberation that go with unschooling and unscheduling. Gail Myles and her family moved to an island to unschool their children:

In August, 1977, I moved with my three sons to an island we own off the coast of Maine. This decision was the result of my husband's and my opinion that they were not learning in public or private schools. Because we were taking them out of N.H. we had no hassle from the school district. I have worked as a volunteer for several years in the Rye schools and informed the teachers and principals of the plans. Many teachers agreed this was a good idea.

I never expected the boys to express any appreciation for this experience. I figured they might be sitting at a lunch with some business friends when they were thirty and mention the year. What I couldn't have predicted is that they would see the difference so soon. They learned to dig clams with the clammers of Maine, the salt of the earth, in forty degrees below chill factors, they lived through situations where everyone takes responsibility for the lives of each other, they came to like and understand opera because it was available to us through Texaco broadcasts, an interest none of us had prior to this, they learned that out of the eight unexpected puppies born, five had to be destroyed because of the food shortage, and probably the best thing they learned was to get along with themselves and each other. They had to, because there was no one else and if you want something from someone you have to give in return. That should take care of this "social life" garbage. To feel your worth in an adult world side by side with hardworking people, is there a better reward? I don't think so. They even had tears at departing from this small coastal community they knew as "in town."

My rewards were beyond measure. No yellow monster took my favorite friends away every morning; when they were exposed to a new vocabulary world I could use it pertinently in everyday happenings; if we wanted to know molecular theory we could work from 9 A.M. to 4 P.M. till it clicked; everything they were exposed to in Calvert Curriculum was learned by all; they spent early evenings putting on operas they made up, shows for Dad's pleasure were presented, sometimes taking three days just to prepare the staging. We read books, books, and books till 1 A.M. and no one had to be up at 6:30 for the monster.

An additional reward was the result of the history, literature, mythology, and architecture we were exposed to; we went to Athens, Greece, in April, a trip we would never have been interested enough in taking or felt a need to take if "doors" hadn't been opened to us. Bud came to love the Parthenon and had to see it.

Tim was a walking encyclopedia on mythology and gave Jack and me the tour in the Archaeological Museum, and Mike was our history guide—we didn't even need a Greek service. Mike is also a gifted writer, and after reading his final composition for Calvert the teacher said she wished she could fly up to meet him, said he knew what writing was all about—she wanted to fly to Troy and Greece as his subject was the Trojan War. He had made her *feel* something inside.

I enjoyed the Calvert system. Their writers are excellent and really speak to the kids. It was a personal relationship in which they looked forward to hearing from someone who was writing to them. Letters were scarce and they learned the value of the written word. But I must say we *used* the curriculum to our needs and interests and only took the grading so that the boys would not be denied the credit upon returning to public school. This was completely their choice—they are encouraged to set policies regarding their futures.

The idea I hate most about public schools is that they should have my children all day when I feed, clothe, doctor, transport, and care most for them, and I am denied those hours with them and the sharing of their learning experiences. I cannot reinforce their education if I am denied the subject matter they are exposed to and am only left with tired grumps who eat, do homework, and flop to bed.

REAL WORLD SKILLS

From the cover story of the April 1980 issue of *Home Educators Newsletter:*

These children [of a home-schooling family] form an exclusive student body as they are each born into the school. They take their places according to ability rather than grade level. They listen to works far above their comprehension, just to be part of the present company. In our own instance, we have one child that keeps all vehicles in top running shape, another who provides milk, eggs, and meat for the table, another who displays beautiful artwork, and another who enjoys gardening.

Katrina spends several hours morning and afternoon doing her farm work, but she is the beneficiary of her own labor, keeps all the records for feed, hay, and other purchases so that she can calculate her profit when animals are sold and what man-hours and money have been expended to gain that profit. I personally am not the least interested in any type of farm work and yet I know that this is developing within Katrina an ability far beyond anything that I could teach her. How much barley will a pig eat in a week, a month, till time for the market? What animals have the quickest turnover? What type of labor hours are necessary to operate a farm? I couldn't answer any of these questions, though Katrina can, and for an eleven-year-old girl I consider that quite an accomplishment. She has a reading assignment just like the other children of 200 pages per week plus a written paper every day. She generally turns in a paper that has to do with her present projects.

It is a rare occasion that I do not get the type of workmanship out of my children that I would get out of some adult. We are presently sectioning off a room in the basement and all the partitions will be built by the children. One startling fact is that John, at age seven, has all his own tools, including a power saw and drill. He builds beautiful miniature log cabins and will be in charge of measuring and cutting boards for the partition project. He is also planning on paneling his own room. . . .

Kevin has repaired all my major appliances since he was kindergarten age. Recently I had to hire a repairman to come and fix my furnace motor, which turned out to be shot and had to be replaced. This repairman hadn't been here for several years and his first question was "Why can't Kevin fix this?" When he discovered the problem he knew that the present motor was beyond repair and he went to get another. However, he brought the burned-out one back because he felt that Kevin could use parts from it.

My dishwasher has been child repaired, my bathroom was child paneled, my toilets were child plumbed. They enjoy developing their abilities, it saves money, and we can use this gained savings for enjoyable activities.

One more wonder that was performed by a child is the light switch which regulates the living-room and hall lights. One switch turns the living room lights on while it turns the hall light off and then turns the hall light on at night when the living-room lights are not needed. An electrician noticed this strange arrangement and said it couldn't be done, but it's been working for a long time.

We have tours through our home occasionally and people never stop marveling at the many things our children know how to do. Kevin built his own motorized three-wheel all-terrain vehicle, as well as helping his dad build a one-man plane. He has developed one patent and is working on another.

People often ask me how I can tolerate the children doing things that are normally only done by adults, and professionals at that. Well, I watch the children carefully and never expect one to do a job which is over his head. I experiment constantly, finding natural abilities and letting them try their wings in harmless, inexpensive ways. If a child shows an ability in a certain area such as plumbing, I try them out taking apart an elbow and putting it back together without a leak. Next comes faucets, or setting a toilet. Next might come the installation of a shower unit, and finally the child is ready to plumb a bathroom. I would have no qualms about letting my thirteen-year-old plumb my entire house. After all, he wired it for D.C. electricity when he was only eight. Our daughter Cathy is remodeling her own home now (she's nineteen), and she has done all her own plumbing, plastering, wallpapering and carpentry. Matter of fact, that's how she helped pay for her college education. She worked as a carpenter in an all-male shop!

Handling money is one of the most useful real world skills and one which gets distorted for many children. Louise Andrieshyn wrote us from Manitoba about her children and money:

Heidi and Michael have just bought themselves ponies with their own money. You'll be pleased to learn that Heidi (10) wrote a cheque for hers.

I don't know what other banking practices are like, but at our credit union any child can have a full-fledged account (and *must* be a shareholder in the corporation in order to have an account). Living in the country, we mail-order shop quite a bit and Heidi's cheques have never been questioned. But perhaps the people who receive them don't know her age! I don't suppose they would ever dream that they were accepting a cheque from a ten-year-old. If they knew, I wonder whether they would refuse to accept it or ask for countersigning?

Since Heidi has a fully personal account, not an "in trust" one, we as her parents are not even allowed to touch her money. We found out the hard way! We went to the credit union to take some money out of her account and they wouldn't let us. They pulled out her file card and showed us her signature saying that only she was able to handle the money in that account. She had signed it when she was 5! I remember distinctly "letting" her sign it, thinking condescendingly how "nice" the experience was for her. Little did I know I was providing her a degree of absolute financial independence.

A sense of the value of money can start very early:

Thought I'd share with you M's "coming of age" as a consumer. M recently turned three. She received a dollar inside a birthday card sent by one of her friends (a 92-year-old). Last year when he sent a dollar I took it without even showing it to her and bought her some balloons with it. This year she opened all her own mail and instantly recognized that it was money and that it was a present for her. She was quite pleased and put it in her wallet which until now was only for *playing* "grownup," and had held only small change. She discussed the dollar, and that she could buy something —whatever she wanted—for herself.

Next day when she got a five-dollar bill in another card we made a fuss again. We discussed the difference in value—on our fingers —of ones and fives, and I thought, "This is going great!"

Next day, when she got a card with a check for *ten* dollars, I thought, "Oh, no, this learning experience is getting out of hand." I hoped she wouldn't realize what a check was so I could spirit it away, but she was too sharp. "More money!" she exclaimed. So we explained what a check was, and traded it for two fives. M had previously studied the one and the five and pointed out that there were different men on them and asked their names (she's very into everything having a "name").

Then M asked me what she could buy with all her "moneys." I suggested she look in the toy catalogues. She got very excited over a construction set (Tinkertoy), and I told her she could look for one like it next time we went to town. So next time Daddy went to town M grabbed her purse and went along to shop for her present to herself. When she found her "struction set" and went to the counter to pay for it—her first purchase—Daddy told her to give the woman a Lincoln, expecting her to get back two Washingtons. Drats!—she gave her a Jefferson! M took it right in stride. Perhaps we should have left it alone, but at home Daddy traded it for two Washingtons. Controlling it again.

After she played with the Tinkertoy set for a couple of days, she expressed disappointment that she couldn't build a house with it. She checked the catalogues and zeroed in on a Lincoln Logs set. The next shopping expedition to town turned one up—for a Lincoln and three Washingtons. We pointed out that she'd spent a lot of money and didn't have that much left. I sense that she has a very balanced feel for money, a good sense of its value, so I'm not worried that she'll either hoard the rest or blow it recklessly.

With all this concern with cash, M didn't lose track of the fact that the money was sent as presents from people who love her. We took pictures of M posed with her presents and a big smile to send along with the thank-you notes.

SPEECH AND LANGUAGE IN REAL LIFE

The difference between learning in and from real life and learning in schools is perhaps most important of all in speech and language. Ivan Illich writes about this in "Vernacular Values and Education," *Teachers College Record,* Fall 1979. (By the time this appears, Illich should have a book in print on the subject of vernacular values.)

In most cultures, we know that speech resulted from conversation embedded in everyday life, from listening to fights and lullabies, gossip, stories, and dreams. Even today, the majority of people in poor countries learn all their language skills without any paid tutorship, without any attempt whatsoever to teach them how to speak. Illich goes on to point out that all over the world, many poor people in nonindustrial countries speak more than one language—a goldsmith he knows in Timbuktu speaks *six*—and that on the whole it is only in nation-states that have had several generations of compulsory schooling that we find most people speaking only one language. For in these supposedly advanced nations, people no longer learn their languages from people who talk to them, meaning what they say, in a context of everyday life, but from professional speakers who are trained and paid to say what others have prepared for them.

Much is said about how inarticulate are today's young. I suspect that an important reason is that so much of the speech they hear, on TV or in school, is not real speech, but canned speech, prepared in advance, and often not even by the speaker. They don't hear many real voices. But it is hearing real voices that makes us want to speak.

A memory. When my sister and I were about four and five, perhaps even less, we visited our grandparents. There was a landing on the second floor, with a railing, through which we could just see down the stairs into the room where the adults sat talking after dinner. After we had been tucked into bed and good-nights said, and the grownups had gone back downstairs, we would slip out of bed, crouch down by the railing, and listen to the grown-up voices. We couldn't catch more than a few of the words, and in any case couldn't understand what was being talked about. But the pull of those voices was fascinating. Usually after a while we would sneak back into bed. But one night we fell asleep there by the railing, where the grownups found us when they went up to bed. I don't remember what came of this, whether we were scolded or punished, and sternly warned not to get out of bed again, or whether the grownups said nothing about it.

Since then I have seen in many other families that it is very hard to keep young children in bed if a group of adults are having lively conversation not too far away. The children will find a hundred different reasons for coming to check out what the grownups are saying.

But, some might say, that's all very fine for privileged families that have interesting visitors. But what about most families, average families? The answer is, first of all, that all people are interesting. As Studs Terkel and Robert Coles have shown in their (very different) books, everyone has many good stories to tell. As long as real people are talking, not just people on TV, children will want to hear their voices and see their faces, and will learn much from them.

8

Living and Working Spaces

SCHOOL OR CLUB?

To a parent who wrote about joining a few other parents in form-
ing their own school, I said:

> Thanks for news of your school. One piece of heartfelt advice.
> People sending their kids to your school must be made to under-
> stand that if there is something they think those children *must* be
> taught or *must* learn, basics or whatever, it must be *their* responsi-
> bility to do that teaching, and to do it in their own home—or at any
> rate, away from the school. The school must be a place where
> people come together to do the things that interest and excite them
> most. Otherwise, you will be torn to pieces with arguments about
> whether the school should teach reading or arithmetic, or teach it
> one or four hours a week, or whatever. Believe me, I speak from
> the bitter experience of many people.

And this would be my very strong advice to any group of
unschoolers who want to start a school as a way of escaping
compulsory attendance laws, or giving their children a place to
meet and be with other children, or for whatever reasons. Okay

to have rules which say, more or less, no fair hurting or bothering other people. Every human society has these, and children expect them and understand them. But the school must not try to *compel* learning. If it does, people will argue endlessly and furiously about what kinds of learning must be compelled. This has happened to small alternative schools again and again.

Nancy Plent wrote about this:

> One more thing I did want to say is about the other mothers I'm meeting. None of us worry about social adjustment stuff; we all know that kids can keep occupied with friends of all ages and with their own interests. But every one of us feels that our kids need more kids. They are feeling "different" and left out, no matter what their situation. E often greets a sunny day with, "Boy, it's a great day to ride green machines! I'll call Tommy and . . . oh, he's in school today." No big thing, maybe, but it happens often, to all of our kids, and we worry about it.
>
> For this reason, the talk always comes around to "maybe if we started some kind of school." We know it is a problem without an answer right now, but we bat it around wistfully all the time anyway. I can only see an answer when we find more people doing it, convince more people that they should do it. I'm giving it all I've got.

It would be a fine thing if in any community there were more places for children, and indeed people of all ages, to get together and do various kinds of things. I talk about what such places might be like in early chapters of *Instead of Education,* and even more in an appendix describing a remarkable place called the Peckham Family Center, which existed for a while in a part of London in the late 1930s. (People are trying to organize a new one in Scotland.)

In some ways, the country clubs that rich folks belong to are a much better model of what we want than a school. Take away the eighteen-hole golf courses, the elaborate tennis courts and other facilities, the palatial clubhouse, and what's left is very close in spirit to what we are after. You don't *have* to play golf just because you go to the golf club. You don't have to *do* anything. There are certain kinds of resources there for you to use, if you want, but you can spend the day there sitting in a chair and looking at the sky. Why not an inexpensive version of the same thing? A country club without the country—or perhaps a different kind of country, just a little patch of field or woods or whatever is handy.

If we can keep the idea of a family club in mind, we will probably make more sensible choices and decisions.

Some years ago a good friend of mine, Peggy Hughes, then living in Denmark, decided to make a 16mm sound film about the Ny Lille Skole (New Little School), a small "school" in which she was working, which I describe in *Instead of Education.* She had done a small amount of black and white photography, but had never even owned a movie camera, let alone made a film with sound.

In time, working almost entirely alone, with occasional advice from the more experienced, she produced a film, about forty-five minutes long, called "We Have to Call It School." I am not unbiased about it; she and I are old friends, I loved the school and the people in it, and for some of the footage I was her sound man. But I think it is the most vivid, touching, and true film portrait of children that I have ever seen. Anyone who likes, enjoys, and respects children will surely be charmed and delighted by it and may learn much from it.

Why should unschoolers want to see a film about school? The answer is in the title. Early in the film is a shot of the children arriving at school in the morning. Over this we hear the voice of one of the teachers, Erik, saying, "We have to call it school. The law in Denmark says that children have to go to school, and if we didn't call this a school, they couldn't come here." But it is not a school in any way that we understand those words. It is a meeting, living, and *doing* place for six or seven adults and about eighty children, aged about six through fourteen. It is more like a club than anything I can compare it to. The children come there when they feel like it, most of the time during the winter, not so often when spring and the sun arrive. Once there, they talk about and do many things that interest them, sometimes with the adults, sometimes by themselves. In the process, they learn a lot about themselves, each other, and the world.

The film is important for unschoolers for many reasons, among them this one. What we need in our communities is not so much schools as a variety of protected, safe, interesting *spaces* where children can gather, meet and make friends, and do things together. Such spaces might include children's libraries (or sections of libraries), children's museums (a wonderful one in Boston), children's theaters (children *making* the drama, not just watching it), children's (or children's and adults') arts or craft centers, adventure playgrounds, and so on. One such space was the Peckham Center. Another such space could be something like the Ny Lille Skole. It's not a matter of copying it exactly, but of catching the spirit of it.

GREENHOUSE

Beth Hagins writes from Illinois about still another child space, the best of the lot, because it is not primarily for children at all, but has its own real and serious work.

> . . . We are working to create a biological research setting for children in the south Chicago area. It's a large solar greenhouse that we have built with people in the black township of Pembroke, Illinois. It's a very rural, low-income community. The quality of life is superbly suited to growing without schooling.
>
> I don't know how to describe the place without sounding like a grant application. I've been "learning" there for the past four years, largely being taught by the older people. They've taught me how to grow, how to make compost, how to conserve, how to slaughter, how to cooperate. I've never been happier learning anywhere. It's even helped put my own formal academic instruction in perspective . . . (Kindergarten through Ph.D.).
>
> The greenhouse manager is a 67-year-old man who's been selling and growing all his life. Our experiments are economic and biological. We are raising laying hens, getting eggs, saving chicken manure, growing worms, fertilizing starter plants, and watching our chickens and plants *flourish* in all the sunlight. We would love to have a few children to work with. We are working to get a few local children involved actively, but it is always more exciting for them to have friends from outside the area coming to learn, too.

. . . It's funny. As I think back on school, the one thing that I feel most molded by was the reward structure for getting A's. Apart from a "B" in sociology as a sophomore in college, I don't think I got anything but A's since fourth grade. I discovered I could get A's in anything, although I am to this day not very quick on my feet in terms of thinking. I suppose that the A's were what opened doors for me, got me into more exciting learning situations—like regional orchestras, national debate forums, and other kinds of special "larger than life" experiences that can stimulate and impress if they do not intimidate. I don't know enough about the deschooling movement to know if this kind of larger association of children is possible. We hope to be able to do something like this with the greenhouse experiments, and to introduce the children to some of the schooled, practicing experimenters who nonetheless share the values of the deschoolers. Many of the solar societies are organized and powered by very wonderful scientists and researchers who would like the opportunity to work on a limited basis with children outside a formal school context.

SPACE UNLIMITED

Harold Dunn of Oregon writes of the hazards of calling any kind of children's space a "school," and about traveling in Mexico with children:

My primary interest is in building nonschool alternatives for kids. Two years ago, when I still believed that Free Schools were the answer, I started a mini-school, with five kids and two adults living with me in my home, a converted school bus parked way out in the Oregon woods beside a small lake. Tuition was free, teaching nonexistent, curriculum based on survival since we had less than $100 a month for all eight of us to live on.

Two of the boys, aged 14 and 15, had spent much of the summer out at my place, always busy and creative in their play. They dreaded the return to public school in September, so we called ourselves a school and just continued on as we had all summer. Only it didn't work out. They became bored, restless, and complained they weren't learning anything.

It took me quite a while to realize that since they were now in "school," they expected somebody to *do* something *to* them. It didn't matter that all summer they had been exploring new realms and expanding their limits with no adult supervision. Now they demanded to be told what to do. Somebody was supposed to learn them something, or else it wasn't a real school and no damn good after all.

I realized then how much we had destroyed for these two boys just by calling ourselves a school. Of course, the destruction happened gradually during all their previous schooling, as they were conditioned to believe that learning is a passive thing, and that school is where it happens.

The three other kids in our school, age 5, 10, and 12, had never been to school, so had no preconceived ideas of what to expect. What a joy it was to watch them explore the world and themselves. Their greatest treasure was my library card, which allowed them to read hundreds of pages each day. They never seemed to get their fill of books, yet they still had energy to cook, bake, chop wood, wash dishes, and clean house. The two oldest girls did far more than their share of the work needed to sustain us all—because they *wanted* to. They were alive, eager, and incredibly inventive. They saw the whole world as open to them, because nobody had taught them there were things they couldn't do.

In a month's time, M (12) went from being a virtual nonswimmer to being the first kid to pass the "Mountain-Man Test," a challenge I had put up to a group of boys that hung out at the lake all that summer. The test consisted of swimming out to the middle of the lake (about 100 yards), alone, at midnight, and diving to the bottom (12 feet), bringing back some mud to prove it. Several boys had tried it, but they all chickened out, even those that were much better swimmers than M. But she stuck with it, working hard to overcome her fears. (It's *dark* down in that lake at night.) And the night she passed the test she announced that since she was now the only member of the Mountain-Man Club, she was changing the name to Mountaineers!

The incredible contrast between these girls, who had no previous schooling, even in free schools, and the two boys so conditioned by their years of public school dogma, was a powerful lesson for me. For many years, I had dreamed of starting a new kind of free school, run entirely by the kids themselves, rather than controlled by the parents or the teachers, as is usually the case. Finally my dream had come true, only to teach me its own absurdity. Any kids truly free to run their own school exactly as they see fit, will immediately declare a permanent vacation, and that will be the end of it. They may get together as before, and do the same things, but they won't call it school unless you make them—and then *you're* running the show, and that's not freedom, even if you're doing it, as I was, "for their own good" to keep them out of public school.

Any kid who has ever been to school knows that "school" is only a special name for a kid's jail, and it's hard for them to imagine having fun, doing what they want, or being creative in jail. So they expect you to tell them what to do, because that's what happens in "school." I find that playing jailer just takes too much energy. I burn out quickly. Yet I can be with those same kids all summer long when they don't expect anything from me, and they give *me* energy. It could go on forever, and I'd never burn out.

Last spring, eleven of us spent two months exploring the deserts of Baja in our school bus. The four school-age boys with us had an incredible learning experience—all the more so because the purpose of the trip was just to have fun.

We speared fish in the warm Gulf waters, hiked deserted sea-shores, climbed cliffs, and explored the ruins of an old silver-mining town. The kids were with us as we learned the secrets of economical grocery shopping in a foreign land, and while we searched through two Baja towns for kerosene.

Together we experienced the adventures of a blowout in the middle of the desert, and a week-long delay due to a broken drive shaft. During that delay D (8) and a Mexican boy were invited to spend all one night shrimping on a Mexican shrimp boat. Everywhere we went, we played with the Mexican kids we met in the parks or on the streets.

But our greatest adventure was when we joined up with a small Mexican circus, and went on the road with them for 15 days, playing the little fishing villages way out on the Vizcaine Peninsula, two days by horrible dirt roads out into the wilderness. Originally we were asked to join the circus because one of our group was a professional juggler. Then gradually the rest of us were encouraged to work up acts and be part of the show. Gilberto, whose family made up the whole circus, taught our kids clowning, tumbling, and whatever else they wanted to learn. All day they practiced and played with Gilberto's kids, developing friendships as deep as any they had ever known. Although they picked up a feel for the

Spanish language, and learned a few words, what they really learned was that words aren't all that important.

During those two weeks we were totally immersed in the life of the circus; several of us found new skills and performed for the first time. C, at 15, has since become a juggler and professional clown.

Later, when it became obvious that our bus was isolating us from even more experiences we might be having, several of us left the main group to hitch or ride the trains and buses. Although our trip cost less than $100/month apiece, I've since been spending about $15/month on my own trips, hitching and hiking around Baja, working for a day or so whenever I feel like it. This is the sort of alternative to school that seems ideal for so many adventure-seeking, broke teen-agers.

FARM SPACE

An article by Jerry Howard in *Horticulture* tells about a food-raising space in a rich Boston suburb:

Bill McElwain, a Harvard man who had taught French, run a Laundromat, and become a discouraged farmer, moved to the prosperous town of Weston, Mass., and saw a lot of fertile suburban land going to waste, on the way to and from his work in Boston (rehabilitating houses in the South End).

He saw suburban teen-agers with few alternatives to football, tennis, drama or boredom, and he saw poor city people paying more for food in Roxbury than he was in Weston. (Bill surveyed the cost of twenty-five identical items in both areas and counted a 13% difference.)

In April, 1970, Bill began with borrowed hand tools and donations of seed and fertilizer. With a handful of dedicated helpers, he cultivated almost an acre; the produce was trucked into Roxbury and distributed free to a children's food program and a housing project. There, residents collected donations that found their way back to the farm.

Within a year, Bill was hired as project director of the new Weston Youth Commission. In 1972, he convinced the town to buy the farmland. He ignited a small but dedicated cadre of supporters, including enough people in the volunteer government to insure the continued support of the town. More kids got involved with the farm, and with the proceeds from the vegetables (now sold in Boston for a nominal $1 a crate) he paid workers a minimum wage. The town put more money and equipment into the project, and by 1975, the farm was growing as much as 100 tons of produce a year. About 25% of this was sold locally; the rest went into Boston.

Bill McElwain was fifty years old when the town bought the farm. He is still project director for the Youth Commission, despite his cavalier view of keeping fiscal records, and he still writes a column for the *Weston Town Crier,* in which he proposes dozens of other activities for the young to take part in.

One fall, for instance, Bill counted 600 maple trees along Weston roadsides. In a year and a half, he and a crew built a sugarhouse near the junior high school (using pine boards milled from local trees); scrounged buckets, taps, and evaporating equipment; and produced a cash crop of 250 gallons of grade A maple syrup. There was cider pressing, orchard reclamation, firewood cutting, crate making, construction of a small observatory, and an alternative course at the high school with regular field trips to Boston's ethnic neighborhoods, and to rural New Hampshire.

Virtually all his plans, large or small, have these common ingredients: they provide young people with paying jobs that are educational, socially useful, and fun; they operate on a small scale, need little capital, and use readily available resources, preferably neglected ones; and they bring a variety of people together to solve common problems in an enjoyable context. Building community is one of Bill's more crucial goals, and he'll seize any opportunity—planting, harvesting, "sugaring off," a woodcarving workshop, or May Day—to bring folks together for a festive occasion.

9

Serious Play

In this chapter parents give us a few glimpses of the ways in which children use play, fantasy, make-believe, poetry, song, drama, and art as a way of exploring and understanding the world. This is a very important part of their life and growth. People have done some persuasive studies to show that children who are good at fantasizing are better both at learning about the world and at learning to cope with its surprises and disappointments. It isn't hard to see why this should be so. In fantasy we have a way of trying out situations, to get some feel of what they might be like, or how we might feel in them, without having to risk too much. It also gives us a way of coping with bad experiences, by letting us play and re-play them in our mind until they have lost much of their power to hurt, or until we can make them come out in ways that leave us feeling less defeated and foolish.

For a healthy and active fantasy life children need time, space, and privacy, or at least only as much companionship as they choose. Obviously school, or any other large-group situation— day-care center, nursery school, play group, etc.—does not allow much of this. Perhaps worst of all, they are usually under the eye and control of adults who, even if they will allow children a fantasy life, feel they have to watch it, understand what it means, judge it, make use of it. It was for just this reason that a well-meaning and quite highly praised book, written about ten years ago, called *Fantasy and Feeling in Childhood,* seemed and still seems to me deeply mistaken. The gist of it (and there may well be many books like it) was that if we, i.e., people who work in schools, paid enough attention to the fantasy lives of children, we could learn to understand them and bend them to our own purposes.

This would be a great mistake and a great wrong. Instead, we should be content to watch and enjoy as much of children's fantasy lives as they will let us see, and to take part in them, if the children ask us to and if we can do so happily and unselfconsciously. Otherwise, we should leave them alone. Children's fantasy is useful and important to them for many reasons, but above all because it is *theirs,* the one part of their lives which is wholly under their control. We must resist the temptation to make it *ours.*

We must also resist the equally great temptation to think that this part of children's lives is less important than the parts where they are doing something "serious"—reading, or writing, or doing schoolwork, or something that we want them to do—or to think that we can only allow them time for fantasy after all the important work is done, as we might give them a little piece of candy after a meal. For children, play and fantasy are one of the main courses of the meal. Children should be able to do them, not just in what little tag ends of time remain after all the "important" work is done, but when they are most full of energy and enthusiasm. We talk these days of "quality time." Children need quality time for their fantasy and play as much as for their reading or math. They need to play well as much as they need to read well. Indeed, we would probably find if we looked into it that children who are not good at playing, dreaming, fantasizing, are usually not much good at reading either.

At any rate, here are some nice accounts of this part of the lives of children.

FANTASTIC WORLDS

A mother writes about the world her son created:

> But at the same time we are, deep inside, ready to "un-school." I
> am absolutely convinced of its rightness. My problem is my chil-
> dren, especially the older one (10). After five years of schooling he
> has made it palatable and even enjoyable by creating a world within
> a world there with a couple of his friends. The schoolwork is no
> problem; he goes so that he can get together easily with 2 or 3 other
> boys for playing baseball or whatever. Also, their world contains
> its own society of "weepuls"—scores of Ping-Pong-ball-sized fuzzy
> creatures of different colors with big feet and tiny antennas. For
> almost a year they had their city covering our 20' × 12' sun porch
> (forced to be dismantled because we are remodeling). I haven't read
> *Gnomes,* but doubt if it could be a more complete study than these
> kids have with weepuls: the cast of characters, layers of their soci-
> ety, their soccer and football fields, space-ports and ships, disco,
> museum, school, movie theater, transportation system, all made in
> detailed miniature with great care and skill; their diet of only
> bananas and banana juice, their death by contact with water, and
> so on. When J went on a scout trip to the snow, the weepul King
> Eeker went with him on skis made out of tongue depressors. The
> weepuls go to school and hide in the desks until break time when
> they come out and make school their place and the boys can do
> what they want with and through them. Homework and boredom
> are put up with for the chance to meet A and K and play with
> weepuls.

Candy Mingins, a teacher, writes about a similar game called
Atlas:

> The family didn't have much money, and did have plenty of Ger-
> man thriftiness—hence the children were not swamped with plastic
> toys and gadgets. . . . They had to create their own play, so C and
> his brother and two sisters (all older) played this ongoing game
> (invented mostly by his brother) for 8 years or more. It was a game
> of the World. Each child had tribes of people made from: tooth-
> paste caps glued to marbles (the Lilliputians); Hi-Q game pieces

(the Microscopians); used Magic Markers with toothpick swords and aluminum foil shields (the Sudanis); cooking oil bottles decorated with paper (the Criscoeans), etc. The tribes fought battles in the garden, conquered territories, kept maps and records, held art shows, had a newspaper, and had their own languages and money systems.

It was an ingenious invention of play, which the children created entirely by themselves, and which lasted through time, always encompassing new interests and ideas as the children grew.

COPS AND ROBBERS

A mother writes about a perennial child's game and her own memories of it:

> Nobody ever told me not to play guns. But, when I was a kid, and the gang played cops'n'robbers, I had a problem because I couldn't "die." Some kid would shoot me, and I would want to fall down and die, but somehow I couldn't, and I would just stand there and look dazed. And if I shot somebody, he would just ignore me because he knew I hadn't really killed him.
>
> After I grew up and had kids of my own, and they had taught me *how* to play cops'n'robbers, I realized that I had been a very schizoid child, very uptight, totally lacking in spontaneity, frozen out of the NOW—and playing guns is a kid's way of getting really "with" other kids and into a very fast-moving, action-packed *present.*
>
> My observation (of about 15 years watching such games) is that only very free-spirited kids can play a really good game of cops'n'robbers, and that many games of cops'n'robbers are ended by a child who *does* have feelings of violence and cruelty and causes an "accident" to happen in which someone is hurt. Usually that child wants to put an end to the game because of jealousy—he *can't* share in the fun; not because he has been excluded by the others, but because he isn't capable of playing.
>
> I don't think "playing guns" usually has anything to do with guns, violence, hostility, or cruelty; it is a game of awareness. Feelings, other than joy, get in the way of awareness, and you can explode your feelings by experiencing the sound of the cap exploding in a cap pistol, for instance.

In playing guns, I believe it goes like this: If I am *aware* of you first, I can shoot you, and you have to die! If I get surprised by you, then I KNOW you are more aware than I am because *you* surprised *me,* so I've got to die. I just give up all awareness (falling in the process) until I feel a surge inside me that says I'm ready to be born again—MORE alive than before! Sometimes you and I catch each other at exactly the same time, and then we have to battle it out —Bang! Bang! Pow! Pow! I got YOU! NO you didn't, I got you FIRST!—until we both know that one of us has bested the other. One of us must die and be born again!

If, instead, one of us gets MAD—then the game quickly ends.

Oh, I love a good, noisy game of cops'n'robbers!

I am an old fossil of almost forty who couldn't play guns now to save my soul, but at least I still remember that I learned something from some kids a long time ago.

I'm trying to *tell* you something that can only be experienced, which tells me that I'm a fool. So, my suggestion is that you find a free-spirited kid (maybe you have one in your home?) and see what you can learn from him.

I believe that it's best to learn to look at the spirit—the feelings expressed—in what your child does, and see through the material object. After all, a child can express his feelings of cruelty and hostility when he pets the dog, and he can express his joy and delight when he shoots his gun. If your child is a joyful child and he WANTS a gun, I think you can trust in his joy, because the Bible says the things of this world are perishable, but the things of the spirit are everlasting, and I, personally, think kids are born knowing this.

Even if a child uses his toy gunplay to drain off his anger and hostility, without hurting anything or anyone in the process, what's the harm in it? My husband says he can remember having those feelings when he played guns as a kid (whereas I never saw such feelings expressed when our kids played guns). He said he thought it was a good thing that he had that outlet, as he had a very unhappy home.

Theo Giesy, a mother of four in Virginia says about this:

Darrin and Danile were introduced to guns by a friend K when they were 2 and 4 respectively. K was 4. One of them would stand on a hassock, the others would shoot him and he would die very dramatically. Then someone else would climb up to be shot and die. K died most dramatically and was most fun. This was repeated as fast as someone could climb up, always with high spirits, fun, and friendliness. Darrin immediately wanted guns and built up quite an arsenal. Shortly after that we moved from California to Michigan. Without K the game changed entirely. Now Darrin and Danile would play house. She would stay home and take care of their babies (her dolls and his dolls) and he would ride the scooter to go off to the woods with his gun to hunt a bear to bring home for them to eat. (All imagination—no one we knew was a hunter.) Darrin was then 2½. At the same time when Darrin was really angry he never thought of guns. His expression of violence was "I'll throw a shoe at you." Guns were part of the world of fun and imagination and had nothing to do with real violence. The "death" of K and Danile and Darrin had nothing to do with hurting anyone.

I thought of that often the next year when Darrin's best friend was not allowed to have guns and they were not allowed to have guns at nursery school. So they built guns out of Tinkertoys or snap blocks. Parents who forbid guns are neither preventing violence nor gunplay and parents who allow guns are not encouraging violence.

HOMEMADE STORIES

The mother of a two-year-old boy told me that she had made up a story in which he was the hero, and all the other characters the animals on their small farm. He loved the story. Later she wrote it down and sent me a copy, saying, "You may find it a bit cute but a 5-year-old boy wondered—in a whisper—all the way through, 'Is it true?' "

Children, whether in city or country, are more likely to be interested in stories in which they play a part, and which are full of things drawn from their everyday life. Parents, or other people who know the children well, are the ideal people to make up such stories. Even if they are not very polished, such stories are likely to be much more interesting than most of the stories in books for little children.

A.S. Neill, at Summerhill, used to make up stories for the children there, in which they were the leading characters, chasing or being chased by various spies, crooks, and villains. And as many know, *Alice in Wonderland* was made up for the real child who was the Alice in the story. So, take a shot at making up stories for your children. As with everything else, as you do it you'll get better at it.

Here is part of my friend's story:

PIG IN THE BED

On Tuesday last week a strange thing went on;
Jack came home early and his parents were gone.
He knew right away that something was up
When he took a look at his friend the pup.
(He was drinking a Coke, taking sips as he spoke.)

"Hey Jack! Look out! Better step aside.
The horse and her colt are going for a ride!"
Jack turned around when the pickup truck
Made the sound that it makes when it's just starting up.

The horse put it in gear and sputtered past,
Then before she started going too fast,
She yelled, "Sorry, Jack, to be taking your car,
But it's been a long time since we've gone very far."

Jack stared, then he wondered, then he said, "O.K.,
But will you try to get back by the end of the day?"

He shrugged and went on down to the kitchen,
But when he got there it was full of his chickens!
"Just fixing a little midday treat.
We get awfully tired of old corn to eat,"
Said the hens as they mixed and blended and baked
Until they came up with banana spice cake.

Everywhere Jack looked in the house, he found animals—even in his bed! How to get them out before his parents came back? Then he hit on the solution:

"I've got it!" said Jack, and he started to scream:
"Up in the barn there's chocolate ice cream!"
The chickens took wing, the pig climbed out of bed.
The cow left the tub and the goats quickly fled.

Up the road the horse was parking the truck.
Jack ran to the freezer. "Whew! I'm in luck!"

He got out two gallons of chocolate ice.
"Plenty for everyone! As long as you're nice."
He passed it out fairly to all on the farm,
To the pig in the pig pen and the cow in the barn.
"Thank heavens you knew just what to do,"
Said the dog, passing his plate. "May I have some too?"
"Certainly," said Jack. "But what will mom say
When she sees I ate two gallons of ice cream today?"

Most parents, whether on a farm or in a city, could spin such
a homemade epic. It doesn't need to scan or rhyme as well as this
—the children who see themselves in the story won't be fussy.

REQUIEM FOR A TURTLE

Small children when left on their own love to make up their own
songs and chants. One mother told me about a chant that her
daughter, when two years and nine months old, had made up one
day while swinging on the swing, and seeing something disappear
with a crunch into the mouth of her cat. The chant went like this:

Oh, we went downtown . . .
Downtown my mother
and Mary Jean went.
We saw some pretty turtles,
some pretty little turtles.
Yes, we did. O yes we did!
Pretty, pretty little turtles . . .
They wiggled and wiggled,
They wiggled their heads,
They wiggled their legs,
And their tails they wiggled, wiggled . . . O!

My mother buyed me
Two little turtles
Two little turtles *and*
One little turtle made

The *other* little turtle
Not lonesome . . . O!
He was s'posed to make him
Not lonesome . . . O!

Did he make him not lonesome? NO!
He climb out, out . . .
He fall on the ground . . . O!
Oh, oh, oh, OH!
He climb out
Over and over AGAIN!
I just can hardly believe it!

I look
And I look
On the ground . . .
I find that little turtle, O!
I can hardly believe it!

But he wiggle and he climb!
He fall out on the table, O!
That ignorant little turtle, O!
He fall out on the floor, O!
The poor little,
The ignorant little turtle, O
And the Poco-cat
Ate him all UP!

Bad, bad Poco!
That turtle scratch him,
He scratch him, that Poco,
In the *stomach*!
I *think*!
I think he scratch Poco
In the stomach!
My *mother* will buy me
Another little turtle. Maybe.
For the GOOD little turtle to play with.
Poor, ignorant little turtle!
Oh, Oh, Ohhh. . . .

(Turned out later the cat *hadn't* eaten the turtle, who was found
under the child's bed.)

A VERY YOUNG ARTIST

A father writes about a "precocious" artist:

> We have one of the happy stories about unschooling. Before M was born we had decided not to send her to school. We moved to the country thinking it would be easier there. Now I realize it might sometimes be more difficult.
>
> We were lucky. The teacher and school board of our local school, where I am janitor, have been tolerant and helpful. The teacher is one of the good ones. M goes once a week on a day of her choosing. Any more than once a week, she thinks, would be awful. One defense that we have thought might help if we are given any trouble about not going to school is that she is bilingual and does learning in her other language at home. (There are laws protecting bilingualism in California schools.) M's mother is Japanese.
>
> M began to draw when she was 6 months old. Everything she did was treated as important art. By the time she was one year old she could draw better than anyone around her. Knowing that she could do something better than anyone, even better than the ever-competent giants around her, emboldened her strokes. In other areas it gave her the confidence to try something difficult, then to continue until she could do it well.
>
> At one year of age she was given an easel and some tempera paints. On her second birthday she got nontoxic acrylics, the medium she has preferred since. She enjoyed painting so much that she began calling herself an artist.
>
> We became curious about other children artists so we checked out the children's art scene in San Francisco where we were then living. We made the surprising discovery that M is a child artist who does not paint children's art. Her work would look absurdly out of place in a show of children's art. Especially so since she began using acrylics because it is always assumed that children's art should be done with watercolors. For obvious reasons acrylics are easier to use than poster paints or tempera but they cost more. I know people who make 5 or 6 times my subsistence wage who tell me they can't afford acrylics for their children. What this really means is that they think children can't do anything worth that much.

Probing deeper in this direction via an understanding of adultism might begin to explain what I mean when I say that much of what is known as children's art is an adult invention.

In all the contacts we have had with the children's art establishments in San Francisco and Tokyo we have had nothing but unpleasant experiences. They are amazed but they are even more skeptical. I think they are hoping she'll turn out to be the 40-year-old midget in one of your books. [Author's note: This refers to an episode in *Escape From Childhood.*] Finally we know they are the enemy. We avoid them, scorn their nonsense books on children's art ("Children will generally not be ready to paint before they are 5 years old"), frown back at the saved missionary smiles they are in the habit of turning on their flock. When they used to say M's work was very good for her age I asked them if they would say Picasso's erotic drawings, done in his latter years, were good for his age.

It is recognized that children have their original imagination destroyed in the socializing process and that as adult artists they must struggle to regain it if they are to create an original vision. There must be some way for people to grow up without losing this although it rarely happens. The most obvious thing to do is to stay out of school and maybe to prevent their exposure to phony children's art. One indication of what might have happened to M if she had been forced to go to school full-time is that when she draws at school her drawings are stiff and uninteresting. They are like children's drawings are supposed to be, cute and easy to patronize. She also prints her signature on them like the other children do. She has always signed her name in cursive and has used nothing but cursive at home since she learned it when she was 4 years old. She's 7 now.

M's conversations about what was going on in the paintings while she was doing them were so interesting that I decided when she was 4 years old to get some of her old paintings out to talk about them with her. She enjoyed seeing her treasures again. About the same thing she said originally was repeated but more concisely. She called them poems. During her fifth year she began writing her poems and stories by herself. One of her 4-year-old poems about a painting described what she imagined she did when she was wandering around the world with us five years before she was born: "When I was in Mama's stomach it was very dark so sometimes I wanted to get out. From a secret door I was looking out of Mama's stomach through her navel. Everywhere Mama went I was watching from my secret door. Each time I looked out she came to a new town. I saw the whole world. That's the place I was born."

With his letter the father sent me some reproductions of M's early work, five paintings done between the ages of 26 and 38 months. They were printed in Japan, perhaps by some museum in connection with a show on children's art. I am guessing, but they look like the postcards of paintings that one can buy in museums. The paintings themselves are stunning. Three of them would stop you dead in your tracks if you saw them in an exhibition of "adult" art. The colors, the shapes, the drawing, the design, the underlying idea of the paintings, are extraordinary.

I am ready to believe that M is an exceptionally talented child. But that is what I felt when I first heard four- to six-year-old children, students of Suzuki in Japan, playing difficult music by Bach, Vivaldi, etc., in perfect time and tune. Perhaps other children might do work of equal beauty and power if their talents were taken seriously and given scope.

10

Learning Without Teaching

Much of the material in this chapter could have gone into Chapter 7, *Learning in the World.* I put it here to make a different point. There I was talking about children (and others) learning outside of school. Here I am talking about them learning without teaching —learning by doing, by wondering, by figuring things out, and often in the process resisting teaching when well-meaning adults try to force it on them. A letter from Judy McCahill in England describes this kind of learning very well:

> I do have the worst time explaining to people how I teach the kids. The trouble arises from the very basic concept, which most people can't grasp, that the kids actually teach themselves. I find it impossible, both timewise and because of my live-and-let-live nature, to give any sort of formal lessons. Recently I thought I would begin giving myself systematic lessons in basic science so that I could teach the kids better, but after three days that failed because I always seemed to have something more important to do than study. So I continue with my major technique of just answering questions as well as I can and helping the kids to ferret out information when they want it.

It interests me, though, how quickly the kids latch onto my *real* enthusiasms and, without anybody intending anything, begin to learn. Last summer I visited the Tate Gallery (a big art museum in London) with a girl who had just finished a year-long course in the history of art. She infected me with her enthusiasm, I attended a slide-illustrated lecture that day, and I examined incredulously the calendar of (free!!!) events the Tate had set up—all sorts of lectures, films, special exhibitions and guided tours.

I've only been back to the Tate once since then, but I brought home a couple of books and gloatingly circled all the events I would attend if I could. (Next week I am going to a performance of *Julietta* by the English National Opera which is connected to a film and lecture on Surrealism at the Tate.) Last month our 18-year-old niece came to stay with us and she and Colleen have gone to the Tate three or four times. She [Colleen] has checked an art book out of the library (never having been interested in art before). And the boys often page through the books, studying the pictures. We have many discussions arising from what the girls have seen at the Tate; Colleen takes notes on the lectures for my benefit. So something new has entered our life, and it was completely accidental.

NO WORDS TO THE WISE

As many may know, in the Suzuki method of violin instruction, at least as first conceived and practiced, the parents of a child, while it is still a baby, begin to play for it, and often, recordings of the easy violin pieces which it will itself learn to play at the age of three. Kathy Johnson and I have talked often (in letters) about Suzuki. Recently she wrote:

You asked me last December to let you know how my home adaptation of Suzuki violin with my two-year-old daughter is working. I hadn't actually brought home the 1/16-size violin then, but in self-defense had to get her one to keep her from having tantrums when my dad and I played. Her being well into the "No" stage now is living proof of why they don't organize a class of young Suzuki violinists until age three.

But I feel you *can* do more at an early age than merely play the record. With no big fanfare, one day when a tantrum started during our duet, I simply suggested she play her own violin—that little one over there in the corner. She gave me a look as if to say, "Oh yes, but of course!" And before the duet was over, she had figured out how to open the case, get the violin out, and saw the bow upside down over the strings a few times. She was delighted.

In the past four months, whenever we saw such a gross mistake on her part, either my dad or I (whoever was closer) would *very briefly* reach down and show her a better way to play as we went along. Of course, she had to learn some rules: not to carry her instrument around the house, especially on noncarpeted surfaces, not to handle the bow hair (or it won't make any sound on the strings), etc. We were amazed how fast she learned to respect her instrument. She even keeps the bow rosined!

She hasn't mastered the technique of playing just one string at a time yet, but she has darn good position, and a wonderful time developing those long full bows.

We were amazed when out-of-town relatives came to visit and our *shy* little daughter brought out her violin to squawk on the strings in front of a roomful of adults. We were all proud—but not as proud as she was! I think the important thing my dad and I learned very quickly was to recognize that moment when she needed help, capitalize on it briefly, then leave her alone to experiment. Praise is used, but in not much greater amounts than Dad and I praise each other. We play for enjoyment. I think she does, too.

She won't stand for a "lesson." Help that is a few seconds too long or in the wrong tone of voice brings loud "No-No's" followed by her putting her violin away and being angry. At this age, there's a fine line between happiness and tears. When she wants, if she wants, we'll see an expert.

A mother writes about another child resisting teaching:

My daughter (3) is in the kitchen teaching herself addition and subtraction on the Little Professor Calculator—a machine I don't really approve of—and every time I give her a gentle hint, she flies into a rage, but when I leave her alone and watch her out of the corner of my eye, I see her doing problems like $3 + 5 = 8$!

Years ago I went to a meeting of Catholic educators, where I heard a talk by a wise, funny old man who had been teaching all his life. One thing he said made us all laugh, and has stuck in my mind ever since: "A word to the wise is *infuriating!*" Yes it is, because it is insulting, and little children pick up this expression of (often loving and protective) distrust or contempt, even when we're not conscious of sending it.

Some years ago I was reading aloud to a small child, as yet a nonreader, perhaps three or four years old. As I read aloud I had the bright idea that by moving a finger along under the words as I read them I might make more clear the connections between the written and the spoken words. A chance to get in a little subtle teaching. Without saying anything about it, and as casually as possible, I began to do this.

It didn't take the child very long to figure out that what had begun as a nice, friendly, cozy sharing of a story had turned into something else, that her project had by some magic turned into *my* project. After a while, and without saying a word, she reached up a hand, took hold of my hand, and very gently moved it off the page and down by my side—where it belonged. I gave up "teaching" and went back to doing what I had been asked to do, which was to read the story.

A father writes:

> It is not possible for an inquisitive child to delve deeply into dinosaurs without wondering about, and learning, how big they were (measurements), how many roamed a certain area (arithmetic), where they lived (geography), what happened to them (history), etc. And, after daddy's knowledge of dinosaurs was exhausted, which happened pretty quickly, a lot of reading was necessary. In short, it simply isn't possible to learn a lot about dinosaurs or anything else without along the way learning and using knowledge and skills that are intellectually prerequisite. After all, the reason that we call "the basics" by that phrase is that they *are* basic, and to worry that a kid will learn just about anything without learning and using the basics is like being worried that he might decide to build a house starting with the roof.
>
> It's hard work, of course, for us to adjust ourselves to the kids' interests. They wake up every morning curious but, alas, rarely curious about the particular topics that we might be prepared to

talk about or might prefer that they be curious about—that's when temptation rears its head and must be suppressed. It's a waste of time and quickly degenerates into intellectual bullying to try to sidetrack a kid onto topics *you* think he should be learning. Of course, going along with the kids' interests may, as it recently did in our family, find you subjected to six straight days of inquiry into space exploration. But, if you will just be patient and observant, the time comes when the kid, because *he* realizes that it's pertinent to learning about his primary interest, will, almost off-handedly (but it sticks), add rocket thrusts, multiply fuel loads, distinguish ellipses from circles, etc. Keep your mouth shut when you are not needed, and be ready to help when you are. The kid will learn.

Perhaps the reason that so many adults—including, I confess, myself—find it hard to refrain from "helping" kids is that it wounds our egos to see how well they get along without us! How can that dumb kid of mine learn so much without a smart fellow like me to teach him? We try in effect to horn in on the kids' sense of pride in accomplishment and, all too often, particularly in schools, we succeed. The results are psychologically and intellectually catastrophic for the victims.

Another father writes:

I have read the books you have written, and between them and Bob (4), I've found, for me, the best way to teach is by example, and the best way to learn is by doing. (Bob continually tells us, "I don't want to know that" when we try to teach him something he doesn't want to learn.) Linda and I are impressed how quickly he picks things up, but what impresses me the most is his ability to just sit and think. I never knew young children did that until Bob showed me. He also repeats and repeats things until he has them. We put him to bed at 9 P.M., and often at 11 we can hear him talking to himself as he goes over things he wants to get straight. This is how he learned the alphabet and how to count to 129. That's his favorite number and he counts to it over and over and over. Somehow he has picked up the idea that a number means a quantity of objects, and I am amazed he has learned that level of abstraction so quickly and completely.

I've tried to let Bob and David learn what they want to at the rates they set, but sometimes it is hard not to teach. There is one story I enjoy, simply because it was the only time I've been successful at teaching when Bob wasn't interested. When Bob was learning to count, he asked me what comes after 113. I didn't answer his question, but instead asked him what comes after 13. Well, he got mad because that's not what he wanted. I remained stubborn and he finally said, "14 comes after 13, what comes after 113?" very indignantly. I immediately said, "114." At first he was disgusted because I didn't answer his question the first time, but then he understood what I had just done. He broke out in a big grin and covered his face. We like to trick each other, and I had just gotten him.

One summer I was visiting an eight-year-old friend and her mother. They lived in a little house on a small side street, really more an alley. Cars seldom come through so kids can play there safely. In one part of the street there are high board fences on both sides, which makes it a good place for small ball games. My young friend and her friends often play their own version of baseball here. For a bat they use a thin stick about three feet long. The ball is a playground ball about six inches in diameter. The rules fit the space perfectly; with that stick, no one can hit that ball over those fences.

The day I arrived, after dinner, she asked me if I would pitch some batting practice. I said, Sure, and we had about forty-five minutes' worth in the alley. Next morning after breakfast she asked again, and we had about an hour more. Some of the time she very kindly pitched to me. I was amazed to find how hard it was to move that squishy ball with that skinny stick.

The point of the story is that in all this I did something about which I felt quite pleased, that I don't think I could or would have done even five years ago. In our almost two hours of play I did not offer *one word* of coaching or advice. The words were more than once on the tip of my tongue, once when she tried batting one-handed (she did better than I thought she would), once when she tried batting cross-handed (she gave it up on her own), and now and then when she seemed to be getting careless, not watching the ball, etc. But I always choked the words back, saying to myself, "She didn't ask you to coach, she asked you to pitch. So shut up and pitch." Which I did.

Nor did I give any praise. Sometimes—quite often, as a matter of fact—when she hit a real line drive, I let out a word of surprise or even alarm, if it came right at me. Otherwise we did our work in silence, under the California sun. I remember it all with pleasure, and not least of all the silence. I hope I can be as quiet next time.

A mother in Ontario describes an extraordinary day in which she and another mother let the children lead the play:

> Last fall we had a school group meeting [of children who on most days were learning at home] twice a week. Mostly 2–4-year-olds and mostly girls with one five-year-old girl and a six-year-old boy. Altogether there were about twelve children. It was quite a delightful group.
>
> This is the day I remember best from that time. We began painting, and working with clay, and playing in the yard in front of the house. As lunch time neared we decided to have a picnic in the little pine forest. (This was one of the favorite nice weather activities.) The little pine trees are about twelve years old and a wonderful size for little people to climb and create fantasy worlds within.
>
> As we were eating, I noticed some tiny green plants growing within the browns, reds, oranges of the fall leaves. I looked closer at the little plants and suggested that the children near me help me look for the various tiny plants growing around us. We found my favorite spring greens—sorrel and peppergrass—and some clover and a couple of plants none of us were familiar with. We nibbled the greens and were pleased with our discovery.
>
> Soon the wonderful game of "roaring lions in the forest" began. The other mother and I sat to rest for a while. One child (3) stayed with us looking at the plants. She was a very quiet child and often stayed by herself very absorbed for long times with her interests while all the others very easily related and played and talked with each other. Sometimes I wondered if she wanted help getting to know others, if she was lonely and frightened in her solitude. But from observing her I'd decided she was actually quite happy on her own a lot. She almost never talked at school, but I knew she could talk because I'd heard her talk to her older sister quite freely. So when she began talking to me about the plants I was delighted. We looked very slowly at many little plants and she pulled some out to look at the roots. Then she looked at the different levels of dead leaves—the brand new, bright crunchy ones were pushed away by

her delicate finger, next there were softer brown ones, then black matted ones, then dirt. We talked throughout this examining of the magic of plants and earth.

When that was complete we moved off to join the others who led us through the pines to the edge of the swamp—cedars and black gooshy mud and water. Someone took shoes and socks off and within a very short time all shoes and socks came off. There was a great deal of splashing and stamping and singing and joy. Someone fell down and got his pants mucky. (I thought—What are his parents going to think?) They were obviously having way too much fun to stop them. Soon all clothes were being taken off and put on the moss under the cedars. And the jolly dance continued. The little girl I described earlier was joining right in with all the others looking quite radiant. One child stayed back from the muck and the wet. He didn't seem disturbed by the others dancing in the muck, but obviously it didn't appeal to him. Exploring the swamp went on until it was time to dry off, get dressed, and go home.

I thought about that day and wondered how most of the parents would have responded. Some might not have allowed the naked water play—others probably would have. Some probably would have felt there wasn't much happening that day as much of it was spent on a long walk. But I was glad that the other mother who was there was as willing as I to follow the little people on their adventure and I loved that day!

FINDING OUT

... A three-year-old has moved into a new house and has played in the sunshine on the new roof. He goes downstairs to supper and when he comes back steps into a changed and darkened world. With a wondering glance he says, "The big shadow is all around." Another three-year-old sees a thin cloud float across the moon. She watches intently, then says to herself, "Like ice, like ice."

This child's vision, quoted in a Colorado (Boulder) magazine called *Outlook,* is echoed by Hanna Kirchner, writing in Poland about the work of the physician Janusz Korczak:

He always stressed that by means of learning the everyday expressions from the obscure language of adults, the child tries to fathom the mystery of life. The child's fragmentary and incomplete knowledge of the world, welded together by imagination, creates a specific "magic consciousness" which, as has been discovered in the twentieth century, exists among children and primitive people and may be associated with the origins of poetry.

She then gives this wonderful quote from Korczak's book *How to Love a Child* (not yet translated into English):

[one child says], "They say there is one moon and yet one can see it everywhere."
"Listen, I'll stand behind the fence and you stay in the garden." They lock the gate.
"Well, is there a moon in the garden?"
"Yes."
"Here too."
They change places and check once again. Now they are sure there must be two moons.

And yet they figure out, sooner or later, and *by themselves,* that there is only one moon.
And Theo Giesy tells this nice story:

When Danile was 6 or 7, she was lying in my bed thinking about money and wondering how $1 would divide among 3 children. She thought about it awhile and said, "You could break it into dimes and give each one 3, that leaves 1 dime, you break that into pennies and give each one 3, and I get the extra penny." That was all her own, I made no comments or suggestions.

When I first taught fifth grade, before I had "taught" the children anything about fractions, or even mentioned the word, I used to ask them questions like this: "If you had three candy bars, and wanted to divide them evenly among five people, how would you do it?" Most of them could think of one or more ways to do this. But after they had "had" fractions, and learned to think of this as a problem that you had to use fractions to solve, most of them couldn't do it. Instead of reality, and their own common sense and ingenuity, they now had "rules," which they could rarely keep straight or remember how to apply.

Since to so many people "learning" means what happens in school, or what is supposed to happen, I would rather use other words to describe what we humans do as a natural part of our living. "Finding out" seems to fit pretty well. Here, a reader talks about this continuous process:

> I am almost a caricature of the congenital unteachable. It may have been something I picked up from imitating my father, for I notice he shares the trait to this day. He is very quick to learn, but utterly resists being taught.
>
> I began to see how much this unteachability pervaded my life when I began about a year ago to see how much of my childhood I could remember distinctly. Probably the extreme example was learning to play the piano. I am told that I started banging away on the family upright at about age four. One day my dad got tired of the noise and said something to the effect of "If you're going to play, why don't you play *something*?" Well, I quit until my parents left the house, and when they came back that afternoon I was already picking out tunes. In a year I played "Silent Night" at church Christmas ceremonies.
>
> *So* much has been like this. I started drawing at about four, also holding the pencil the wrong way. People said that I would never be able to draw that way. After selling dozens of paintings and drawings, I still hold it that way—I don't like the other way, as it produces a more unsteady hand for me. When, at about twelve, I wanted to write books, my dad gave me an old Royal and left me alone. I learned to type at good speed with one right-hand finger.
>
> Then there were swimming lessons, which almost permanently made me hate swimming. A couple of years afterward, when I *wanted* to swim with my friends, I jumped in and swam as if I had always done so.
>
> I taught myself auto mechanics on my first car, after being told for years that I was low in mechanical ability. I became a good carpenter's apprentice in two months, building one and a half houses with just one carpenter working at the same time. I surprised them all (except my parents—who had been listening) when I switched from an undergraduate education in pre-law to master's

work in engineering, putting to rest the old thing about how artsy-booksy types cannot cope with numbers.

How did I get through schools? Only one way—by taking the offensive. Way back around fifth grade, my parents supplied us kids with the Golden Book Encyclopedia. I lapped up each book as it came home from the supermarket. Not long after that I was tested for reading at school and was found to be reading five years ahead of my grade. What is more, the Golden Book Encyclopedia gave me two invaluable things which freed me from much of the meaningless work the schools had cut out for me. One, I acquired from the encyclopedia a working familiarity with many aspects of science, history, geography, and art—such that I still "leaned on" this knowledge during exams as late as, say, tenth grade. Moreover, it taught me an understanding of how the world works, so that I could figure out what I did not actually know.

I recall what I did in fifth grade to free up more time to study airplanes, which I was then immersed in as a subject. The teacher wanted us to come up with five new words a week which we were supposed to define as a vocabulary lesson [Author's note: as if anyone ever learned words this way]. Trouble was, words did not come to me at this steady pace. So, one day, I reached into the dictionary for two hundred-odd words and did a year's assignments in one bored stroke. Then I went back to gobbling up new and historical words as part of the new book I was writing on airplanes.

When I went back to grad school I again entered on the explicit understanding that I would take some required courses and do some required research for the chance to be allowed hunks of free time to pursue an area that no one at the school even understood. It worked. So well, in fact, that I literally walked into a job working with the guy who my previous research had shown to be tops in the field.

And now I find some strange truths. With the top-notch people that make up our company, *what counts is the ability to teach oneself* [Author's emphasis]. As my employer puts it, "Though we may seem to know a lot around here, we succeed because we start out by admitting our ignorance, and then setting out to overcome it."

This points up one important idea, the "need to know." People often say of me that I "know" a great deal about this or that; but often I have only average knowledge or less. In any given context, however, I can identify what I need to know next, and self-reliance has taught me to immediately acquire the knowledge in ways which do not essentially differ from one case to the next. Thus it occurs to me that if people recognized knowledge as being important *only in relation to actual goals*—narrow or broad in scope—rather than being some kind of unquestionable goal in itself, they might better know how to go about acquiring it.

I know more than a few individuals who share my experience. Their existence assures me that a market exists for free schools offering not "teachers" but *the resources necessary for self-teaching.*

THE SHORT, HAPPY LIFE OF
A TEACHING MACHINE

When the Santa Fe Community School was just starting, a young inventor, who hoped to market one of the "teaching machines" then in fashion, lent one of his models to the school. It was a big metal box, that sat on top of a table. Through a window in the front of the box, one could see a printed card. Beside the window were five numbered buttons. On the card one might read something like this: "An apple is a (1) machine (2) animal (3) fruit (4) fish (5) musical instrument." If one pushed button #3, a little green light went on above the buttons, and a new card appeared behind the window. If one pushed any of the other buttons, a red light went on. Like most teaching machines, it was only a fancy way of giving multiple choice tests.

On the day the inventor brought the box to school the children, aged 5 through 8, gathered around to see how it worked. The inventor showed them how to use it, and for a while the children took turns pushing the buttons and answering the questions on the cards. This only lasted a short while. Then the children began to say, "Open the box! We want to see inside the box!" Someone opened up the front panel, showing the cards, mounted on a revolving drum. Beside each card were five little holes, and a metal plug to stick into the hole matching the "right answer" to the question on the card.

The children considered all this a minute, and then fell to work —*making cards.* After a while they all had some cards to load into the machine. Bargains were struck: "I'll play using your cards if you'll play using mine." One child would load up the machine with his cards, and put in the answer buttons, then another child would come and take the test, then they would trade places. This went on for perhaps a day or so, all very serious.

Then, so the friend told me who was teaching there at the same school and saw all this, the game began to change. There was much loud laughter around the machine. The teachers went to see what was going on. What they saw was this. A child would load the machine, as before, and another child would take the test. Up would come a card saying something like, "A dog is a (1) train (2) car (3) airplane (4) animal (5) fish." The child taking the test would press button #4, the "right answer," and *the red light would go on.* The child who had made the card, and others watching, would shriek with laughter. The child being tested would push the buttons, one by one, until he hit the "right" one and the drum turned up the next card. Then, same story again, another right answer rewarded with the red light, more laughter. When one child had run through all his rigged cards, the other would have a turn, and would do exactly the same thing.

This happy game went on for a day or two. Then the children, having done everything with the machine that could be done with it, grew bored with it, turned away from it, and never touched it again. After a month or so the school asked the inventor to take his machine away.

This little incident tells us more about the true nature of children (and so, all humans) than fifty years worth of Pavlovian behaviorist or Skinnerian operant conditioning experiments. Maybe Psychologist and Pigeon is a good game, for a while at least. But all human beings soon want to play Psychologist; no one wants to be the Pigeon. We humans are not by nature like sheep or pigeons, unquestioning, docile, happy to work the machine as long as it lights up its green lights or rolls out its food pellets. Like these children, we want to find out how the machine works, and then *work it.* We want to find out how things happen, so that we can make them happen. That is the kind of creature we are. Any theory of learning or teaching which begins by assuming that we are some wormlike or ratlike or pigeonlike creature is nonsense and can only lead (as it has and does) to endless frustration and failure.

LEARNING A NEW LANGUAGE

Young children who come into contact with people who speak more than one language will learn to speak all of those languages, usually without much trouble. Older people, who have a great deal of trouble, are amazed by this. To explain it, they invent fancy theories about children having a special aptitude, or their brains being somehow different from adults'.

The real explanation is simpler. The child, who in his home speaks language A, but meets outside the home other children who speak language B, does not in any way set himself the task of "learning language B." In fact, he does not think of himself as "speaking language A," or indeed any language. He just speaks. He tries to understand what people are saying, and to make them understand what he wants to say, and the more he does this, the better he gets.

Now, all of a sudden, he meets some people whom he can't understand at all, and who can't understand him. What he wants and tries to do is understand those people, at least a little, *right now,* and to make them understand him, at least a little, *right now.* That is what he works at, and since he is smart, tireless, ingenious, not much discouraged by difficulties, and not at all worried about "failing" or looking foolish, and since he gets instant responses to tell him whether or not he is understanding or being understood, he very quickly gets good at it.

His parents think how wonderful it is that he is learning language B so quickly. But he is not trying to do that. He would not understand what it meant to "learn a language," and would not know how to do such a task even if people could explain to him what the task was. He is just trying to communicate with those people he meets.

After my father had retired from business, he and my mother began to spend the winter half of each year in Mexico. My father, who had been—just barely—a good enough student to graduate from a "good" college, told himself sternly, and kept telling himself for six years and more, that he ought to "learn Spanish." My

mother, who had not gone to college, and had been a poor student
—she had always been terribly nearsighted, but beyond that was
bored to death by the tasks of school—could not have cared less
about "learning Spanish." What she wanted, like little children,
was to be able to talk to these people around her, who were not
at all like any of the people she had ever known, and who interested her very much. She had always had a small child's keenness
of observation and sharpness of mind, and now, like a young child,
she began to try to talk to the people around her, to ask the names
of things, to ask *how* to ask the names of things. The people she
talked to, enchanted as people always are by someone who makes
a real effort to speak their language, talked back, showed her
things and told her their names (as they did to me when I visited),
gently corrected her mistakes in pronunciation or usage, not so
that she would speak "correctly" but only so that she would be
better understood, and helped her in every way they could. The
result was that very soon she could talk easily and fluently with
people on many subjects.

At the same time, my father, who thought of himself as trying
to "learn Spanish," which meant to learn to speak it correctly, so
that *then* he could talk to the people around him, never learned
more than twenty or so words in all the years he lived in Mexico.
Now and then my mother tried to get him to say a few words to
the people he met. He couldn't do it. He was struck dumb by his
school-learned fear of doing it wrong, making a mistake, looking
foolish or stupid. He backed away from all these human contacts,
telling himself all the while that he really ought to learn Spanish
but was just too old, didn't have the aptitude, and so on.

LEARNING MUSIC

The October 5, 1977, issue of *Manas* magazine quotes, from the
book *Piano: Guided Sight Reading,* by Leonard Deutsch, this
interesting fragment:

> The famous Hungarian and Slovak gypsies have a centuries-old
> musical tradition. This colorful folk has brought forth numerous

excellent instrumentalists, notably violinists. They learn to play much as an infant learns to walk—without teaching methods, lessons, or drills. No written music is used. The youngster is merely given a small fiddle and *allowed to join the gypsy band* [Author's emphasis]. He gets no explanations or corrections. He causes no disturbance, for his timid efforts are scarcely audible. He listens: he tries to play simultaneously what he hears, and gradually succeeds in finding the right notes and producing a good tone. Within a few years he has developed into a full-fledged member of the band with complete command of his instrument.

Are these gypsy children particularly gifted? No, almost any child could accomplish what they do. The band acts as teacher talking to the pupil in the direct language of music. The novice, by joining the band, is immediately placed in the most helpful musical atmosphere and psychological situation; thus, from the beginning, he finds the right approach to music activity.

In contrast, an extremely intelligent and capable friend, not at all daunted by most forms of learning, and a lover of music, once told me that she wished she could read music, but that ever since she had been taught music in school, the task had seemed hopelessly mysterious, terrifying, and impossible. I asked her if she could think of any special part of it that seemed harder than the rest. Like most people in that position who are asked that question, she made a large gesture and said, "All of it. I just don't understand *anything* about what those little dots mean on the page." I asked if it was the rhythm or the pitch that seemed most mysterious. After some thought, she said, "The pitch." I then said (there was a piano handy), "If you like, I think I can show you in a few minutes how to find any written note." She agreed. Within half an hour she was very slowly playing, by herself, a piece out of a beginning piano instruction book.

Five things made it possible for me to help her find out how to do this. (1) It was her idea, her interest; *she* wanted to do it. (2) I was at all times ready to stop if she wanted to. She knew I would not, in my enthusiasm for teaching, push her into the confusion, panic, and shame into which eager or determined teachers so often push their students. (3) I accepted as legitimate and serious both her anxiety and her confusion. Even in the privacy of my own mind, I did not dismiss any of her fears or questions as silly. (4) I was ready to let *her* ask all the questions, to wait for her answers, and to let her use my answers as she wished. *I did not test her understanding.* I let her decide whether she understood or not, and if not, what to do about it, what question to ask next. (5) I was not going to *use* her to prove to her or myself or anyone else what a gifted teacher I was. If she wants to explore written music further, fine. If she wants to ask me for more help, that's fine too —though even better if, as I suspect, she can do it without my help. But if, having proved to herself that she *can* figure out what notes mean, she doesn't want to do more of it—well, that's fine too.

In an article entitled "Violinist Par Excellence," in *Music Magazine,* February 1980, a great violinist talks about teaching:

> Nathan Milstein says his own family in Odessa was not particularly musical. "They became musical eventually," he laughed. "But I don't think a musical family makes much of a difference." His mother wanted him to play violin not because she was musical, but because, as he said once, she "wanted to calm me down and she thought the violin would do it."
>
> Later, he taught his younger brother how to play the cello. "It wasn't difficult. If somebody's smart and knows music, he can do it. I could teach him because I played the same family of instrument: violin, cello, it's the same, only you put your fingers further apart. People exaggerate everything."
>
> Like many artists, Milstein suspects that even the role of teachers is exaggerated. "A teacher doesn't help much. Not many teachers do. Young people often think that if they go to a teacher, the teacher will tell them how to play. No! Nobody can tell you. A teacher may play very well in one way, but his student might not be able to play as well if he is taught to play the same way. That's why I think that the teacher's business is to explain to the pupil, especially the gifted ones, that the teacher can't do very much except to try to open the pupil's mind so that he can develop his own thinking. The fact is that the pupils have to do it. They have to do the job; not the teacher."
>
> Looking back, Milstein admits that none of his teachers were particularly helpful in this way. "But you see," he explains, "I was

always very curious and experimenting. Instinctively I thought that if I will not help myself my teacher will not help me."

. . . The worst teachers, in Milstein's opinion, are those who are not performers themselves. "Performers can give students more than any professor who is in the Curtis Institute or in the Juilliard School," he says vehemently. "Because you can only give something to a young person from your own experience. Teachers who don't perform, who never studied for a career, how do they know? I know of famous teachers in America that are ruining young people. Ruining!" By contrast, Milstein does not think that a very gifted person will be ruined by not having a teacher. . . .

SELF TEACHING

A teacher in Vancouver writes:

I saw an interesting thing this past week. I was down at a little storefront place called the Community Computer Institute (a small business which rents time on computers—the little personal ones —for very good rates: they also have self-teaching programs which you can use to have the computer teach you how to use the computer). While I was there an older man and a young boy, about 11, came in and were looking around. The kid was fascinated and the man was a little perplexed and amazed, "They're finally here . . . my, my . . ." However, the kid began to show the man some games on one of the simpler computers and within a few minutes both were engrossed in a major "Star Trek" game. After the game the kid explained some rudimentary principles of programming to the man, who by this time was very interested.

So was I, because here was a classic example of a teaching/learning situation between two people without regard for age, roles, or formal structure. I felt very good watching this whole episode and wondered what kind of things we could invent to facilitate this kind of thing happening throughout the city. I tried to explain this to some of the teachers I work with and they just ignored me. "That's not real learning and it just gets in the way of teaching them math skills." Here was an 11-year-old kid who had taught himself more about computers than I know, just by hanging around this place before it officially opened (so they let him use the computers for free) and by reading simple articles about programming. And they tell me that it's not real learning!

A mother writes more about "real learning":

The best thing I wanted to share with you is that E is reading. I was prepared to see him a nonreader still at the age of 10, 12—who could tell? He was fascinated with the shapes of letters on his father's truck when he was two, picked out letter shapes in sidewalk cracks, read short words on signs, played games with beginning sounds (his idea, not mine) and generally always liked words.

Getting from that stage to actually reading books left a blank in my mind. If he didn't want me to help him, didn't sit down and work at it, how was he doing to read beyond the shopping center signs stage? It must be at this stage that school people nervously rush in with methods and phonics rules, and at times I had to stop myself from doing the same. Teaching habits die hard. He knew so much! But he wasn't pulling it all together, wasn't even interested in opening a book to see if he could read the whole thing. I was dying of curiosity to see if he could, but I kept biting my lip every time a "lesson" threatened to come out.

He started about three months ago curling up with a comic book in the magazine section of the supermarket every week. Sometimes he'd buy one, and after we read it to him once, he'd take it off to a corner and study it for a while. He began "reading" them in bed. I knew something was happening because he got very quiet at these times, never asked me what a word was, and never made comments on the pictures. It became clear to me that reading was a private thing to him. After a while, he picked out easy books for bedtime reading and offered to read them to me. There were very few words he didn't know, and I'll never know how he learned the others. But it doesn't matter. He did it because he wanted to. I just hope I can keep on resisting all the pressures to do otherwise and let him set his own priorities.

One of our readers tells us about his brother's learning:

My brother is an electronics technician, by trade, and an electronics whiz by vocation. While still a teen-ager he *taught himself* all the mathematics, language, etc., necessary and built many complicated things—an oscilloscope, a computer, etc. He is now making a lot of money (I am not!) as a skilled technician (I am not!) while continuing to develop his own very creative ideas in electronics in his free time, with his own equipment, at home.

TEACHING VS. LEARNING

In "Vernacular Values and Education," (*Teachers College Record,* Fall 1979), Ivan Illich wrote of a man he had visited:

> This man . . . had ceased to be a parent and had become a total teacher. In front of their own children this couple stood *in loco magistri.* Their children had to grow up without parents, because these two adults, in every word they addressed to their two sons and one daughter, were "educating" them—they were at dinner constantly conscious that they were modeling the speech of their children, and asked me to do the same.

Vol. 3, Nos. 5 and 6 of *The Home and School Institute Newsletter* talks about things people can do with children at home. At first glance, many of them seem very sensible and pleasant, things that many loving and observing mothers have been doing for years. Thus:

BEDROOM—READING

Dress Me and Body All (vocabulary builders). There are words that attach to clothing—shirt, blouse, sock, shoe, etc.—and there are words attached to body parts—foot, arm, head, knee, etc. The bedroom is a fine place to learn these words; say the words aloud as clothes go off parts of bodies, print the words on large pieces of paper and label clothes in closets and drawers. . . .

Well, yes, perhaps. It all depends on the spirit in which this is done. If you like babies and little children, and on the whole I do, it is fun to talk to them about the things you are seeing or doing together. In *How Children Learn* I said that many mothers (or other adults) getting a small child ready to go out might say something like:

> ". . . Now we'll tie up this shoe; pull the laces good and tight; now we'll get the boots; let's see, the right boot for the right foot, then the left boot for the left foot; all right, coat next, arms in the sleeves,

zip it up, nice and tight; now the mittens, left mitten on the left hand, right mitten on the right hand; now comes the hat, on it goes, over your ears . . ." This kind of talk is companionable and fun, and from it the child learns, not just words, but the kinds of phrases and sentences they fit into.

But I'm afraid that the real point of this, that the talk *was* companionable and fun, a way for the mother to express in words some of her love for the child and pleasure in its company, may have been lost. In this mother's voice, as I hear it in my mind's ear, I can hear tones of pleasure and excitement, the words matching the action, perhaps a sympathetic grunt as she tugs at a stuck zipper or pulls on a boot, the whole thing underlined with many an affectionate squeeze or pat. This is not at all the same thing as saying, as we put on the child's coat, "Coat! Coat! Coat!" so that the child will "learn that this is a coat." The difference is between talk which is done for the pleasure itself, with learning only a possible and incidental by-product, and talk which has no purpose other than to produce learning.

From what I read elsewhere in this *Home and School Institute Newsletter,* it looks as if they have fallen solidly on the wrong side of this line. Thus:

> *Subject Bounce.* Over a fast breakfast or a sit-down dinner, play this "talk" game that prepares children for putting their thoughts into writing. Toss out a subject, start with simple ones that children know about—summer, friends, breakfast, school. The child then comes up with a statement about it; examples, "Summer is the best season," or "Friends like the same things you do." As children build sophistication, their subjects and statements get more sophisticated, too.

Awful! Reading this, I understand and share the real horror that Illich felt at his friend's dining room table. Years before I began teaching, I spent an evening with parents of young children in a home in which nothing was said or done without some kind of "teaching" purpose. Every word or act carried its little lesson. It was nightmarish, the air quivered with tension and worry. I could not wait to leave.

Life is full of ironies. I wrote *How Children Learn* hoping to help introduce the natural, effortless, and effective ways of learning of the happy home into the schools. At times I fear I may only have helped to bring the strained, self-conscious, painful, and ineffective ways of learning of the schools into the home. To parents I say, above all else, don't let your home become some terrible miniature copy of the school. No lesson plans! No quizzes! No tests! No report cards! Even leaving your children alone would be better; at least they could figure out some things on their own. Live together, as well as you can; enjoy life together, as much as you can. Ask questions to find out something about the world itself, not to find out whether or not someone knows it.

THE PRICE OF TEACHING TRICKS

Dr. Gregory Bateson, one of the most learned and creative intellectuals of our time, who in his life has studied and written a great deal in anthropology, psychology, and other fields, has summed up much of his life's work and thought in the book *Steps Toward an Ecology of Mind* (Ballantine). In one chapter, discussing the difficulties of communicating with dolphins and other animals, he says,

> . . . [There are] very special difficulties in the problem of how to test what is called the "psychology" (e.g., intelligence, ingenuity, discrimination, etc.) of individual animals. A simple experiment . . . involves a series of steps: (1) the dolphin may or may not perceive a difference between the stimulus objects, X and Y. (2) The dolphin may or may not perceive that this difference is a cue to behavior. (3) The dolphin may or may not perceive that the behavior in question has a good or bad effect upon reinforcement, that is, that doing "right" is conditionally followed by fish. (4) The dolphin may or may not choose to do "right," even after he knows which is right. Success in the first three steps merely provides the dolphin with a further choice point. . . .
>
> Precisely because we want to argue from observation of the animal's success in the later steps to conclusions about the more elementary steps, it becomes of prime importance to know whether

the organism with which we are dealing is capable of step 4. If it is capable, then all arguments about steps 1 through 3 will be invalidated unless appropriate methods of controlling step 4 are built into the experimental approach. Curiously enough, though human beings are fully capable of step 4, psychologists working with human subjects have been able to study steps 1 through 3 without taking special care to exclude the confusions introduced by this fact.

In other words, as a rule, when psychologists ask a human subject to do some task, and the subject does not do it, they tend to assume it is because he cannot do it. This makes it quite easy for subjects, especially if they are people from whom the psychologists expect little, to fool their testers. In *Dibs—In Search of Self* (Boston: Houghton-Mifflin Co., 1965), Virginia Axline tells about a very capable six-year-old boy who had been able to make a number of experts in such matters think, wrongly, that he was autistic, illiterate, and all but incapable of speech. In *The Naked Children* (New York: Macmillan Co., 1971), Daniel Fader tells of some black students in a Washington, D.C., junior high school who by their behavior and test scores had tricked their teachers into thinking, again wrongly, that they could barely read, could not speak Standard English, and indeed could speak little English of any kind.

Bateson goes on to say:

> Let me now consider for a moment the art of the animal trainer. From conversations with these highly skilled people—trainers of both dolphins and guide dogs—my impression is that the first requirement of a trainer is that he must be able to prevent the animal from exerting choice at the level of step 4. It must continually be made clear to the animal that, when he knows what is the right thing to do in a given context, that is the only thing he *can* do, and no nonsense about it. In other words, it is a primary condition of circus success that the animal shall abrogate the use of certain higher levels of his intelligence.

My uncle by marriage, Grove Cullum, an officer in the U.S. Cavalry, expert horseman and lover of horses, made this point more bluntly. One day in conversation I happened to make some remark about horses being intelligent. "Goodness, no," he laughed, "they're not intelligent. If they were, they'd never let us ride them."

In 1959 or so, teaching fifth graders in a very exclusive private school, which with rare exceptions would not even admit children with I.Q.'s of less than 120, I wrote, "School is a place where children learn to be stupid." I could see it was so, but didn't know why. What was it about even this very high-powered, child-centered, "creative" school, that made children stupid? I came to feel, as I wrote in *How Children Fail,* that it was fear, boredom, and the confusion of having constantly to manipulate meaningless words and symbols. I now see that it was that, but far more than that, the fact that *others had taken control of their minds.* It was being *taught,* in the sense of being trained like circus animals to do tricks on demand, that had made them stupid (at least in school).

On the basis of much experience, Bateson says this is true of all creatures, and I agree. The elephant in the jungle is smarter than the elephant waltzing in the circus. The sea lion in the sea is smarter than the sea lion playing "My country, 'tis of thee" on some instrument. The rat eating garbage in the slums is smarter than the rat running mazes in the psychology lab. The crawling baby, touching, handling, tasting everything it can reach, is smarter than the baby learning, because it pleases his mother, to touch his nose when she shows him a card with NOSE written on it.

The most important question any thinking creature can ask itself is, "What is worth thinking about?" When we deny its right to decide that for itself, when we try to control what it must attend to and think about, we make it less observant, resourceful, and adaptive, in a word, less intelligent, in a blunter word, more stupid.

This may be the place to answer a question that by now many people have asked me: what do I think of baby training books— teach your baby this, teach your baby that, make your baby a genius. I am against them. The tricks they tell parents to teach their babies to do are not necessary, not very helpful, and if continued very long, probably very harmful. The trouble with teaching babies tricks, even the trick of reading, is that the more we do this, the more they think that learning means and can only mean *being taught by others to do tricks,* and the less they want to or can explore and make sense of the world around them in their own ways and for their own reasons.

I don't doubt for a second that the experts in teaching babies tricks can indeed teach them an impressive variety of tricks while they are still quite young. But this has little or nothing to do with true learning or the capacity for it. Intelligence, as I wrote in *How Children Fail,* is not the measure of how much we know how to do, but of how we behave when we don't know what to do. It has to do with our ability to think up important questions and then to find ways to get useful answers. This ability is not a trick that can be taught, nor does it need to be. We are born with it, and if our other deep animal needs are fairly well satisfied, and we have reasonable access to the world around us, we will put it to work on that world.

11

Learning Difficulties

DISABILITIES VS. DIFFICULTIES

I have included this short chapter, which may someday be part of a longer work on this subject, for several reasons. In the first place, parents who teach their children at home may find now and then that some of them do things like writing letters or spelling words backward or showing some confusion about right and left. Such parents should not become alarmed, or assume that something serious is wrong with their child, or that they must throw the whole matter into the hands of "expert" specialists. In the second place, parents who have already sent children to school may be told that their children have such problems. Such parents, again, should not panic, and should be extremely skeptical of anything the schools and their specialists may say about their children and their condition and needs. Above all, they should understand that it is almost certainly the school itself and all its tensions and anxieties that are causing these difficulties, and that the best treatment for them will probably be to take the child out of school altogether. In the third place, parents should resist the general claim on the part of schools that only they are competent to teach children because only they are able to tell which children have learning disabilities and if so, what must be done about them.

To school people and others who talk to me about "learning disabilities," I usually ask a question something like this:

"How do you tell the difference between a learning *difficulty* (which we all experience every time we try to learn anything) and a learning *disability*? That is to say, how do you tell, or on what basis does someone decide (and who is the someone?) whether the cause of a given learning difficulty lies within the nervous system of the learner, or with things outside of the learner—the learning situation, the teacher's explanations, the teacher him/herself, or the material itself? And if you decide that the cause of the difficulty lies within the learner, who decides, and again on what basis, whether or not that inferred cause is curable, in short, whether anything can be done about it, and if so, what?"

If any readers ask these questions of schools, I would like very much to know what answers they get. I have never received any coherent answers to these questions. What I usually get instead are angry insistences that learning disabilities are "real," that is to say, built into the nervous systems of children. Here are some of my reasons for thinking they are not, and instead, what may be some of their true causes, and what we might sensibly do about them.

NOBODY SEES BACKWARDS

A few years ago a national magazine ran a full-page ad for some organization dealing with so-called "learning disabilities." At the top of the ad, in large letters, were the words, SEE HOW JOHNNY READS. Then a photo of an open children's book printed in very large print, large enough so that people reading the ad could read the book. The story was "The Three Little Pigs." But many of the letters in the story had been shifted and turned around in odd ways. Some were upside down or backwards. Sometimes two adjacent letters in a word had been put in reverse order. Sometimes an entire word was spelled backwards. Then, beneath the photo, again in large letters, the words THINK HOW

JOHNNY FEELS. Then some text about all the children suffering from "learning disabilities" and all the things the organization was doing to cure or help them.

The message was plain. We were being asked to believe that large numbers of children in the U.S., when they looked at a book, saw something like the photo in the ad, and so, could not read it. Also, that this organization could and would do something about this—it was not clear just what—if we gave it enough support.

I looked again at the children's book in the photo. I found that I could read it without much trouble. Of course, I had two advantages over this mythical "Johnny": I could already read, and I already knew the story. I read it a bit more slowly than I ordinarily would; now and then I had to puzzle out a word, one letter at a time. But it was not hard to do.

This was by no means the first time I had heard the theory that certain children have trouble learning to read because something inside their skins or skulls, a kind of Maxwell's Demon (a phrase borrowed from physics) of the nervous system, every so often flipped letters upside down or backwards, or changed their order. I had never taken any stock in this theory. It failed the first two tests of any scientific theory: (1) that it be plausible on its face; (2) that it be the most obvious or likely explanation of the facts. This theory seemed and still seems totally implausible, for many more reasons than I will go into here. And there are much simpler and more likely explanations of the facts.

The facts that this theory set out to account for are only these: certain children, usually just learning to read and write, when asked to write down certain letters or words, wrote some letters backwards, or reversed the order of two or more letters in a word, or spelled entire words backwards—though it is important to note that most children who spell words backwards do not at the same time reverse all the individual letters.

I was too busy with other work to take time to think how to prove that this theory was wrong. But for a while I taught in a school right next door to what was then supposed to be one of the best schools for "learning disability" (hereafter LD) children in New England. I began to note that in that particular learning hospital no one was ever cured. Children went in not knowing how to read, and came out years later still not knowing. No one seemed at all upset by this. Apparently this school was felt to be "the best" because it had better answers than anyone else to the question, "Once you have decided that certain children can't learn to read, what do you do with them all day in a place which calls itself a school?" Later, when I was working full-time lecturing to groups about educational change, I had other contacts with other LD believers and experts. The more I saw and heard of them, the less I believed in them. But I was still too busy to spend much time arguing with them or even thinking about them.

Then one morning in Boston, as I was walking across the Public Garden toward my office, my subconscious mind asked me a question. First it said, "The LD people say that these children draw letters, say, a P, backwards because when they look at the correct P they *see* it backwards. Let's put all this in a diagram.

P | q

1 | 2
3 | 4

q

"In space #1 is the correct P which the child is asked to copy. In space #3 is the backwards P which he draws, because (we are told) this is the way he sees it. All right; in space #2 we will put what the child supposedly sees when he looks at the correct P in space #1." (The wavy line represents perception.)

Then came the $64 question.

"Now, what does the child see when he looks at the backwards P in space #3, the P that he has drawn?"

I stopped dead in my tracks. I believe I said out loud, "Well, I'll be d——!" For obviously, if his mind reverses all the shapes he looks at, the child, when he looks at the backwards P in space #3, *will see a correct P!*

So our diagram would wind up looking like this:

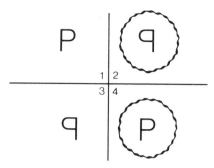

This imaginary child, if he did what the LD experts say he does, would look at P#1, see P#2, draw P#3, and *looking at that, see P#4.* What he had drawn would not look *to him* like what he was trying to copy. He would think to himself, "I made a mistake," and would draw his P the other way around. At least, he would do so if, as the LD people claim, his drawing was an accurate copy of what he perceived. Even if his mind reversed every shape it saw, *a backwards P would still look backwards to him!* To put it still more broadly and fundamentally, we cannot tell by looking at the shapes people draw whether they perceive shapes backwards or not, *since they would draw the same shapes in either case!*

So the "perceptual handicap," "he-draws-backwards-because-he-sees-backwards" theory goes down the drain. It does not explain what it was invented to explain. Nor does it explain anything else—this event, the child drawing the letters backwards, is all the evidence that supports it. Why then does this obviously false theory persist? Because, for many reasons, it is very convenient to many people—to parents, to teachers, to schools, to LD experts and the giant industry that has grown up around them—sometimes even to the children. The theory may not help anyone learn to read, but it keeps a lot of people busy, makes a lot of people richer, and makes almost everyone feel better. Theories that do all that are not easy to get rid of.

But then, why does the child draw the P backwards? If he is not, as I have shown, reproducing the shape that he perceives, what is he doing?

The answer is plain enough to anyone who has watched little children when they first start making letters. Slowly, hesitantly, and clumsily, they try to turn what they see into a "program," a set of instructions for the hand holding the pencil, and then try to make the hand carry out the instructions. This is what we all do when we try to draw something. We are not walking copying machines. When we try to draw a chair, we do not "copy" it. We look at it awhile, and then "tell" our hand to draw, say, a vertical line of a certain height. Then we look at the chair again, then back at the paper, then "tell" our hand to go halfway up the vertical line, and from that point draw a line of a certain length in a certain direction. Then we look back at the chair for more instructions. If, like trained artists, we are good at turning what we see into instructions for our hand, we will produce a good likeness of the chair. If, like most of us, we are not good at it, we will not.

In the same way, the child looks at the P. He sees there is a line in it that goes up and down. He looks at the paper and tells his hand, "Draw an up and down line," then draws it. He looks back at the P, then tells his hand to go to the top of the up and down line and then draw a line out to the side. This done, he looks back at the P, and sees that the line going out to the side curves down and around after a while and then goes back in until it hits the up and down line again. He tells his hand to do that. As you can tell watching a little child do this, it may take him two or three tries to get his pencil all the way around the curve. Sometimes the curve will reverse direction in the middle, and that will have to be fixed up. Eventually he gets his line back to the up and down line.

At this point, most children will compare the two P's, the one they looked at and the one they made. Many of them, if they drew their P backward, may see right away that it *is* backwards, doesn't look quite the same, is pointing the wrong way—however they may express this in their minds. Other children may be vaguely aware that the shapes are not pointing the same way, but will see this as a difference *that doesn't make any difference,* just as for my bank the differences between one of my signatures and another are differences that don't make any difference.

In thinking that this difference doesn't make any difference, the children are being perfectly sensible. After all, they have been looking at pictures of objects, people, animals, etc., for some time. They know that a picture of a dog is a picture of a dog, whether the dog is facing right or left. They also understand, without words, that the image on the page, the picture of dog, cat, bicycle, cup, spoon, etc., stands for an object that can be moved, turned around, looked at from different angles. It is therefore perfectly reasonable for children to think of the picture of a P on the page as standing for a P-shaped object with an existence of its own, an object which could be picked up, turned around, turned upside down, etc. Perhaps not all children feel this equally strongly. But for those who do, to be told that a "backwards" P that they have drawn is "wrong," or that it isn't a P at all, must be very confusing and even frightening. If you can draw a horse, or dog, or cat, or car pointing any way you want, why can't you draw a P or B or E any way you want? Why is it "right" to draw a dog facing toward the left, but "wrong" to draw a P facing that way?

What we should do, then, is be very careful *never* to use the words "right" and "wrong" in these reversal situations. If we ask a child to draw a P, and he draws a T, we could say, "No, that's not a P, that's a T." But if we ask him to draw a P, and he draws one pointing to the left, we should say, "Yes, that's a P, but when we draw a picture of a P we *always* draw it pointing this way. It isn't like a dog or a cat, that we can draw pointing either way." Naturally, there's no need to give this little speech to children who never draw letters backwards. Indeed the chances are very good that children who start off drawing certain letters backwards would, as with errors in their speech, eventually notice the difference between their P's and ours and correct it, if we didn't make such a fuss about it. But if we are fainthearted and feel we have to say something about backward P's, it ought to be something like the above.

However, I strongly suspect that most children who often reverse letters do not in fact *compare* shapes. Like so many of the children I have known and taught, they are anxious, rule-bound, always in a panicky search for what the grownups want. What they do is turn the P they are looking at into a set of instructions, memorize the instructions, and then compare the P they have drawn against the instructions. "Did I do it right? Yes, there's the line going up and down, and there's the line going out sideways from the top, and there it's curving around and there it's coming back into the up-and-down line again. I obeyed the rules and did it right, so it must *be* right."

Or perhaps they may try to compare shapes, but are too anxious to see them clearly. Or perhaps, as with anxious people, by the time they have shifted their eyes from the original P to the P they have drawn, they have forgotten the original P, or dare not trust the memory of it that they have. This feeling of suddenly not being able to trust one's own memory is common enough, and above all when one is anxious. Now and then I find myself looking up a phone number two or three times in a row, because each time I start to dial the number I have the panicky thought, "Did I remember it right?" Usually I can only break out of this foolish cycle by saying to myself, "Right or wrong, dial it anyway." It usually turns out to be right. But I can understand how a certain kind of self-distrusting person (by no means rare) might go through this process a great many times. I am sure that many of the failing students I have taught have had somewhere in their minds the permanent thought, "If I think of it, it must be wrong."

It is possible, too, that a child, making up a set of instructions for his hand, might try to use the ideas of Right and Left, but with some of the confusions I will talk about later in this chapter, so that "right" when he was looking at the P might mean the opposite of "right" when he was drawing it. The fact remains that whatever may be children's reasons for drawing letters backwards, there is no reason whatever to believe that seeing them backwards is one of them.

STRESS AND PERCEPTION

We can tell a good deal about the competence of a particular group of experts by the kinds of research they do or do not do.

In World War I we first began to see evidence that prolonged anxiety, stress, and fear can have great destructive effects on the human nervous system. The trenches were a kind of satanic laboratory of stress. More soldiers than ever before lived for much longer times than ever before in cold and wet, under the constant threat of death, often under continuous heavy bombardment. Under these conditions many suffered a disorder which doctors called "shell shock." Some became totally blind, or deaf, others became paralyzed, shook all over, lost all control over their muscles and limbs. The authorities first suspected faking, but it was soon clear that these soldiers were not faking. The only cure for these ailments, which in many cases looked like "physical" disorders, was to take these men out of stress, away from the front. After some time in a safe and calm place, they regained to varying degrees their sight, hearing, and use and control of their limbs. Many were even able to go back to the front.

In World War II this happened again. Many of the British troops who spent days on the beaches at Dunkirk, under continuous bombardment from both guns and planes, broke under this stress in exactly the same way. The doctors of World War II called their condition "psychoneurosis." The cure was basically the same —to remove the afflicted men from the scene of stress and danger.

In the years since then, all kinds of other evidence has begun to accumulate that stress can cause what seem to be physical disabilities. In my own work I began to see, not only among the children I taught, but in myself as I struggled for the first time to learn a musical instrument, that anxiety could make it much harder for the children, or myself, to think, to remember, or even to see. In *How Children Fail* I described how one day, under pressure, I totally lost for a short time the ability to see meaningfully. Five years later, in *The Lives of Children* (New York: Random House, 1969, George Dennison described, in the most painful and almost clinical detail, the effects of stress and fear on one of his pupils.

So it was reasonable to suppose, when educators began to claim that some children might be having trouble learning because of "perceptual handicaps," that they might look for possible connections between such inferred handicaps and children's fears and anxieties. As far as I have been able to learn, very few of them have yet done so.

Not long ago I was one of many speakers at a large conference of specialists in "learning disabilities." Before more than a thousand people I reviewed the evidence for a connection between anxiety and perceptual or other learning disorders. I spoke of the medical experience of two world wars, and of my own experience as a teacher and as a beginning learner of music. Then I asked for a show of hands response to this question: "How many of you have heard of—only heard of, not done—any research on possible connections between perceptual handicaps in children and their anxiety, however measured? How many have heard of any research to find whether and to what degree lowering measurable anxiety in children might lessen the incidence of perceptual handicaps?"

In that roomful of over a thousand experts in this field, *only two people* raised their hands. What the others may have known, I do not know. But only two raised their hands.

I asked what they knew. One told me of research I had long known about, done by a man who, at least until very recently, had no degrees in psychology and no standing whatever in the educational "establishment." He had found high correlations between children's anxieties and perceptual handicaps, and that lowering the anxieties did indeed greatly lower the incidence of such handicaps. (He also found that diet was very important.)

The other man who raised his hand did not speak. But later, he wrote me a letter. He is, and has been for some time, a professor of education at a leading university in the very city in which this conference was held. He too had suspected the kind of connection I talked about. He then had worked out a way of teaching reading that he thought might lessen this anxiety, had used this method to teach a group of students officially labeled "perceptually handicapped," and had found that after quite a short time in his class, in the opinion of their regular teachers, his students were much less handicapped than they had been before. This, I would add, in spite of the fact that his classroom was nowhere as stress-free as I others I have known, or as he himself might have made it if he had not been under pressure to show some fairly quick results.

There were other questions I have asked at other places and times, but did not think to ask there. When I first heard that boys were supposed to be four or five times as likely to have "perceptual handicaps" or "learning disabilities" as girls, I asked in a letter published in a national magazine whether any research had been done to look for possible connections between this four- or five-to-one ratio and the sex of the teacher. I have yet to hear of any. And it would surely be interesting to see what connections there might be between the incidence of "perceptual handicaps" in children and the measurable anxiety *of their teachers.* But again, as far as I know, no such research has been done.

Meanwhile, we have every reason to be very skeptical of the expertise of people who fail or refuse to ask such questions.

One more note about the LD conference. On one of the many tables displaying books and pamphlets were copies of a newsletter published by one of the leading LD associations. Reading one, I came across a most extraordinary sentence, in an article by a former president of the association. In it she said that LD "professionals" should insist very strongly that the causes of these disabilities were always neurological. She admitted that there was so far very little evidence to support this idea. Then she added these remarkable words: "We must not take the absence of evidence as the evidence of absence." In other words, just because there is no evidence to support our theory doesn't mean that we shouldn't continue to push it.

RIGHT AND LEFT

Many adults get very upset and anxious about right and left. If a child writes a letter backward, or reads off some letters in the wrong order, or does anything else to suggest he is confused about right and left, adults begin to talk excitedly about "mixed dominance" and "perceptual handicaps" and "learning difficulties." The child is quickly labeled as "having a serious problem." Specialists (if the family or school can afford them) are called in and told to take over.

A child once asked me a question that not only completely surprised me, but also suggested that when children are confused about right and left, the reason may not be in them but in us, the adults, and the way *we* talk about right and left. In short, the child's confusion may make sense, and if we only understood that, we might easily straighten it out.

I was in an early elementary classroom, working on something with some children in a corner of the room. I needed something in my desk, and asked a child please to get it for me. He said okay, and asked where it was. I said, "In the top right-hand drawer." There was a pause. Then he said, "Whose right hand, mine or the desk's?"

For an instant I was baffled. Then I saw, and understood. When he looked at the desk, it was as if he saw a living creature looking at him. So I said, *"Your* right hand." Off he went, brought back what I had asked for, and that was that.

Later, I thought that many young children must be animists, and see objects as if they were living creatures. I wondered how many of them might have had that same question in their minds, without ever asking it. And if they didn't ask it, how did they ever learn the answer? Probably from experience. They went to the desk, looked in *its* right-hand drawer, found nothing, looked in *their* right-hand drawer, found what they wanted, and so learned which was meant, like the infant I described in *How Children Learn,* who at the table asked people to pass the salt, pepper, butter, etc., so that by seeing what was passed she could find out what those words meant.

But some children might not interpret the desk experience in that way. They might assume that the adult had made a mistake about the drawer. Or they might think that they themselves had made a mistake about which was right and which was left. The kind of children who worried about mistakes, because their parents or teachers worried, might be particularly ready to blame themselves for any confusion.

Only recently, as I began to think more about this, did I realize that our adult rules about right and left are even more confused than I had thought. Thus, when we ask a child to get something out of our right-hand coat pocket, we mean the coat's right hand, not the child's. When we talk about the right headlight of a car, we mean the car's right hand. But the right-hand entrance to a house is *our* right hand, not the house's. We adults talk sometimes as if things were people, and sometimes as if they were not, and there's little rhyme or reason in the way we do this. Why should a car or boat or train have its own right side, but not a house?

In the theater, of course, the confusion about whether the audience's or the actors' right or left is meant led people to invent the words "stage right" or "stage left" to mean the right or left of the actors as they looked at the audience.

Under photos of groups of people we see, "Reading from left to right, Jones, Smith, Brown, etc." A child being shown such photos might hear someone say, "That's me over on the right." Our right as we look at it? Or the right of the group? So the people on the right are *really* on the left, and vice versa. Some children might see this as more of the world's delightful nonsense. But other children might think in panic and terror, "Why don't they make up their minds which way they want it? How do they ever expect me to get it straight?"

We might well ask, how do any of us ever get it straight. Most of us learn it the way we learn the grammar of our language, which is so subtle and complicated that (I am told) no one has yet been able to teach it to a computer. Children learn very early that the words "I, you, she, etc." refer to different people depending on who is saying them. Not an easy thing to figure out, when you come to think about it. Yet no one ever explains that to them. Nor do they say to themselves, as they grow up, "*I* refers to the person who is talking, *you* to the person or persons talked to, *we* to both of them together, and *he, she, they, or it* to the people or things talked about." They just use the words that way, and it works.

In the same way, most children don't think to themselves, "Cars, boats, coats, trains, planes, all have their own right hands, while books, photos, desks, houses do not." They just learn from experience which is which, and don't worry much about the contradictions, just as most French children don't worry about why a house should be feminine and a building masculine, or a coat masculine and a shirt feminine.

In short, most children master the confusion of right and left because they never become aware of it, any more than I did until just a few days ago. Others may become aware of the confusion but are not troubled by it and don't feel any need to set it right or make sense of it—it's just the way things are. But some children are philosophers. They examine everything. They expect and want things to make sense, and if they don't, to find out why not. Still others are threatened and terrified by confusion and paradox, above all, by seeing people act as if something made sense when it obviously doesn't. At some deep level of their being, they wonder, "Am I the one who's crazy?"

I suspect that most of the children who have persistent trouble with right and left in school or in life are of this latter kind. After a few right-left mistakes, which they make only because they have not yet learned our crazy right-left rules, they begin to think, "I must be stupid, I never can figure out right and left." Soon they go into a blind panic every time the words come up. They work out complicated strategies of bluff and avoidance. When people ask about right and left, they learn to get other clues—"You mean the one by the window?" etc. (Since this article appeared in *GWS,* many adults have told me about the tricks and devices they must rely on to keep from mixing up right and left.) In general, they assume that there is something wrong with them.

If this is true, what might we do about it? One thing we should *not* do is to set out to "teach" the rules of right and left. Most children have always figured out right and left without much teaching, other than being told when very little, "This is your right hand, this is your left foot, etc." Let them go on learning it that way. But if a child seems to be confused or anxious about this, then we can begin to make the rules more explicit. We can say, "I mean *your* right hand, not the desk's," or "I mean the *coat's* right hand, not yours," perhaps adding, "I know that sounds a bit crazy, but that's just the way we say it, don't worry about it, you'll get used to it."

EAST AND WEST

Thinking about right and left brought back an old memory. Years ago a teacher of geography told me of a most interesting and surprising discovery. Teachers who teach young children about maps and directions find that some pick it up quickly. But others, when shown a map and asked to point east, act like the children I described in *How Children Fail*—wave their hands in all directions while carefully reading the teacher's face for cues, watch their smart classmates, bluff, fake, wait it out, and so on. Most teachers let it go at that, thinking, "Good students, bad students, you get all kinds."

But somewhere a teacher noticed something. A few children, shown a map and asked to point east, almost always pointed wrong, *but always in the same direction.* Looking into it further, people found that a small percentage of people, some children, some adults, had a very strong sense of direction. It was as if they had a compass in their minds, or as if under their feet the ground was everywhere marked with direction lines. Whether their compass and direction lines were correctly labeled, whether the east they pointed was in fact true east, my informant did not tell me. But, asked to point a given direction, they always pointed the same way.

My mother had that kind of sense of direction. Driving without a map on strange, winding, suburban roads, when the rest of us had long since lost our bearings, she always knew about where we were, which way we were headed, and which way we needed to go to get where we wanted. An inborn gift? Perhaps, though it can probably be learned. At any rate, for children with such a gift, the question, "Which way is east?" can only mean, "Which way is *true* east, or *world-east*?" If we understood this, we could make the distinction (which we ought to make anyway) between *world-east* and *map-east.* Once children understood the relation between maps and the territory being mapped, which we could help them see by making maps of their room, the house, the yard, the block or neighborhood, etc., we could then ask questions like, "If you were here"—showing a point on the map—"and began to walk east, show me on the map where you'd be going." Or we could take the walk first, and then see on the map where we had walked. After doing this a few times, a child would be able to show map-east, map-north, etc.

I talked to a teacher friend (math) about this. He laughed and said that when he was a child he thought for quite a few years that north, world-north, was straight up, and world-south straight down, since all the maps he had seen were in school, on the walls. In time, he figured it all out for himself, *by* himself.

Recently these thoughts about east and west have led to a new thought. Suppose there were some people who thought that right and left, like east and west, referred to something in the world itself, in short, that right meant world-right and left meant world-left. How could they ever figure out, from our talk about right and left, which was which? One minute world-right would seem to be this way, the next minute that way. We can hardly imagine their confusion and, probably, terror. Most of them would soon decide that they were just too stupid to figure out what seemed so easy for everyone else. Yet they, or we, might quickly clear up all that confusion by just asking a couple of the right questions.

What to do, if children seem to have these confusions? Above all, keep calm. If a child shows confusion about right and left, don't panic, give him plenty of time to work it out for himself. Some small things we could do might help. When we first start telling children which is our right hand and which our left, it would probably be a good idea for both of us to be facing the same way, the child standing in front of us or sitting on our lap. At some point, facing the same way, we might both hold a toy in our right hand, and show that when we are facing the same way, the right hands are on the same side, but that when we turn to face each other, the right hands are on the opposite side. It would probably be better not to talk much about this as we did it. Just show it now and then, as another interesting fact about the world.

Beyond that, we should not assume, just because children do know that this is their right hand and this their left, that they understand all about right-hand drawers and coat pockets—all our strange rules about right and left. For some time, when we talk about such things, we should be sure to point out which side we mean. If the child seems to take all this in stride, we don't need to say anything and would be wiser not to. But if the child seems unduly puzzled or anxious about this, then we could make the right-left rules more explicit.

12

Children and Work

ON FINDING ONE'S WORK

In his book *Growing Up Absurd,* (New York: Vintage Books, 1956), published in 1956 and even more up-to-date now than then, Paul Goodman asked (italics his): "But *the question is what it means to grow up into such a fact as 'During my productive years I will spend eight hours a day doing what is no good.'* " Later, in an essay printed in a collection of his works entitled *Nature Heals* (New York: Free Life Editions, 1977), he wrote:

> Brought up in a world where they cannot see the relation between activity and achievement, adolescents believe that everything is done with mirrors, tests are passed by tricks, achievement is due to pull, goods are known by their packages, and a man is esteemed according to his front. The delinquents who cannot read and quit school, and thereby become still less able to take part in such regular activity as is available, show a lot of sense and life when they strike out directly for the *rewards* of activity—money, glamour, and notoriety. . . .
> It is disheartening indeed to be with a group of young fellows

who are in a sober mood and who simply do not know what they want to do with themselves in life. Doctor, lawyer, beggar-man, thief? rich man, poor man, Indian chief?—they simply do not know an ambition and cannot fantasize one. But it is not true that they don't care; their "so what?" is vulnerable, their eyes are terribly balked and imploring. (I say "it is disheartening," and I mean that the tears roll down my cheeks; and I who am an anarchist and a pacifist feel that they will be happier when they are all in the army.)

Paul Goodman was writing here about poor boys. But even in the more hopeful sixties it was just about as true of affluent youth. In those days I was often asked to speak to high school assemblies, mostly in rich suburbs of big cities. What I almost always talked about was the difference between jobs, careers, and work. A job, I said, was something that you did for money, something that someone else told you to do and paid you for doing, something you would probably not have done otherwise, but did only to get the money. A career was a kind of ladder of jobs. If you did your first job for a while, made no mistakes and caused no trouble, whoever gave you that job might give you a new job, better paid, maybe slightly more interesting, or at least not so hard-dirty-dangerous. Then, if you did that job okay for a while, your boss might then give you a slightly better job, and so on. This adds up to what is called "a career."

By "work" I meant and still mean something very different, what people used to call a "vocation" or "calling"—something which seemed so worth doing for its own sake that they would gladly choose to do it even if they didn't need money and the work didn't pay. I went on to say that to find our work, in this sense, is one of the most important and difficult tasks that we have in life, and indeed, that even if we find it once we may later have to look for it again, since work that is right for us at one stage of our life may not be right for us at the next. I added that the vital question, "What do I really want to do? What do I think is most worth doing?" is not one that the schools (or any other adults) will often urge us or help us to ask; on the whole, they feel it is their business only to prepare us for employment—jobs or careers, high or low. So we will have to find out for ourselves what work needs to be done and is being done out there in the world, and where and how we will take part in it.

As I said these things, I looked at the faces of my hearers, to sense how they felt about what I was saying. What I saw, and usually heard in the question periods that followed, made me feel that most of these students were thinking, "This guy must have just come from Mars." Work worth doing? Work that you would do even if you didn't need money, that you would do *for nothing*? For most of them it was not just impossible, it was unimaginable. They did not know, hardly even knew *of,* any people who felt that way about their work. Work was something you did for external rewards—a little pay, if you were like most people, or wealth, power, fame if you were among the fortunate.

Among all the young people I talked to, there was never, anywhere, a hopeful, positive, enthusiastic response to what I said. I cannot remember even one among all those students, the most favored young people of the (then, at least) most favored nation in the world, who said or later wrote to me, "Mr. Holt, here's what I am interested in and care about, how can I find a way to work at it?"

FINDING TRUE WORK

I was on my submarine, the U.S.S. *Barbero,* heading west for Pearl Harbor, when we first heard the news about the atomic bomb. I knew enough to know that before long any country that wanted could and would make them. It seemed clear to me that the only way to prevent the worldwide spread of nuclear weapons, and in the end nuclear war, was to have some sort of world government. When we came back to the U.S. in October, to "mothball" our sub, I tried to find out about any other people who might be working in some way for world government. By the middle of the following summer I decided that I had to find a way to do this work full-time. I went to the three world government organizations to ask for a job. Two had nothing. The third had nothing at the moment, but said that in the fall the young man working in their mailroom would be going back to college and that I could have his job for $35 a week. I said I would take it. In the fall I began work, making up and sending out packages of literature, stamping the mail, keeping the membership card files, running the Addressograph machine, and doing any other odd jobs that turned up. One day I was told that the Junior Chamber of Commerce in Bayonne, New Jersey, had just asked for a speaker, on a day when all our other speakers were busy. Would I do it? I gulped and said I would. It was the first of about six hundred speeches that I was to give for the organization. Later I left the mailroom and began to work as a "field organizer," traveling about, giving speeches and trying to start local chapters.

In 1952 I left the organization, spent much of the next year living and traveling cheaply in Europe, and came home, thinking that I might try to go into farming, since even then I was very interested in what we now call ecology. My sister, who had been trying without success to persuade me to be a teacher, did persuade me to visit a small co-ed boarding school, the Colorado Rocky Mountain School, that John and Anne Holden had just opened in Carbondale, Colorado. Since the school planned to do much of its own building and food-raising, she thought I might be able, while working and being paid, to learn many things I would need to know if I did go into farming. Thinking, "It can't hurt to look," I went to the school two weeks after it had opened and spent a day there, living the life of the school, going to some classes, talking to the students, helping some of them with their work, and playing informal soccer with them.

I liked it. My insides sent me the same message they had sent years before, when for the first time I went down into a submarine: "Right now, this is the place for you." Next day, just before I left, I said to John Holden, "You know, I like it here, and I'd like to stay and work here." He made what some might have taken as a rather negative reply: "Well, we'd be glad to have you, but the trouble is, we haven't any place to put you, and we haven't any money to pay you, and we haven't anything for you to do." In return I said, "Well, if you get some sort of roof over my head, I don't much care where you put me, and if you're feeding me I can probably live without money, for a while at least, and I'm pretty sure I can find something to do." It was an offer he couldn't refuse. He laughed and said, "If you're willing to come out here on that basis, come ahead."

Two weeks later I was back. For a month or two I lived in a little building, once a granary, that they were turning into an infirmary. I slept on a cot near a table saw, stepped over piles of sawdust to get to it, lived out of my suitcases. I found plenty to do. I began cooking breakfast for the school every day, tutoring individual students in economics, trigonometry, reading, and coaching soccer. When another teacher left to get married, I took over her room and salary (about $1750/yr.) By the next year I was teaching regular classes in English and math, and was the school business manager. A year later they hired a full-time business manager, but I then started teaching French as well as the English and math. I taught there four years, worked very hard, had a good time, learned a great deal.

The point of these stories is that many of the people who are doing serious work in the world (as opposed to just making money) are very overworked and short of help. If a person, young or not so young, said to them, "I believe in the work you are doing and want to help you in any and every way I can, and I'd be glad to do any kind of work you ask me to do or that I can find to do, for very little pay, or even none at all if you can give me room and board," I suspect that many of them would say, "Sure, come right ahead." Working with them, the newcomer would gradually learn more and more about what they were doing, would find or be given more interesting and important things to do, might soon become so valuable that they would find a way to pay her or him. In any case, he or she would learn far more from working with them and being around them than in any school or college.

A FALSE START

I have a close friend whom I have known since he was in high school. His marks were good, his parents had money, so when he finished high school he naturally went to a "good" college. Since English had been his best and easiest school subject, he majored in English. Four years and $20,000 later he had his B.A. degree.

What next? Well, his marks were still good, he still had time, his parents still had money, so he went to a "good" graduate school to get a Ph.D. in (now necessarily) English. During these years we remained good friends. One day, when he had completed all the course requirements for a Ph.D. and was finishing his thesis, I asked him, "When you get through with all this stuff, what are you going to do?" The question seemed to surprise him. After a pause, he said, "I don't know, teach English in some college, I guess." I said, "Is that what you really want to do?" This question surprised him even more. After another pause he said, "No, not particularly, but what else *can* I do?" That surprised *me*. Is that what a Ph.D. is supposed to do for you?

He began to teach English at a small state university, in the Western mountain country he loved. He soon found that his students were at college only to get the ticket, and were not in the least interested in anything he had learned and wanted to teach. All they wanted to know, and very politely asked, was, "What do we have to do to pass the course?" This took all the point out of teaching. For a while he tried to put in his class time, collect his paycheck, concentrate on the farming, hunting, fishing, hiking, camping, and skiing that he really loved, and not worry about his students and what they liked or didn't like. It didn't work. He stuck it out for some years, every year hating it more. Finally he quit. Today, after some difficult years, he is a carpenter and small builder and contractor, doing careful and skilled work in a town where there is enough demand for it to keep him busy. He has found his work. But it still seems too bad to have spent fifteen years of his life and $40,000 of his parents' money just to find out that he didn't want to be an English professor.

Even then, he was fortunate in having enough money behind him so that he could run the risk of leaving his job and looking for work worth doing. Most people can't. A young woman about to graduate from a school of education once said to me, "Well, I've learned two things here, anyway—that I don't like children and I don't like teaching." I asked why she went on with it. She said, "I have to, I've spent too much time and money learning to do this, I can't turn around and start learning to do something else."

Ten years ago many students used to ask me whether they

should go to, or stay in, or go back to college. I used to say, and say now, that a college degree isn't a magic passkey that opens every door in town. It opens only a few, and before you spend a lot of time and money getting one of those keys, it's a good idea to find out what doors it opens (if any), and what's on the other side of those doors, and to decide whether you like what's on the other side, and if you do, whether there may not be an easier way to get there.

GROWING UP, PERHAPS NOT ABSURD

How much it can mean to a young person to feel that there is work worth doing out there in the world can be seen from these excerpts from letters from a Massachusetts high school senior. During the summer after a very unhappy and unsuccessful year in eleventh grade, she wrote:

> I developed a very negative attitude about school but I was still very distressed and concerned about my performance in school. I was still very interested in learning but in the classroom I found learning very dull. I was enrolled in classes in which everyday attendance was mandatory, but I began cutting classes. I was not alone. A whole crew of us used to hang out in a dingy girl's room. The school doesn't have a lounge so this room had to do. Well, my whole school year was a disaster. I dropped out of all my classes except for two when the 4th term rolled around. I scheduled these classes for the morning and so I could leave the school before 11:00 nearly every day. . . .
>
> I was studying my third year of Spanish but I dropped out at the end of the third term because I could not learn in an atmosphere which I felt was hostile (toward me).
>
> . . . I often resorted to smoking marijuana during school. It broke up the monotony of a school day. Pot didn't interfere with my studying. I found I could concentrate remarkably well while I was high. But I must say it totally ruined my attitude, especially when it came time to decide whether or not I should go to the next class.
>
> . . . My relationship with my family suffered. . . . I was going around with older kids outside of high school. . . . My parents felt these kids were responsible for my attitude change. Perhaps they

were to some extent. A few of them had dropped out of high school and none of them went to college except for one kid who stopped going after two years. They didn't seem to be headed anywhere. . . .

Well, here I am. I hope to go on to college yet with my high school record I don't know. Kids have a tendency to goof off during their senior year. I am going to have to work hard to make up for last year's mistakes. But . . . I feel alienated in school, at home, and even with my "friends."

. . . I would like to know if you have any suggestions. I am interested in ecology, conservation, English, writing, history, gardening, photography (I don't have a camera, though), silver jewelry making (I have already completed a beginner's course), alternative energy sources (solar energy especially). . . .

In reply, I suggested that during the summer she visit the New Alchemy Institute in Woods Hole, Massachusetts. The New Alchemists, as they call themselves, are a group of people, led or perhaps I should say assembled, guided, directed, inspired, and coordinated by John and Nancy Jack Todd, who are trying to find ways in which human beings can live, in modest comfort, in a gentle, stable, and enduring relationship with the earth. The Institute is a small experimental farm and research facility, in which people experiment with solar greenhouses, fish-farming, intensive food raising, tree raising, windmills, composting, biological pest control, worm raising, etc. As small as it is, it seems to me one of the most important groups of people working anywhere. It is not at all an exaggeration to say that the health and happiness of our country, our planet, and the human race, may depend a great deal on what they are able to learn there.

At any rate, the student did visit them. In December of that same year she wrote again:

My main purpose for writing you is to thank you for your advice. I had written that I was interested in organic gardening and you suggested that I should visit the New Alchemy Institute. Well, my mother and I took you up on your suggestion one Saturday and although I did not get a chance to talk with any of the Alchemists, I thoroughly enjoyed exploring the farm. I went to a seminar on raising earthworms and saw a movie about the present plight of small farmers in this country.

Last spring an article on the New Alchemy Institute was featured in the Boston *Globe*. . . . I brought it into the Alternative School Room to show my friend and Alt. advisor. I also showed him your letter and I must say with no exaggeration the man was delighted. . . . He had not visited the Institute but in spring he may arrange to take a group of Alt. students for a visit. . . .

During the summer I suffered from an extremely bad attitude about school. I wanted to complete my last year of high school by means of a totally alternative learning process. But I decided upon entering school in September that if I was to have a satisfactory academic record for college, I must work within the system. The trip to the New Alchemy Institute made a permanent impression on me and influenced my decision to major in Life Sciences and Agriculture in college. Well, not only did I wish to improve my academic standing for college, but I also wished to prove to myself that I was still capable of being a good student despite my changed attitudes toward a structured and traditional education. Last year's failures in school nearly ruined my self-esteem.

I enrolled in five major subjects (not including phys. ed.) though I needed only five credits and a year of gym to graduate. I'm presently enrolled in an honors Spanish III Course, Latin I, Marine Biology and Animal Behavior, Economics, and an advanced placement English course! Believe me, that is quite a change in academics from the previous year. In order to carry this workload I had to quit Alternative School. No one told me that I had to leave the program, but I decided it was best. . . . Well, I've survived and after the first term I had earned a place on the honor roll.

THE MOST DIRECT WAY

An article from *Sports Illustrated* (December 17, 1979) shows how a person can zero right in on his chosen work:

One of the youngest and most successful design teams in contemporary ocean racing [has] Ron Holland, 32, as its equally unlikely chief. Holland failed the most elementary public exam for secondary schools in his native Auckland, New Zealand, repeatedly flunked math (considered by many to be a requisite in yacht design) and has no formal qualifications whatsoever in naval architecture. He even elected not to complete a boatbuilding apprenticeship. Yet today everybody wants a Holland design.

. . . At 16 he walked out of secondary school—"too academic," he says—and told his mother later. Even then he seemed to know that his future lay in boats. Until a primary schoolteacher introduced him to Arthur Ransome's *Swallows and Amazons,* a classic children's tale about a sailing holiday off England's Norfolk Broads, Holland had read nothing. Teachers had sent him to remedial reading classes. But after *Swallows and Amazons* he became a bookworm. He had been sailing since he was seven, when his father bought him a seven-foot dinghy, undaunted by the fact that in his first race he finished fourth and last.

Holland got into the boating industry as an apprentice, and quickly chucked that job because the boss would not give him time off to go ocean racing. . . .

He spent nearly three years working with American designers, first Gary Mull and finally the flamboyant Charlie Morgan.

It was in 1973, after less than three years of intermittent design experience, that Holland changed course again. He left Morgan to campaign his own quarter-tonner, *Eygthene,* in the world championships at Weymouth, England. It was a radical design—based, Holland admits now, on intuition, not "plain arithmetic." *Eygthene* won.

And just in time. With Laurel, whom he had married in 1971, he was living aboard the cramped quarter-tonner. A potential sale had just fallen through. He had no money in the bank.

Ron Holland sets a good example for people trying to find their work. If you know what kind of work you want to do, move toward it *in the most direct way possible.* If you want someday to build boats, go where people are building boats, find out as much as you can. When you've learned all they know, or will tell you, move on. Before long, even in the highly technical field of yacht design, you may find you know as much as anyone, enough to do whatever you want to do.

Of course, if none of the people doing your chosen work will even let you in the door without some piece of school paper, you may have to pay time and money to some school to get it. Or, if you find out that there are many things you want or need to know that the people working won't tell you, but that you can find out most easily in school, then go for that reason. At least, you will know exactly why you are there. But don't assume that school is the best way or the only way to learn something without carefully checking first. There may be quicker, cheaper, and more interesting ways.

Here are some other examples. This from *Solar Age,* December 1979:

> At age 22, Ken Schmitt is head of Research and Development for Alternative Energy Limited (AEL), a small new, company . . . which plans to sell [alcohol] stills beginning some time next year. . . .
>
> At 17, he owned a construction company, which "gave me the capital to experiment." Schmitt has experimented with solar energy systems for the last two years. His pilot plant for methanol (wood alcohol) synthesis may be the forerunner of a plant that will produce half a million gallons per day for Los Angeles motorists; and five foreign countries may buy rights to use a pyrolysis process he developed.

And from *The Boston Monthly,* December 1979:

> The head of the Boston Computer Society, a group that regularly publishes a newsletter and holds meetings to learn and exchange computer ideas and information, is 16 years old. Technicians for many of the local computer stores are high school students. Computerland in Wellesley has a volunteer expert with a terrifying knowledge of computers who works with their customers in exchange for unlimited computer time—he is twelve years old.

SERIOUS WORK

A family I know has been traveling around the country in a converted bus, staying for a while in towns that interest them or where they know people they like, then moving on. Not long ago the father wrote:

> A friend had just become "owner for a week" of a grocery store because the owner needed a vacation. S, the friend, decided he would capitalize on the opportunity and try to get a month's worth of "ownership" out of a week. He hired me to do several electrical

and carpentry jobs while the boss was gone. An impression must be made. Many improvements. Check writing power—hire—fire—chief for a day!

We had to be there early and work before the store opened. I shook the kids up at six, we unplugged the bus, and were off. The kids followed me into the store toting tools. S said they could play in the store and the idea of having a supermarket all to yourself carried quite a charge. Supermarkets almost always come fully equipped with people—most of whom are adults. Children who are there are seldom wanted or welcome. They are usually being admonished by mother for handling the sacks of candy placed carefully within their reach by knowing management.

Well, not the case this morning—the store was theirs. They roamed the aisles for a while contemplating the space. Within half an hour everyone felt at home and C sat down with K at a table in the deli and started reading her a book they had brought from the bus.

Soon S arrived in a panic! The fresh juice-making operation in the back room was two hours behind because the shipment of containers hadn't come. A big selling item for the store was fresh-made juices of several kinds, made from fresh produce early each morning. Panic—the crowds would hit and there would be no juice. Money would be lost, good will would slip. Being "owner for a week" S had fewer learning sets than your average supermarket manager so he said, "Who wants a job?" F and G (the boys) were low on funds—"We do." "Wash your hands and come with me." They went back to the little juice factory in the back room and S introduced the new help to the juice man.

I stopped by about half an hour later and saw an amazing operation. I have never seen F and G work so hard with such enthusiasm. F was filling bottles with carrot juice and G was wiping, labeling, and pricing. The juice man was pouring bushels of carrots into a big peeling machine and then on to a grinder and then to a two-ton hydraulic press. Gallons and gallons of carrot juice were flowing and the boys' eyes were wide and their hands were a blur. Before today carrots existed either one every few inches in a row in the ground or in one-pound plastic-wrapped bundles. These machines ate carrots like a giant dinosaur. The pace was intense. The juice man had his routines down pat and the kids picked up the rhythm. It was a dance and you had to keep in step. Commands came in three-word sentences and they were obeyed. No time for discussion or explanation—real work—a real product—a real classroom. Sacks of carrots became 85¢ bottles of juice in minutes. G said, "I don't care if S pays us or not, this is fun."

Three hours later I was done, the store was open and they were still having fun. Three large garbage cans of dry carrot pulp sat outside the juice room door. F's shirt and pants were orange and drenched. G was restamping a case of bottles he had marked 58¢ instead of 85¢. No hassle over the mistake—just stamp them again. After all, the juice man had to throw out a whole batch of carrots that got to the shredder before they were peeled. Mistakes are part of what people do. Unfortunately in schools full of desks, they are forbidden.

I was having my breakfast on the bus when they finished and they popped in, each carrying a fist full of three dollars. They had worked harder in that three hours than I had ever seen them work before and they were ecstatic. They had new knowledge, new dignity (they saved the day) and some negotiable legal tender. My prize was to have been there to see it.

From a mother:

J (4) took another quantum leap. We're market gardeners. He asked for and has his own plot, marked off with string (to his specs) for which he raised plants in the greenhouse and in which he's raising radishes for money. This is all on his own, but we try to help carry out his suggestions and ideas. Including when he's asked me to thin his radishes as he was "too tired." However, yesterday while I was working steadily transplanting, he took up a hoe and hoed every part of the garden that needed it *because he saw it needed to be done* [Author's emphasis]. It took about an hour of hard work in which he did as good a job as I. Usually when he does something well I find myself commenting with some praise, but this time it would have been obviously, even ridiculously, superfluous. As if I would tell my husband he was a good boy for working so hard. J was at that time in that enterprise my equal. I was thrilled.

A mother writes from Manitoba:

One of the best times we had in the euphoric first two months out of school, was a marathon session in the biochemistry lab where I work. I had a 48-hour experiment going which had to be checked in the middle of the night. J went in with me the first night and we had trouble with one of the machines, a fraction collector which moves test tubes along under the end of a length of fine tubing which slowly spits out the stuff to be collected. We stayed there until 5 A.M. and J occupied himself almost the whole time with a stopwatch checking the rate of drips from the tubing, the rate of movement of the tubes, and the rate of a monitoring pen on another machine—all work that was necessary for getting the job done—and he revelled in it.

We left the building just as the last stars were leaving the sky. Sheep and cattle were grazing quietly on nearby university pastures. Only the birds provided sound. J was amazed that he had really passed through all the dark hours without sleeping. I thought of all the kids who could not have the kind of exhilaration he had just had because of their confinement to hours dictated to them by schools.

We slept all that morning and went back to the lab for checks during the afternoon and again at night and the following day. J wanted to stay with it right to the end and did. He learned all sorts of things in that short span of time about units of volume and time, about multiplying and dividing, about fractions, about light absorption, magnets, solutions and probably other things. The same boy had been completely turned off by school math and was regarded by some as "slow" and "lazy."

A mother writes from New Hampshire:

T, A, and I . . . earn almost all of our money by seasonal orchard work—picking apples 2 months in the late winter. We leave home and work in various parts of [apple country].

. . . A started picking of her own accord one day when she was 5. She put her raincoat on backwards, using the hood as a bucket to hold the fruit until she emptied into the boxes. She was very proud of herself. She worked all day and picked 3 bushels. The next rainy day we made a quarter-size bucket out of a plastic waste basket and a pant leg. The cloth bottom opened up for emptying like our buckets. T made her a 10-foot ladder (he makes and sells apple-picking ladders). She picked from the bottoms of our trees and we paid her what we earned per bushel before deductions for food and rent.

Now, 5 years later, she has a custom-made half-size bucket and a 14-foot ladder. She works 2 hours or more most days, picking to the same quality standards we use. She keeps her own tally. She pays about ½ of her own living expenses from her earnings when we're on the crew. She handles the ladder well, picks as much of the tops as she can.

How much to pay her and how much to expect her to work have been areas of confusion. It didn't seem right to continue to pay her, in effect, more per bushel than anyone else by not deducting any expenses. But if we deducted her full expenses, she wouldn't earn anything (yet). So we compromised. Earning money is not her main motivation but she likes to get paid and it seems good for her to have money to spend. If she continues to increase her production she'll soon be able to pay her full expenses on the crew and have a good amount left over.

In many poor cultures the kids' earnings help support the whole family. We have to earn enough to live on the rest of the year. So it seems possible that as she gets older she might pay her expenses the rest of the year too, or contribute toward things we'll all use. We are not part of a tradition where the kids work a lot or contribute much to the family's survival. And we are not so close to the line that our survival depends upon her contributions. So when we're in doubt we take the more regular (like our own upbringing) course. I believe she's working a good amount of her own accord when we're on crews. She says she wants to get so she's paying all of her expenses on the crews.

I don't believe in compelling kids to study some subject they don't want to, but I do believe in insisting they do some work, in relation to their abilities and the needs of the family. Since they start with a compelling desire to do what the older family members do, this is no problem. Now sometimes she objects to some chores (it's boring, so-and-so doesn't have to). We insist. If you want to be warm, too, you have to carry firewood, too. She seems to see the justice of it and gives in pretty easily.

She helps with pruning, too. Has her own saw and with direction will sometimes prune a whole tree. But it is a harder skill to learn.

I think living on a work crew has been really good for our family. It helped me set limits and encouraged us to accept time away from each other, but still allowed us to be together when we needed it. Very young, A accepted that I had to work and learned to amuse herself very well. I think that kind of solitude is very important for everyone. She became less clinging and demanding and I learned

I could choose which demands I would meet. Before crew life I felt I should give her everything she was asking for. As a result of working with her near I learned that she could accept it and *benefitted* when I sometimes let her work it out herself. This led to both of us feeling our own individuality and made our close times closer. And brought my way of being with her into accord with T's way. Her attitude toward work (and mine) have benefitted from the work situation. Most of the crew, most of the time, are working with a willing attitude and there's a lot of enthusiasm that is catching. She works harder and longer with T, who enjoys pushing himself, than with me.

Since I have been the bookkeeper on the last few crews her interest in math has grown sharply. She helps with the payroll and counts out everyone's final net pay. She seems to have a good solid concept of reading and math. She doesn't gobble them up in quantity but when she's interested in something she follows it through.

I wrote in reply:

You wonder how A compares with other kids her age? My guess would be that she compares very well, probably smarter, more self-reliant, more serious, considerate, self-motivated, independent, and honest.

People get smart by giving constant attention and thought *to the concrete details of daily life,* by having to solve problems which are real and important, where getting a good answer makes a real difference, and where Life or Nature tells them quickly whether their answer is good or not. The woods are such a place; so is the sea; so is any place where real, skilled work is being done—like the small farm where Jud Jerome's daughter worked, like your own orchards.

Two summers ago I spent some time working with a small farmer in Nova Scotia, the neighbor and friend of the friends I was visiting. He had a large garden where he grew almost all his own vegetables, had about 20 acres in hay, raised Christmas trees. He also owned woodlots, from which he cut wood, for his own use and to sell. He was 72 years old, and did all this work himself, with the help of two horses. The skill, precision, judgment, and economy of effort he displayed in his daily work were a marvel to see. The friend I was visiting, a highly intelligent and educated man, no city slicker but a countryman himself, who had long raised much of his own food and killed, butchered, and cured or frozen much of his own meat, said with no false modesty at all that if he farmed for fifteen or twenty years he might—with plenty of luck and good advice—eventually learn to farm as well as this old neighbor.

LEAF-GATHERING

Children show me again and again that they love to be really useful, to feel that they make a difference.

Two years ago, as I write this, I began a mini-experiment in urban agriculture. Each fall, when the trees in the Public Garden have lost their leaves, men blow them into big piles and later take them away. While the leaf piles are still there, I collect several garbage cans full and make a packed-down pile of them in the little sunken patio behind my basement apartment. Every day I pour over them the water I use for washing, dishes, shower, etc., and use the rotted leaves to feed the worms I am raising.

As soon as the leaves were thick on the ground this fall I began collecting. Many early mornings, I put two plastic garbage cans on a small garden cart, took a leaf rake, trundled the cans into the Public Garden, raked up a pile of leaves, and filled the cans, jumping up and down in them from time to time to pack the leaves well down. Then I rolled cart and cans to the sidewalk behind my apartment, dumped the leaves over the wall into the patio, and later gathered them into piles which I packed down with weights.

One morning I collected and piled up more than a dozen loads. Feeling rain in the air, I thought I would make a couple of trips and bring in four more cans full, while the leaves were still dry. When I reached the Public Garden I saw four boys (8, 9, 9, and 10, as I later found out), gathering leaves and putting them into the now dry sunken pool that surrounds a small monument. They spotted me and rushed over to ask if they could borrow my garbage cans to fill up with leaves, which would be quicker than dumping one armful at a time. I said that was a good idea, but that I needed the cans, because I was going to fill them up with leaves and take them home. What for, they asked. To make them into rich dirt, I said. They thought about this for a moment. Then they asked if they could borrow the "wheelbarrow." I said, Sure, but that when my cans were full I would need it back. They agreed and went off with the cart, which they used to take their leaves to the empty pond. When I was ready I called to them and they brought the cart back. I took the cans home, dumped the leaves over the wall, and went back for more.

This time the boys came over to ask if they could help by loading into my cans some of the leaves they had put in the pond. I said that there were plenty of leaves left on the ground, and that I didn't want to take leaves away from their nice pile. They insisted that they wanted to do it, so I thanked them and said to go ahead. While they filled the cans, I raked up more leaves. Back they came in a few minutes with full cans, all talking and asking questions. I jumped up and down on the leaves inside the cans; the boys were amazed to find how much the leaves packed down. Then I began to fill the cans with the leaves I had raked. The boys asked if they could help me do that. I said, Sure. As we worked I told them I was going to use the leaves to feed the worms I was raising. They were fascinated by this. What kind of worms? How many did I have? Where did I get them? How much did they cost? What did they eat? How did I feed them? What did I keep them in? Why was I doing this?

When the cans were full and loaded on the cart the boys asked if they could help me take them home. I thanked them again and said, Fine. With very little arguing, they organized a four-man cart-pushing team. Two pushed, and two stood up at the front corners holding on, "guiding it," as they said. By this time they were so curious about the leaves and the worms that I decided to show them to them. They had been told to stay in the Garden, but I said that since I lived only a couple of blocks away we would be right back and I was sure their mothers wouldn't mind. So they pushed the cart to the wall where I unload. One asked me to lift him up so he could see the leaf pile in the patio. I did, and he was amazed to see how big it was. Soon they all climbed or were lifted to the top of the wall, and watched while I dumped the leaves. When the leaves stuck a bit in the can, one of them helped pry them loose. All the while they asked questions about me. What did I do? I said I wrote articles and books. What kind of books? Books about children and school. And so on.

When we went indoors two boys insisted on carrying the empty garbage cans downstairs, while a third pulled the cart up some steps—a hard struggle—and put it away. Then we went out to look at the leaf pile. I found a worm and showed it to them. There was a chorus of "Yuk! Slimy!" But in only a second or two they all wanted to hold one. I also found and showed them some egg cases, and one of them spotted a tiny worm, newly hatched, hardly bigger than a thread. They were fascinated by this, all four talking and asking questions at once. Soon they asked if they could each have a worm. I said, Sure, got one for each, gave each a little hunk of dirt to keep the worm in, some leaves to wrap the dirt in, and a paper bag to carry it.

As we walked back to the Public Garden they asked about how worms made more worms. I told them that worms were bisexual, boys and girls at the same time, and that any two worms could come together and fertilize each other, after which both of them could produce egg cases. Soon we were back at the monument and their leaf pile. After a bit more talk I said that I was sorry but that I had to go home and do some other work. I hated to leave these bright, friendly, curious, enthusiastic, helpful children. I loved working with them and showing them things and answering their questions. I think they were just as sorry to leave me. I remember, when they were pulling the loaded cart (which was quite heavy) toward my apartment, one of them said, to the others, not to me, and in the kind of voice that can't be faked, "This is *fun*, doing this!" They all agreed—much more fun to be helping a grownup do serious (even if mysterious) work than just playing around in a leaf pile. I hope they may have more chances to work with me, or some adult who cares about what he or she is doing. I hate to think of them ever becoming like the bored, sullen, angry, destructive teen-agers who hang out every day at the Boylston Street entrance to the Public Garden.

The other day a young person wrote me saying, "I want to work with children." Such letters come often. They make me want to say, "What you really mean is, you want to work *on* children. You want to do things *to* them, or *for* them—wonderful things, no doubt—which you think will help them. What's more, you want to do these things whether the children want them done or not.

What makes you think they need you so much? If you really want to work with children, then why not find some work worth doing, work you believe in for its own sake, and *then* find a way to make it possible for children—if they want to—to do that work with you."

The difference is crucial. The reason my work with the leaves and worms was interesting and exciting to those boys was precisely that it was *my* work, something I was doing for *my* good, not theirs. It was not some sort of "project" that I had cooked up because I thought they might be interested in it. I wasn't out there raking up leaves in the hope that some children might see me and want to join in. I never asked them to help, never even hinted; they *insisted* on helping me. All I did for them—which may be more than many adults might have done—was to say that if they really wanted that much to help me, then they could. Which is exactly the choice I would like to see the adult world offer to all children.

VOLUNTEER WORK

A twelve-year-old wrote us about being an office volunteer:

> In July 1978 my mother was asked to work at the Childbirth Education Association office. At that time we had a three-month-old baby named C. So my mother asked me if I would like to go to the office to mind C while she did her work. But when I went in, it seemed that C slept most of the time except when she was hungry. So I started to do a little work. Mrs. L. gave me some little jobs to do. Her daughter R (who is now a very good friend of mine) helped me to get into bigger things. She taught me to make registration packets. Even now I do about 100 a week at home. She taught me to run the folding machine so that we were able to fold the papers for the registration packets and also for the Memo. We enjoyed that a lot. I can even do it better than my mom because she gets the papers stuck sometimes. I also learned what to say when I answered the phone, even though I had a hard time getting "Childbirth Education Association" out in one breath and I sometimes disconnected people instead of putting them on hold.
>
> I can't forget the literature orders. That was the best. We really

had fun doing those. Finding the right papers and counting them out. Writing out bills and addressing the envelopes was lots of fun. R and I both knew what literature was there and what wasn't, so we could answer questions about what was in stock better than our moms.

I also had to do the postage meter at the end of the day. I always tried to use Mrs. L's adding machine to figure out the totals, but sometimes I would have to use my brain; then I didn't like it so much.

But it wasn't all work; sometimes R, her brother and I would play a game or go to the library. I really looked forward to coming in to the office. But soon the bad part came. I had to go back to school. So as soon as I got my school calendar I sent in a paper with all the days I had off from school so I could come into the office.

Now I am waiting for the summer to come so I can go into the office and help out.

Not long ago in our office we had so many letters from people asking about *Growing Without Schooling,* and about teaching children at home, that we could not answer them all. In the magazine I asked readers if some of them, who could type and also had a cassette tape recorder, would help with this. Many offered to do so, among them the mother of L, the Down's syndrome child about whom I wrote earlier. She asked if it would be okay, for the letters she was doing, if L addressed (in handwriting) the envelopes. I said, Fine. I sent them a tape of letters, which came back soon afterward, the letters typed, the envelopes neatly addressed. Then I sent them a big stack of letters from all over the country, that we had already answered, but that now needed to be broken down by states so that we could send them to people in the various states for a closer follow-up. Along with these I sent a tape of instructions. About this, L's mother wrote:

> . . . L was thrilled with the whole project, and most impressed with being addressed by name on the tape. She took to the sorting and filing with gusto. I hadn't mentioned that this was another part of our "program," again one where I had tried to convince the schools to do something "real." They kept trying to get her to alphabetize on paper, and I wanted them to give her index cards, recipes, etc.,

or folders. No use. So when we started our planning this year, I had her make up a bunch of file folders, for each course or planned activity, and she puts receipts, brochures and stuff in them. Also we keep her papers for figuring out money, arithmetic problems, sentences, etc. Also, since I need some shape for my days and am a chronic list-maker, we'd make up daily schedules (especially so she could go about her work without having to check with me every minute, something she really enjoys—the independence, I mean). These schedules, if more than routine, go into the folders.

So she was already used to that. She made up the folders (with my help in listing the states and assorted abbreviations). The first round, I went through the letters and underlined the state. The second time around I just screened them to be sure there *was* an address and that it was legible, but didn't note them—she figured them out herself. Anyway, L loves the job, and can't wait to get started, at night even, after supper. All this seems ideal for L's purpose—some work experience, plus the exposure to the filing, alphabetizing, state names and abbreviations, etc., all without any formal "instruction," just doing it—the perfect way, but hard to find, especially for her. [Author's note: In a later letter, she said that L had a paying part-time job.]

13

Home Schooling and the Courts

Since schools have been losing so many unschooling cases, and getting so much bad publicity, we might well ask why they keep taking parents to court. There are probably many reasons, which vary from school to school. But the most important reason of all these is that the schools, and often their lawyers, simply don't know the law. They can usually quote the compulsory school attendance laws of their state, but they know little or nothing about what the courts have ruled about the meaning of these laws.

Not long ago I spoke to a large meeting of educators from southeastern Massachusetts. This is fairly affluent country, so the school people there are probably about as well informed as anywhere. At one point I asked people to raise their hands if they had even a rough idea of what was meant or referred to in the phrase *Pierce* v. *Society of Sisters.* I had expected to see perhaps a dozen hands. Not one was raised. But this U. S. Supreme Court decision of 1923 is perhaps the most fundamental of all rulings on this question.

More recently, when I was testifying before the Education Committee of the House of Representatives of the Minnesota legislature (see Chapter 15), a member of the legislative staff read to the committee a summary she had prepared of court decisions on compulsory schooling. It was not bad as far as it went, but it was at least *two years* out of date—it mentioned neither Sessions, Perchemlides, Giesy, nor the very important Hinton case in Kentucky. And it left out some other and very important earlier rulings in favor of home school families.

Most judges in family or juvenile courts, where many unschooling cases will first be heard, probably don't know this part of the law either, since it is not one with which they have had much to do.

This means that when we write up home schooling plans, we are going to have to cite and quote favorable rulings. The more of this we do, the less schools will want to take us to court, and the better the chances that if they do we will win. Under our adversary legal system the task of courts is not so much to decide what "justice" is, as to decide which of the parties before them, in terms of existing laws, court decisions, etc., has the strongest argument. The courts will not do our legal work for us. If we don't cite favorable court cases in our plans or briefs, judges (who may very well not even have heard of them) are not going to put them in their rulings. But once we put before a court an argument or a legal precedent, the court cannot ignore it, but must either agree with it or find a stronger argument to oppose it. Otherwise, it runs the risk that its ruling will later be reversed by a higher court.

Now and then I discover a wonderful book, which I want to recommend to all home schoolers, only to find that it is long out of print. One such book is *The End of Obscenity* (New York: Random House, 1968) by Charles Rembar. (It might be in a library or law library.) It is the best book for laymen, at least that I have seen, about how constitutional law *works.* I learned an immense amount from it about how judges think, and about how lawyers go about making cases that they think may convince judges.

Rembar was able to persuade the courts to overturn definitions of obscenity that had been established in statutes and upheld by courts for many years. In other words, he was trying to persuade the courts essentially to reverse themselves on an important point of law—something they very rarely do. And by an amazingly ingenious series of arguments he was able to do it.

The chief lesson of Rembar's book is that if you want the courts, or a court, to reverse rulings that have been well settled in law, you have to present them with arguments they (and the courts before them) have not heard before. You can't go before them and say what has been said before, in the hope that *this* time they will say Yes where previously they had always said No. You have to give them a reason for saying Yes that the earlier courts did not have.

This is why it is important to know, in as much detail as possible, what the courts have said about home schooling.

THE STATE OF IOWA V. SESSIONS

Here are excerpts from the ruling of the District Court of Iowa in and for Winneshiek County, in the case of The State Of Iowa, Plaintiff, versus Robert Sessions and Linda Sessions, Defendants.

FINDINGS OF FACT

1. Robert Sessions and Linda Sessions were each charged under Section 299.1 in that each did unlawfully fail to have his or her 7-year-old son, Erik Sessions, attend a public school and/or obtain equivalent instruction elsewhere.

2. They were tried under that charge in Magistrate's Court. They were each found guilty and were sentenced to pay a fine of $50 and costs were assessed against them. . . . Appeal was thereafter filed. . . .

6. The defendants requested the board of directors of the Decorah Community School District to approve their home teaching program. The board refused, and the matter was appealed to the State Department of Public Instruction, and a decision was rendered by the board . . . sustaining the position of the Decorah board and stating in substance (a) that the Sessions met the first test, that is, or an equivalent instruction program . . . (b) the Sessions did not meet the second test, that is, the requirement of "providing instruction by a certified teacher." . . .

7. Thereafter, the Sessions filed a petition for declaratory ruling

with the state board in which clarification and guidance of interpretation was asked in the following form: "Precisely what must we do to comply with the 'instruction by a certified teacher' clause of 299.1 of the 1977 Code of Iowa?"

On May 10, 1978, the board answered the query in letter form stating in substance . . . (c) ". . . the appropriate standard to be used to determine the amount of instruction required by a certified teacher is that portion of a normal day during which instruction occurs in the public school district of residence . . . strongly imply the necessity of teacher presence or close proximity throughout the instructional process." This letter and information reached the defendants some time after their conviction.

8. Defendants assert the unconstitutionality of the charge in that: (a) the law is vague on standards of public instruction. (b) It violates the 1st and 14th Amendments. (c) Denial of due process by the action of the Decorah Community School District Board. . . .

The Court enters the following:

CONCLUSIONS OF LAW

3. Defendants further assert unconstitutionality by virtue of alleged violations of the 1st and 14th Amendments to the United States Constitution. Defendants in effect assert that their right to freedom of religion has been denied by denying the defendants their right to educate their child as they desire. The defendants cite the compelling case of *State of Wisconsin* v. *Yoder,* 406 US 205, 32 Lawyers Ed. 2d 15, 92 Supreme Court 1526, and other citations in substantiation of their position. . . . The Court feels that under the very concept of the *Wisconsin* v. *Yoder* case cited by the defendants, that adequate showing has not been made to put the defendants' opposition on a religious plane. In the cited case the Court said in substance: ". . . a way of life, however virtuous and admirable, may not be interposed as a barrier to reasonable state regulation of education if it is based on purely secular considerations; to have the protection of the religious clauses of the 1st Amendment, the claims must be rooted in religious belief . . ."

This is not to say an individual or individuals must be a part of an organized religion to come under the concept of the cited case. But rather under the record in this case the defendants have not presented to the Court sufficient evidence to sustain their argument under the 1st Amendment. . . .

6. Defendants urge the position that truancy violation being a criminal charge, the burden is on the plaintiff to prove all of the elements of the crime beyond a reasonable doubt. This proposition is surely an accurate statement of the law. Applying this to the case before the Court, the burden would be on the State to show each of the following elements: (1) That the defendants failed to have their child attend school in a public school district; and (2) Failing to have the child attend public school, they did not cause said child to attend upon equivalent instruction by a certified teacher elsewhere.

The first element was proved. As to the second element, the State held that the parents did procure a program indicating an equivalent education. The query remaining then: Was the equivalent instruction provided by a *certified teacher elsewhere*?

. . . The Court's ruling in this case is not to be construed as the Court's passing upon the quality of education in the Decorah school system. . . . The Court's function is essentially to determine whether or not the defendants have committed the crime alleged and are guilty thereof.

7. Finally the Court legally concludes that the burden is above set forth under the second element, "failing to have child attend public school, did they cause said child to attend upon *equivalent instruction by a certified teacher elsewhere*?" In this connection the Court must conclude that based upon the entire record, the State has failed to prove the alternate or second element, that is, that the schooling for Erik is not the equivalent by [sic] a certified teacher elsewhere. The Court concludes that there is a reasonable doubt as to the question of the certified teacher, and that as a consequence the defendants should be acquitted of the criminal charge.

In so ruling the Court has considered of great significance the element of equivalency, the sincere effort on the part of the defendants to comply, the difficulties and long delay in their getting a response to their query on a certified teacher (in fact no response was received until after their conviction), the inherent nature of the statutes contemplating a private tutorial situation as an alternate [sic] to public school attendance, and finally the conclusion that the legislature created a public school requirement with alternatives. These alternatives may not be arbitrarily denied, but if the statute is to have a viable Constitutional aspect of validity, it must be a determinable, workable statute with the opportunity for a legitimate exception.

The Court can understand the concern over the propriety of "opening the door" for many attempted exceptions. However, the Court feels that this is not a real threat under the statute and reasonably within the spirit of the statute. Exception as contemplated by the statute adds strength, not weakness, to the law.

8. Finally the Court merely concludes that the second and alternate element of the crime has not been proven beyond a reasonable doubt.

NOW, THEREFORE, IT IS THE JUDGMENT AND DECREE OF THE COURT:

1. The judgment and sentence of the Magistrate is reversed.
2. The defendants are hereby acquitted of the charges filed against them.
3. Costs are assessed to the plaintiff.

Frank D. Elwood, Judge
First Judicial District, Iowa

This is clearly one of the most important decisions on compulsory schooling that has yet appeared. To be sure, the court ruled on very narrow grounds. But that is why the ruling is so important. There is little in it that most judges, whatever might be their views on compulsory schooling, would be likely to disagree with. It is a decision which many courts, at least in those states where the law provides specifically for alternatives to schooling, may accept as a reasonable precedent. It holds that in all such cases (1) the burden of proof is not on the parents but on the schools (2) to show beyond reasonable doubt (3) that what the parents propose to do at home will be worse than what the schools are actually doing (not just talking about doing). Few school systems will in fact be able to show this, either to a judge or a jury.

This gives good reason to hope and believe that in states whose laws provide for alternatives to schooling any parents who prepare their case with sufficient care can probably win a favorable ruling from a court, if the schools push them that far.

It is worth noting, too, that this Iowa court held it very much against the State, i.e., the schools, that they did not cooperate with the Sessions in their efforts to find out precisely what the schools would accept as "equivalent." This means that when parents ask the schools what they would have to do to make their home-schooling program "equivalent," the schools must answer. If the parents then do what the schools said they had to do, courts are unlikely later to rule against their program.

It is also worth noting that this court said that people do not necessarily have to belong to some organized religious group to claim the protection of the freedom of religion under the First Amendment. It is not clear what evidence the Sessions, or some other family, would have had to present to make and sustain such a claim. But this altogether proper vagueness in the law about what is meant by religious belief may make it possible for many more people to take their children out of schools on religious grounds.

PERCHEMLIDES V. FRIZZLE

On November 13, 1978, Judge Greaney of the Massachusetts Superior Court handed down a ruling favorable to an unschooling family named Perchemlides. Some of the most significant parts of this (very long) ruling follow:

II. CONSTITUTIONAL AND STATUTORY CLAIMS

Central to the Perchemlides' complaint is their assertion that under the United States Constitution, parents derive certain rights and accrue certain protections to choose an alternative to public school education for their children. It is important to note at the outset the exact point of the argument. Plaintiffs do not argue that there exists a federally protected right to *home* instruction, *per se,* but rather that federal protection attaches to a home education alternative which is supplied by state statute and state court decisions. In reply, defendant willingly concedes that parents have a "fundamental right" to send their children to non-public schools as long as those schools meet valid educational standards set by the state. . . .

For reasons discussed below, I conclude that although it is the right and duty of the superintendent or the school committee to inquire into, and either approve or disapprove home education plans, the parents' constitutional right to decide how their own children shall be educated places reasonable limitations on that inquiry and thus circumscribes the discretion of the local authorities. Due in large part to the novelty of this situation for the Amherst school system, and to a genuine misunderstanding about the scope of parents' rights to home educate their children, the superintendent and the school committee have, in the Court's opinion, applied some standards to the review of the plaintiff's plan which are inappropriate, and the matter must be returned to them for further consideration.

A. Constitutional and Statutory Protection of the Right to Home Education.

On a number of occasions, the United States Supreme Court has held that certain personal rights can be deemed "fundamental" or "implicit in the concept of ordered liberty" and are included in a guarantee of "personal privacy" that emanates from the more specific guarantees contained in the Bill of Rights. Because the Constitution does not mention "privacy," courts and commentators have disagreed about the precise constitutional source of the guarantee. Older decisions . . . looked to the concept of liberty contained in the first section of the Fourteenth Amendment. *Pierce* v. *Society of Sisters,* 268 U.S. 510 (1925); *Meyer* v. *Nebraska,* 262 U.S. 390 (1922). More recent cases, while not entirely abandoning this ground, have drawn upon the First, Fourth, Fifth, and Ninth Amendments in various contexts. *Roe* v. *Wade,* 410 U.S. 113, 152–53 (1973). Whatever the precise constitutional source of the individual right to privacy, the Supreme Court has stated that the right not only protects against the unjustified disclosure of personal matters, but also protects the individual's "interest in independence in making certain kinds of important decisions." *Whalen* v. *Roe,* 429 U.S. 589 n.26 (1977).

It has become an axiom of constitutional law that one such kind of decision that individuals may make without unjustified government interference deals with matters relating to "child rearing and education." *Smith* v. *Offer,* 431 U.S. 816 (1977); *Carey* v. *Population Services International,* 431 U.S. 678 (1977); *Whalen* v. *Roe, supra; Paul* v. *Davis,* 424 U.S. 693 (1976); *Wisconsin* v. *Yoder,* 406 U.S. 205 (1972); *Griswold* v. *Connecticut,* 381 U.S. 479 (1965);

Pierce v. *Society of Sisters, supra.* The Supreme Court has repeatedly reaffirmed the authority of the *Pierce* holding that "the fundamental theory of liberty upon which all governments in this Union repose excludes any general power of the state to standardize its children by forcing them to accept instruction from public teachers only." *Pierce* v. *Society of Sisters,* 268 U.S. 510, 535. The nature of the parents' right on a constitutional level, and the fact that it draws support from several branches of the Bill of Rights was concisely expressed in these terms by Justice Douglas concurring in *Roe* v. *Wade:*

The Ninth Amendment obviously does not create federally enforceable rights. It merely says, "the enumeration in the Constitution of certain rights shall not be construed to deny or disparage others retained by the people." But a catalogue of these rights includes customary, traditional, and time-honored rights, amenities and privileges. . . . Many of them, in my view, come within the meaning of the term "liberty" as used in the Fourteenth Amendment . . . [one] is *freedom of choice in the basic decisions of one's life* respecting marriage, divorce, contraception, *and the education and upbringing of children . . .* [Judge Greaney's italics].

Thus, parents need not demonstrate a formal religious reason for insisting on their right to choose other than public school education since the right of privacy, which protects the right to choose alternative forms of education, grows out of constitutional guarantees in addition to those contained in the First Amendment. Non-religious as well as religious parents have the right to choose from the full range of educational alternatives for their children. There will remain little privacy in the "right to privacy" if the state is permitted to inquire into the motives behind parents' decisions regarding the education of their children. As plaintiffs here point out, the plaintiffs in *Pierce* included a secular military academy, and the holding in that case did not mention religious beliefs of the Free Exercise clause of the First Amendment. See also, *Farrington* v. *Tokushige,* 273 U.S. 284 (1927); *Meek* v. *Pittenger,* 374 F. Supp. 639, 653 (E.D. Pa. 1974).

Without doubt, then, the Massachusetts compulsory attendance statute might well be constitutionally infirm if it did not exempt students whose parents prefer alternative forms of education.

B. Scope of the State's Regulatory Powers.

. . . Just as the Court in *Roe* v. *Wade* recognized that the state has important interests in regulating the abortion decision, the state has an important interest in regulating the education of school-age children. The defendants accurately point out that attempts by parents to deny that the state has any right to set educational standards for school-age children have been consistently rejected by the federal courts. . . .

The Perchemlides do not dispute that under the police power the state is obliged to see that children are educated and to set reasonable standards that define and limit the term "education." Neither do the Perchemlides seek to do that which is proscribed by *Wisconsin* v. *Yoder*—to "substitute their own idiosyncratic views of what knowledge a child needs to be a productive and happy member of society" for the standards set by duly elected and appointed officials. On the contrary, the plaintiffs appear essentially willing to conform their home education program to the state's bona fide academic and curricular standards. [Author's note: As to which of these standards are in fact bona fide, see Judge Meigs's ruling in *Hinton* v. *Kentucky State Board of Education,* also very much worth quoting in any home education proposal.] . . .

The state may not, however, set standards that are so difficult to satisfy that they effectively eviscerate the home education alternative [Author's emphasis]. . . . [the state] may not use regulations or standards as a means of discouraging alternatives which are not identical to the public schools. *Farrington* v. *Tokushige,* supra; *State* v. *Whisner,* 351 N.E. 2nd 750 (S.Ct. Ohio 1976). . . .

It follows from the very nature of the right to home education that the school committee or the superintendent may not reject a proposal submitted by parents on the ground that the home environment is *socially* different from the classroom environment. . . . Under our system, the parents must be allowed to decide whether public school education, including its socialization aspects, is desirable or undesirable for their children. . . .

III. JUDICIAL REVIEW

. . . Given the competing interests present in this case . . . the proper role of the court is as follows: *First,* it must measure the substantive standards used by the superintendent and the school committee against the constitutional limitations already outlined. *Second,* it must analyze the procedural due process aspects of the case to determine how much process is due the parents and whether they obtained the process due. *Third,* once satisfied that constitutional standards have been employed and due process protections accorded, the reviewing court should do no more than examine the school committee's articulated reasons for its decision to see whether it can determine "with some measure of confidence whether or not the discretion . . . has been exercised in a manner that is neither arbitrary nor capricious" and whether the decision to deny the home education request "was reached for impermissible reasons or for no reason at all." *Dunlop* v. *Bachowski,* 421 U.S. 560, 57173 (1975).

IV. FINDINGS AS TO STANDARDS AND PROCEDURAL DUE PROCESS

. . . The school committee members and superintendent have stated that "in evaluating plaintiffs' proposed plan, defendants applied the same standards used in approving any other form of alternative education. Such plan had to be equal in thoroughness and efficiency and in the progress made as that of the public schools." That is the statutory standard used in evaluating *private school programs.* Nothing in the statute makes this standard directly applicable to the "otherwise instructed" language in which the Supreme Judicial Court, in the *Roberts* case, found a right to home education. Indeed, the way the statute is written indicates that applying criteria used to evaluate private schools may not be appropriate to a home education request. The statute very carefully delineates the type of schools that form a permissible alternative to public day schools and then reserves alternate education as a separate, distinct classification in this language: ". . . or of a child who is being otherwise instructed in a manner approved in advance by the superintendent or the school committee."

There are certain ways in which individualized home instruction can never be the "equivalent" of any in-school education, public or private. At home, there are no other students, no classrooms, no pre-existing schedules. The parents stand in a very different relationship to their children than do teachers in a class full of other people's children. In view of these differences, to require congruent "equivalency" is self-defeating because it might foreclose the use of teaching methods less formalized, but in the home setting more effective than those used in the classroom. For example, certain step-by-step programs of graded instruction, involving the use of standardized texts and tests periodically administered, might be unnecessary when the parent-teacher enjoys a constant communication with the child, and so is able to monitor his or her comprehension and progress on an individualized level impossible in a school setting.

In summary, the record shows that school committee members had somewhat contradictory notions about what standards to apply to the Perchemlides's application, and that most of the committee members relied upon impermissible standards, to one degree or another. Much of the difficulty encountered by all parties in this situation could be avoided were the school committee and superintendent to draft broad standards setting out their expectations for home education programs. Although I decline to rule that such standards are required in this context, it is significant that federal courts have viewed, in other contexts, "the establishment of written, objective and ascertainable standards" as an "intricate [sic] part of Due Process." *Baker-Chaput* v. *Cammett,* 406 F. Supp. 1134 (D. N.H. 1076), and cases cited. . . .

Some of the reasons cited for the rejection of the Perchemlides's plan, such as lack of group experience, improper motive, and bad precedent, clearly intrude too far on the parents' right to direct their children's education. Other strictly academic standards used may have been perfectly appropriate, but even here it is impossible to know whether the authorities disapproved the plan because Richard could not be expected to learn as much as he would in public school, a permissible reason, or because the actual program of study was not a carbon copy of the public school curriculum, a requirement which is not imposed by statute and intrudes too far on the right to home education.

We print these words from Judge Greaney's ruling so that from now on people will quote freely from them in any home education plan they draw up. These words, in short, are not here just to make people feel better but to be used.

We have quoted the parts of the ruling that are most important and helpful to us. But any who fear that they may be in conflict with the schools would probably do well to read the entire ruling (available from Holt Associates, 308 Boylston St., Boston MA 02116). It is an excellent lesson in how thorough and careful judges think.

No more than lawyers do judges like to lose. For a lawyer, losing is having a court rule against you; for a judge, it is having a higher court reverse you. Judge Greaney has taken great pains to build a ruling that will stand.

What has this to do with us? Lawyers, in preparing legal briefs, try to construct an argument so solid that, in effect, all the judge has to do is sign it. Our task is to put into every home education proposal a legal argument that is so strong that the schools' lawyers will not be able to overturn it in court, or better yet, will not even wish to try. The more we can learn to think like a careful judge, the better our chances of winning in court if we have to go there, or of staying out altogether.

VIRGINIA V. GIESY

The following excerpts from a recent Virginia court may be useful to unschooling parents in a number of states.

VIRGINIA: IN THE JUVENILE AND DOMESTIC RELATIONS DISTRICT COURT OF THE CITY OF NORFOLK
COMMONWEALTH OF VIRGINIA V. THEO GIESY NO. A 08203-A
COMMONWEALTH OF VIRGINIA V. DANIEL GIESY NO. A 08202-1
April 4, 1979
Johnny E. Morrison, Assistant Commonwealth Attorney, for plaintiff.
Thomas B. Shuttleworth for defendants.

. . . The statute involved in this case (Sect. 22-275.6) directs the defendants, as parents, as to each child, to "cause the child to attend school or receive instruction as required by this article."

. . . Section 22-275.1 of the same Article spells out the options available to the parents . . . (1) to send their children "to a public school," or (2) "to a private, denominational or parochial school," or (3) to have such children "taught by a tutor or teacher of qualifications prescribed by the State Board of Education and approved by the division superintendent in a home."

The parents in this case . . . have elected course (2), a private school, and maintain that they are in *bona fide* compliance therewith.

The defendant parents, in compliance with course of action (2) have established their own private school. It is denominated "The Brook School," after Mrs. Giesy's maiden name. It has a faculty of essentially one teacher, Mrs. Giesy. It has a student body of four, the four children of the family.

The Commonwealth maintains that this is no true school, but a mere subterfuge of a school, in violation of the Compulsory School Attendance Law and is established as a device to circumvent that law; and that the defendants are, by virtue thereof, criminally responsible.

With respect for the Commonwealth's position, examination of the Commonwealth's own laws on the subject is in order. They are embraced within Title 22, entitled Education, of the Virginia Code.

. . . As to course of action (2), private schools, those for primary and secondary education contemplated by the case at bar, the statutory law of Virginia provides only a wall of silence.

. . . The legislative wall of silence is not deemed to be accident or oversight, but rather an eloquent expression of formal state policy.

As in the case of the silence of Congress, failure of the General Assembly to exercise the power of regulation is deemed to be an expression of its will that the subject should remain free from restrictions. See 16 Am. Jur. 2d, Const. Law Sect. 209.

. . . As to private schools, the law provides no guidance—no definition, no delineation of institutional parameters, no prescription as to faculty, students, curriculum or accreditation—nothing whatsoever.

What constitutes a private school may be determined by academicians or citizens, but the state refrains from participating in such determination.

The mission of the Court is to construe the will of the legislature. Where the legislature provides no law to construe, the Court refrains from construction. The Court does not make law.

. . . So The Court is without legal ability and is without legal authority to say that the Brook School constitutes a private school or to say that it does not constitute a private school.

It may or may not, and reasonable minds may differ.

The issue before the Court is narrow—whether by placing their children in the Brook School the defendants are in violation of Section 22-275.6 and guilty of a crime.

There is no proof that they are guilty beyond a reasonable doubt, and we therefore dismiss the case.

James G. Martin, IV
Judge

HINTON V. KENTUCKY STATE BOARD OF EDUCATION

From the *New York Times,* January 26, 1979:

> An estimated 5,000 Christian fundamentalist schools that have sprung up in the past few years are claiming the right to keep the state completely out of their affairs. . . . They do not want to be told what textbooks to use, what educational policies to adopt or even that they must be licensed. . . .
>
> Representatives of 20 non-accredited Christian schools in Kentucky fought a 1977 ruling by the State Board of Education that parents who used such schools were liable to prosecution and their children subject to being listed as "habitual truants." They hired William B. Ball of Harrisburg, Pennsylvania, a lawyer who is a frequent defender of religious freedom.
>
> At least for the moment, they have won. Despite powerful opposition from many political leaders, a Kentucky Circuit Court Judge, Henry Meigs, ruled on October 3 that the state had no right to make its regulations mandatory. Judge Meigs said the board must refrain from limiting the schools' choice of textbooks and from forcing teachers to be certified. The state has appealed. . . .

Here are excerpts from Judge Meigs's ruling:

FRANKLIN CIRCUIT COURT
CIVIL ACTION NO. 88314
DIVISION 1
Filed Oct. 4, 1978
Reverend C. C. Hinton, Jr. et al. (Plaintiffs) v. Kentucky State Board of Education, et al. (Defendants)

It would not be difficult to find in the record of this case abundant support for a conclusion that the regulatory scheme fashioned by the State Board, and sought by it to be imposed upon these plaintiff schools under the dubious authority of "approval" (KRS 156.160) is far beyond Constitutional limits of legislative delegation. . . .

[Plaintiffs'] incontrovertible proof shows—and the demeanor of the witnesses confirms—irreconcilable philosophical differences between their educational concepts, notions of textbook and curriculum content and teacher qualification. These differences are not fanciful or arbitrary, but very real and substantial, having a foundation in firmly held religious belief. . . . Expert testimony in this case certainly established that there is not the slightest connection between teacher certification and enhanced educational quality in State schools. . . .

The State is unable to demonstrate that its regulatory scheme applied to the *public* schools has any reasonable relationship to the supposed objective of advancing educational quality. . . . Plaintiffs, on the other hand, have shown that without benefit of the State's ministrations their educational product is at least equal to if not somewhat better than that of the public schools, in pure secular competence.

. . . Action and threatened action of the State against these plaintiffs or any of them heretofore enjoined temporarily, is now hereby enjoined [Author's note: i.e., forbidden] permanently, all at defendants' costs.

Given under my hand this 4th day of October 1978.

Henry Meigs

Judge, Franklin Circuit Court.

The board of education appealed the case to the Supreme Court of Kentucky *(Kentucky Board of Education* v. *Rev. C. Harry Rudasill, et al.).* The Kentucky Supreme Court upheld the lower court, saying that the state cannot force private schools to meet the accreditation standards regarding courses, teachers and textbooks that it sets for public schools, but that it could monitor the schools' performance through a standardized achievement testing program. In effect, the ruling shifts the burden of proof from the schools, which previously had to show they were worthy of accreditation, to the state, which now can act against the schools only if it demonstrates they are inadequate.

The decision, written by Justice Robert Lukowsky, focused on the state constitution, specifically Section 5 which never has been tested in Kentucky courts and which says in part: ". . . Nor shall any man be compelled to send his child to any school to which he may be conscientiously opposed."

Home schoolers and would-be home schoolers in other states should read not only the compulsory school statutes in their states, but also their state constitutions, to see what these may have to say about rights of parents, religious freedoms, etc. In some states the clauses governing these matters in the state constitution may be more explicit and more favorable than anything in the U.S. Constitution. In any case, we should as far as possible try to get decisions based upon such clauses, for the state will probably not appeal these decisions in the federal courts, where our chances may be less good.

A CANADIAN RULING

IN THE PROVINCIAL COURT (FAMILY DIVISION) OF THE COUNTY OF LAMBTON, THE LAMBTON COUNTY BOARD OF EDUCATION VS. MIREILLE BEAUCHAMP

. . . Mrs. Beauchamp contends her son is "legally excused" from attendance under further provisions of the [Education Act of Ontario] and for that reason is not guilty of the offence charged.

Section 20(2) of the Act provides that:

A child is excused from attendance at school, *inter alia,* if (a) He is receiving satisfactory instruction at home or elsewhere.

Mrs. Beauchamp urges that her son is in fact receiving satisfactory instruction at home at her hands employing correspondence materials from Christian Liberty Academy which is located in Prospect Heights, Illinois.

. . . In full and able written argument, neither counsel has been able to refer the Court to reported cases in the Province of Ontario interpreting or applying the relevant provisions of the Ontario Act.

. . . Historically, it appears that the defense of alternate education entered the statutes primarily as a concession to the establishment and operation of parochial or denominational "separate" schools, but it also has been widely used in the establishment of nonsectarian private schools.

. . . It seems clear to me that the Ontario statute does not limit the defense of alternative education in such a way as to preclude home instruction, nor obviously does it purport to prevent the inclusion in alternative education of the inculcation of religious tenets and values training, whether those principles be held by a minority or a majority of the populace.

The various legislatures, however, have clearly intended to place limits on the exercise of this right of alternative education, and such, no doubt, was a partial intent of the legislature of Ontario in enacting Sections 20, 23(2), 25(4), and 29.

The language of the legislation does not make the extent of the expressions of this intent obvious, in that it does not specify or spell out exactly what form of education is an acceptable alternative. It appears reasonable to infer that the legislature of this province intended to ensure that the alternative program be of a quality comparable to that of the public school system, however.

In his argument, counsel for Mrs. Beauchamp noted that there appears to have been no attempt by ministry officials through guidelines, regulations, or through directives in this particular area to define what was or could be satisfactory education at home.

In some provinces, the determination of equivalency of the alternate education is reserved to officials of the Ministry of Education and is expressed through the issuance of a certificate or ministerial opinion. This is not the case in Ontario where it appears clear that the courts do not lack jurisdiction to make this determination in the face of an executive decision, as is the case in the Province of Alberta as seen in the case of *The Queen* v. *Wiebe,* [1978] 3 W.W.R. 36; but on the other hand, that the Court itself must make this determination based on evidence adduced.

. . . Mrs. Beauchamp's evidence consisted of the reading of a paper delineating her concerns with and rejection of aspects of the public educational system, and expressing her intent and philosophy with respect to the education of her children. Mrs. Beauchamp is obviously an able, intelligent and sincere person whose views would be shared in whole or in part by a not-insignificant number of Canadians. . . .

I have no doubt that the legislature of Ontario, in enacting *The Education Act,* intended a purpose with which the majority of the population agrees, and that it is to maintain at least a minimum degree or standard of education for its citizens; and to that end, the state is accorded the right to interfere with the rights of parents to educate their children as they wish.

Obviously, there will always be persons who for religious, cultural, or other sectarian purposes reject all or part of the public educational system, and pressing against them will be the intent of the state to protect their children from what may be the ignorance, excess, or folly of their parents which may in turn deprive their children of the right to full and free development and may result in them becoming a burden and a charge upon society as a whole.

It is very important that there be a fine balance between these contending rights and interests.

. . . At issue in this case is not a parent's right to insist on the inclusion of religious and moral precepts in the education of his or her child. That right is at this time well established, provided the parent is sufficiently able and determined. The issue is the adequacy of the alternative educational system provided to that child in all its other aspects.

On the other hand, I am satisfied that those seeking to invoke the compulsive powers of the state in the face of the alleged failure of the parent or guardian to provide an adequate alternative and thereby to impose the sanctions of quasi criminal legislation, have a substantial burden of proof. . . .

In this case the evidence tendered on behalf of the Lambton County Board of Education falls short of establishing beyond a reasonable doubt that Mireille Beauchamp is guilty of the offense charged. . . . I must conclude that as the law of Ontario now stands, that the educational authorities must conclusively prove their case through the introduction of substantial, detailed, and expert testimony if necessary.

This may impose a very difficult onus on the educational authorities and perhaps present an extraordinary challenge to the courts, but I have no alternative in this matter before the Court than to find Mireille Beauchamp not guilty of the offense charged, and I so find.

[Signed] Judge David F. Kent.

MICHIGAN V. NOBEL

From an important decision on December 12, 1979:

IN THE 57TH DISTRICT COURT FOR THE COUNTY OF ALLEGAN

Mr. Peter Nobel and Mrs. Ruth Nobel are charged with a violation of the Compulsory Education Laws of the State of Michigan pursuant to 1976 Public Act 451, Sec. 1561, MCLA 390. 1651; MSA 15.41561, for failure to send their minor children to public school. . . .

At the trial, the Defendants did not dispute the fact that they were not sending their children to public school or to a private school outside the Nobel home. However, the Nobels contend that they are not guilty of the offense charged because they were educating their children at home in a "satellite school" of the Christian Liberty Academy, headquartered in Chicago, Illinois, pursuant to the dictates of their conscience and in furtherance of sincerely held religious beliefs. The Nobels assert for those reasons that the Statute in question as applied to the facts of this particular case is unconstitutional, insofar as it requires certification, for violation of the First Amendment to the United States Constitution guaranteeing the free exercise of religious beliefs.

Peter and Ruth Nobel have been educating their children at home utilizing materials and assistance provided to them by the Christian Liberty Academy of Chicago, Illinois. The children had previously attended a private school, but that school no longer meets the religious standards of the Nobels.

Mrs. Nobel received a Bachelor of Arts degree from Calvin College in elementary education. Mrs. Nobel has had several years of teaching experience prior to September 1, 1978, and while she has never applied for a teacher's certificate, did receive a provisional teaching certificate pursuant to her degree in elementary education at the time of her graduation.

Mrs. Nobel refuses to obtain a teaching certificate because of her religious beliefs. Mrs. Nobel testified that her daily life was governed by her understanding of the world of God as contained in the Bible and it is her firmly held religious belief that parents are responsible for the education and religious training of their children and that the parents must not delegate that role and authority to the government or any State, that for her to accept State certification would, according to her religious beliefs, be placing her responsibilities for education of her children in a position subservient to that of the State in violation of her religious beliefs. . . .

Testimony of Mrs. Nobel at trial indicated that her religious beliefs would prevent her from sending her children to the public schools because public school education directly conflicts with her belief in God and her interpretation of the teachings of the Bible and her religious beliefs in general.

Mrs. Nobel further testified that she could not send her children to any certified private school in the area because they too failed to meet her standards of religious training and education.

Pursuant to her religious beliefs, Mrs. Nobel began a program of home education which consisted of the same basic subject material as is taught in the public schools. . . . No evidence was offered or shown to indicate that this curriculum was deficient in any way.

Dr. George L. Hopkins of Florida, an educational psychologist, administered intelligence and psychological testing of the Nobel children. Dr. Hopkins's qualification as a psychological and educational testing expert was stipulated to by the parties herein as were the findings of the test results.

Dr. Hopkins's evaluations indicated that each of the five Nobel children are above average intelligence, that each has obtained an educational level ahead of other children in their chronological age group. . . . In addition thereto, Mrs. Nobel was tested and found to possess the intelligence as well as the training and appropriate psychological makeup to perform well as a teacher.

The evaluations also indicate that the children were well socialized and are emotionally and psychologically well adjusted. An "offer of proof" from the Reverend Paul Lindstrom of the Christian Liberty Academy was also read into the record indicating that the course of study which the children were engaged in through the Academy was geared to the religious convictions of the Nobels.

Professor Donald Erickson of the University of San Francisco testified as an expert witness. *His testimony indicated that there was no evidence whatsoever that a teaching certificate proved teacher competence or that it has been empirically shown that a teacher's certificate enhances the quality of the educational process received by the students. He indicated that students in private schools consistently do better on standardized tests than public school students even though many private schools do not require certification of their teachers* [Author's emphasis].

Dr. Erickson indicated that very few parents would choose to educate their children at home and the expense to the State to insure that home education was adequate would not be an undue financial burden or otherwise on the State.

Pursuant to a hypothetical question using the facts of this case, Dr. Erickson was of the opinion that the education the children were receiving was adequate and that in his opinion the "certification" of Mrs. Nobel was unnecessary to meet any State interest in education of the children under the circumstances of this case. . . .

The testimony established that the Nobel home was maintained in a neat and sanitary condition and that there was no objection on the part of the Nobels to any State inspection of the home or to State educational testing of her children. . . .

The Attorney General of the State of Michigan in an Opinion dated September 27, 1979, being Opinion 5579, addressed the following question: Whether a parent may provide for his or her child's education at home without having a certified teacher present. . . . In his Opinion he recognizes as an exception to the Statute private home schools that have a certified teacher or tutor present and concludes that any private home school must utilize certified teachers and that it is his opinion that a parent may not provide for his or her child's education at home without having a certified teacher providing instruction and courses comparable to those offered in the public school district in which the child resides.

It should be noted, however, that the issue of religious freedom was not addressed by the Attorney General when such exercise of religious beliefs precluded the certification of the parent teacher. This Court must therefore address that issue.

The First Amendment to the United States Constitution states that "Congress shall make no law respecting an establishment of religion, or prohibiting the free exercise thereof . . ." The free exercise clause was made applicable to the States, through the "concept of liberty" embodied in the (Fourteenth) Amendment. *Cantwell* v. *Connecticut,* 310 U.S. 296, 303 (1940). The United States Supreme Court has adopted a broad definition of what constitutes "religion" for the purposes of free exercise analysis. In *United States* v. *Ballard,* 322 U.S. 78 (1944), the Court indicated that proper inquiry is limited to whether or not the adherent was *sincere* in his or her beliefs.

The definition of religion is currently broad enough to include many beliefs which are not conventional, traditional theism. *United States* v. *Seeger,* 380 U.S. 163, 166 (1965). "Sincere and meaningful belief which occupies a place in the believer's life parallel to that filled by orthodox belief in God." *Welsh* v. *United States,* 398 U.S. 333 (1970). The Court has noted that nontraditional beliefs, including secular humanism, atheism, and nontheistic faiths, are all "religion" for the purpose of free exercise analysis. The Supreme Court in *Fowler* v. *Rhode Island,* 345 U.S. 67 (1953), held that it was "no business of the courts to say that what is a religious practice or activity for one group is not religion under the protection of the First Amendment."

Mrs. Nobel refused to be certified even though she is clearly an experienced and otherwise qualified elementary school teacher because it would violate her religious beliefs.

Freedom of religion is, of course, a fundamental constitutional right which occupies a "preferred position" in our constitutional framework. *Murdock* v. *Pennsylvania,* 319 U.S. 105, 115, (1943).

The government can only punish acts taken pursuant to sincerely held religious beliefs in extraordinary circumstances. Criminal or civil sanction of religion-based action must be based upon a compelling State interest. Furthermore, there must be no "less restrictive means" available to achieve the legitimate State interest while maintaining the integrity of the citizens' religious beliefs. *Sherbert* v. *Verner,* 374 U.S. 398, 407 (1963); *Wisconsin* v. *Yoder,* 406 U.S. 205, 214 (1972).

Therefore, the State must have a compelling State interest, and no narrower alternatives, in applying the teacher certification requirement for home education to the Nobels under the facts of this particular case. The burden of proof in any criminal case is upon the State to demonstrate that there is a compelling State interest, and that no narrower alternative to the government action could be taken. (*Sherbert* v. *Verner,* 374 U.S. 398, 407 [1963].)

No evidence has been introduced in this case that would demonstrate that the State has a compelling interest in applying teacher certification laws to the Nobels or that the education interest of the State could not be achieved by a requirement less restrictive on the religious beliefs of the Nobels. . . .

The evidence indicates that the Nobels' educational program is meeting all of the State compulsory education requirements except for the certification of the teacher therein.

The Supreme Court of Kentucky found the certification procedure unnecessary as the State failed to show that there was any overriding State interest in such uniform requirements being applied without exception.

The State's case here is based solely on the need for uniform application of the certification requirement for home instruction, not lack of teaching ability.

The evidence clearly establishes that the Nobels have met the purpose of the Statute as stated by the Attorney General. For her to accept certification would not make her a better teacher, nor would it make her children learn more easily, nor would it make her children more intelligent, nor would it provide any additional benefits for her, her children, or the State, but it would, indeed, interfere with her freedom to exercise her religious beliefs. . . .

The Nobels have a documented and sincere religious belief and this Court won't and no Court should interfere with the free exercise of a religious belief on the facts of this case.

The interest of the State in requiring certification on the facts as contained in this particular case must give way to the free exercise of religious belief.

THEREFORE, the charges against the Nobels are dismissed and a Judgment of acquittal will enter.

[Signed] Gary Stewart, District Judge.

THE LAW SUMMED UP

Here, in sum, is the meaning of these rulings:

1. Parents have a right to educate their children in whatever way they believe in; the state cannot impose on all parents any kind of educational monopoly, of schools, methods, or whatever. *Pierce* v. *Society of Sisters, Farrington* v. *Tokushige,* and most recently *Perchemlides.*

2. The state may not deprive parents of this right for arbitrary reasons, but only for serious educational ones, which it must make known to parents, with all the forms of due process. Again, *Perchemlides;* also *Nobel.*

3. A state that would deny parents these rights by saying that their home education plan is inadequate has a burden of proof to

show beyond reasonable doubt that this is so. Parents are assumed to be competent to teach their children until proved otherwise. This Assumption of Competence is kin to and part of the general Assumption of Innocence (of the accused) which holds in all criminal proceedings. *Sessions.*

4. In order to prove that the parents' education plans are inadequate, the state must show that its own requirements, regulations, etc., are educationally necessary and do in fact produce, in its own schools, better results than the parents get or are likely to get. *Hinton et al.* (Ky.); also *Nobel.*

14

Legal Strategies

LOOKING UP THE LAW

A father phoned me a few years ago. For many good reasons he was thinking of suing his local school. Looking for a good lawyer to represent him, he asked advice from a nationally famous expert on constitutional law. This lawyer recommended a lawyer friend. When the father interviewed that lawyer, he was surprised and discouraged to find that he planned to turn most of the work of the case over to a young assistant, who, though knowing little or nothing about the law in this area, would charge the father $50 for every hour of work. The father mentioned a book that he thought had an important bearing on the case; the lawyer had never even heard of it. Later the father said to me, "I'm not going to pay him fifty dollars an hour to read that book. I can't afford to educate him at that price."

Quite right. People who make $100 or more an hour can afford to pay other people $50 an hour to do legwork and research for them. People who make $5 or $10 an hour must do that legwork and research themselves, and use the $50-per-hour person to do *only* those things that they can't do for themselves. Take this book the father wants the lawyer to know about. The best bet for him is to read the book, copy the pages he thinks are most important, sum up the rest, and have the lawyer read the copied pages and the summary. It will take the lawyer only a few minutes and cost the father only a few dollars.

For some time, we unschoolers are not likely to find many lawyers, anywhere in the country, who know as much about the law on unschooling as we know *or can easily find out.* This is not an issue about which most lawyers have concerned themselves. We cannot rely on them to work out good strategies and write good briefs for us—at least, not at a price that most of us can afford. We are going to have to do much of the research, decide what legal action we want to take, what kind of decision we hope to get from the courts, and put together all our necessary supporting evidence, citations, quotes from rulings, etc. Only after we have prepared the strongest possible case should we think about hiring a lawyer to polish it up and steer it through the courts.

How then do we learn the law? When I suggested in an early issue of *GWS* that people write their state legislators to find out their state laws on compulsory schooling and related matters, one of our readers replied:

> I would suggest that it's more educational and satisfying to go to the local library and look up the laws for yourself than to ask your state legislator (who will have to do just that, as he certainly will not be familiar with them . . .). Any large public library, like the main library of a large city system, or the public library in the county seat, will have volumes of all the laws of one's home state. Once you find the Education or Schools section, there is usually a subsection entitled "School Attendance." After each of the specific laws, court cases relating to that law are listed and commented on, but while you're in the law books, you'll want to look at the index at the back—which is usually quite extensive—for cross-references to subjects like "home study," "private school," "tutoring," etc., which will lead you to other laws dealing with these.
>
> Often, the education laws are also bound in a separate volume as well (e.g., Baldwin's *Ohio School Law*) which contains a "text" section setting forth all of the laws in a more readily understood, almost narrative form—which, however, you'll want to cross-check

with the statutes themselves. Finally, while you're in the local library, you might want to look at a commentary on the state's laws, called (state name) Jurisprudence, which will give you a concise overview of the statutes and related court cases.

For the court cases themselves, you have to go to a law library. Some are maintained by local bar associations, but often bar admittance to the public. If this is the case, go to the nearest law *school* library and make yourself at home. You can either register at the desk as a nonstudent, or just walk around pretending you're a student. You can look up (with a bit of assistance at first) any case cited in your state laws (or elsewhere for that matter) and read and copy (for a fee) the entire text of the decision. You can get the texts of the big pro-home study decisions (*People* v. *Levisen,* Ill. and *State* v. *Massa,* N.J.) just for your own edification.

Two short comments on this. Commentaries on state law may have some other name than (state name) Jurisprudence, but if so, the library will tell you what to look for. And most city halls, county courthouses, etc., have law libraries open to the public. Anyone in the legal section of your city or county government would be able to tell you whether there is such a library, and if so, where it is.

Our reader continued:

Another thing a law library will have is complete sets of state law volumes for each state. Let me relate how I used these just last week. A man in Mass. wrote me that he's asked a lawyer if there were any loopholes in Mass. law regarding home study. The lawyer found one, which this man is now using. The man did not quote the law to me, and I was anxious to see how closely it paralleled our own state's loophole; this took less than five minutes. I then skimmed the cases cited throughout the section (after each of the laws) and found one described as relating to home study *(Commonwealth* v. *Renfrew).* I read the entire decision in this case, which cited and thus led me to several other important Mass. cases (as well as some from other states).

I took our reader's good advice, and did what I had often urged others to do—get information for themselves, instead of depending on some expert. I went to the main Boston library, asked at the information desk where I would find state laws, was sent to a reference room, asked again there. They told me to look up in a law index, which they showed me, the numbers of the particular laws I was interested in, then come back and fill out a slip for the books themselves. The law books used to be on open shelves, but people stole them, so now they were all on reserve. I picked the index that seemed easiest to use, made up my list of statutes, took them to the desk, and soon had the law books. In another minute I was reading the laws.

A word about those books of legal commentary. They are a handy way to find out in a hurry what was decided in a particular case. But in a matter that closely concerns you, like home schooling, it is better to get and read the whole decision, if you can, for several reasons. In the first place the summary and commentary on the case must reflect to some degree the editor's own bias. I have seen summaries of pro-home study rulings that were in fact less strong than the rulings themselves, or that made the rulings seem less important than they actually were. In the second place, you may find arguments in the complete ruling, but not included in the commentary, that may be very useful to you in a number of ways in preparing your case. Even the most skillful commentator cannot condense a ten-page ruling into a half-page summary without leaving out much of importance.

In a later letter our friend referred to an important Massachusetts case, *Commonwealth* v. *Renfrew* (1955) 126 N.E.2d 109, 332 Mass. 492, and then explained what those numbers mean: *volume* 126 in the *Northeastern Reporter* (N.E.), *Second Series* (2d), *page* 109; the same case is also cited in volume 332 of the Massachusetts State Reporter, on page 492. Other states and regions will have comparable volumes and abbreviations, and librarians will be able to tell you what they mean.

Another reader wrote later:

> Anyone who is really interested in the general background of what the courts have said in relation to various claims by parents who were tried for failure to comply with their state's compulsory attendance laws can get an excellent overview in 65 ALR 3d 1222. This numbering system is also very simple: ALR stands for Ameri-

can Law Reports, 65 means volume 65, 3d means this is the third set of books (there is also ALR 1st and ALR 2d), and 1222 is the page number where the report starts.

Laws recently passed, or recent court rulings, will not yet be in the law books. For these, you must go to the source. Last year, the General Assembly of North Carolina (1979 Session) passed laws freeing private schools from almost all state regulations. When we heard this, we wrote to the Clerk of the Senate in Raleigh, and also to the North Carolina State Library, describing the legislation and asking for a copy. Within a few weeks, both responded. Each sent a different bill—there were two highly similar bills passed the same day, identical except that Senate Bill 383 dealt with "religious schools" and Senate Bill 526 with "certain qualified nonpublic schools." However, all a school has to do to "qualify" is to receive no funding from the State of North Carolina.

The legislation requires the schools to keep attendance, immunization, and standardized test records, and send to the state a "notice of intent to operate." It says, "any such school may, on a voluntary basis, participate in any State operated or sponsored program which would otherwise be available to such school." The final paragraph is "No qualifying nonpublic school, which complies with the requirements of this Article, shall be subject to any other provision of law relating to education except requirements of law respecting fire, safety, sanitation and immunization."

PREPARING A CASE

MAKING USE OF OFFICIAL GUIDELINES

States, and in many cases school districts, will probably have statements of purposes, objectives, methods, etc. Parents will do well to get hold of them, and try to word their own educational plan so that all parts of these statements are covered. If state law or policy requires the teaching of state history, as in many states it does, then you should have something about state history in your program. If state law or policy requires that schools teach children about the dangers of alcohol, as I believe it does in New York, then you should have something written down about that. The point is to give the district and/or state authorities the least possible excuse for disapproving your program.

For instance, the Vermont State Department of Education has developed a list of "Basic Competencies" in reading, writing, speaking, listening, math, and reasoning, and a "Pupil Progress Record" to be maintained for each student. Interested people can get the record, manual, and teacher's guide from the state. It would be a good idea for home and study plans to refer specifically to the skills described, and to state how they plan to touch on each aspect. One Vermont mother has said her eleven-year-old found it easy to meet the requirements.

Parents may not always find it possible to phrase or adjust their home program to fit district or state policy—the differences of philosophy may be simply too great. In that case, there is nothing to do but say that you disagree with them, and why, in as much detail as you can. David Armington, an old friend, and a very able and experienced elementary school teacher, and also teacher of teachers, sent some comments on the proposed *Home Study Guidelines* of the New Hampshire State Board of Education. What he says about the nonneutrality of schools on what are in fact matters of religious concern seem to me of the greatest legal importance. Parents preparing a statement for schools and/or a legal brief would probably do well to include some such statement. Here are some of his remarks:

> . . . I find the proposed guidelines quite irrelevant to situations in which parents or guardians want to take over the educational function because the program of the school clearly violates, or is incompatible with, their deeply-held beliefs and values. . . . It is simply not true that the schools are, or ever could be, value-free or value-neutral, for even a stance of steadfast neutrality or objectivity communicates a value. It is simply not true that we keep religion out of the schools. Identifiable creeds and churches, yes. Religion, no. For education is essentially religious, because at its center is the individual human soul.
>
> I have often thought that if you closed your eyes and dropped your finger on a map of the United States, it would hit a community

where the differences on questions of education are as great as, or greater than, the differences on questions of religion. Yet in that community, if it's a smallish one, you would find several churches but only one school! One might be inclined to say that such differences are really only differences of detail, of method, of technique; different routes to objectives we all share. This is not true. I am not talking about alternative methods for teaching reading, or whether to teach old math or new math, or whether to offer sex education, environmental studies, and four years of French.

I am talking about different educational objectives, different values and priorities, which can reflect different views about the role of the school and of education in our society.

A classroom in which children are expected to compete with each other is very different from one in which competitions arise naturally and spontaneously from the cooperative life of the group.

A classroom which measures children against each other or against outside standards is very different from one in which each child is encouraged to assess himself.

A classroom in which children learn by doing is very different from one in which they learn by being told.

A classroom in which the work is fed to children in tiny sequential bites is very different from one in which children tackle problems in full and lifelike complexity.

A classroom in which the children share significantly in planning what happens to them is very different from one in which things are planned for them. . . .

A classroom that encourages self-discipline is very different from one in which the teacher disciplines. . . .

TAKING A STAND ON TESTING

Many families report that their local schools, though willing to let them teach their children at home, insist that every so often the children take standardized tests. I feel very strongly that while parents may be wise, for the sake of harmony, to make small concessions to the schools about curriculum, they should resist as strongly as possible any demand by the schools that their children's growth and learning be measured by standardized tests, for at least these reasons: (1) Even in the narrow areas which they cover, the tests do not measure well what they claim to measure; 2) the tests do not touch those many areas outside the narrow school curriculum in which children may be learning a great deal.

The Summer 1979 issue of *The Testing Digest* reports that in July 1978 the National Educational Association, to which most American teachers belong, endorsed a resolution on testing. Parents who are in conflict with their schools on this issue, or fear they may be, may find it helpful to quote the resolution in their home-schooling plan. It reads as follows:

> The National Education Association recognizes that testing of students may be appropriate for such purposes as (a) diagnosing learning needs, (b) prescribing instructional activities, (c) measuring student progress *in the curriculum content utilizing tests prepared or selected by the classroom teacher* [Author's emphasis].
>
> The Association opposes the use of tests that deny students full access to equal educational opportunities.
>
> The Association opposes the use and will continue to seek the elimination of standardized tests, which are:
>
> a. Damaging to a student's self-concept and contribute to the self-fulfilling prophecy whereby a student's achievement tends to fulfill the negative expectations of others.
>
> b. Biased against those who are economically disadvantaged or who are culturally and linguistically different.
>
> c. Used for tracking students.
>
> d. Invalid, unreliable, out-of-date, and restricted to the measurement of cognitive skills.
>
> e. Used as a basis for the allocation of federal, state, or local funds.
>
> f. Used by book publishers and testing companies to promote their financial interests rather than to improve measurement and instruction.
>
> g. Used by the media as a basis for invidious public comparisons of student achievement test scores.
>
> h. Used to test performance levels as a criterion for high school graduation.

QUESTIONING NEED FOR CERTIFICATION

In the Kentucky and Michigan cases quoted in the previous chapter, the courts ruled that the state had not been able to show any evidence that certified teachers produced better results than uncertified. On this matter, a reader sent us further evidence, which many families may find useful:

> You bring up the lack of proof that certified teachers get better results. I know of one quite opposite proof. When Arizona began a statewide third grade reading test, the first year they had questions included about the teachers' training in Reading. It was glaringly clear from the answers that the more courses teachers had in Reading in college, the worse their class results were. The worst scores in the state were in a school in a good economic district where all the primary teachers had master's degrees in Reading (mostly, of course, from Arizona universities). Members of the education establishment, including Reading professors, obviously were unhappy about this news and the publicity it received. The next year, the information about the teachers' "credentials" no longer accompanied the test scores
>
> This information was learned from and can be verified by the Reading Reform Foundation, 7054 E. Indian School Rd., Scottsdale AZ 85251.

QUESTIONS TO RAISE

In his wonderful book *How to Survive in Your Native Land,* James Herndon writes:

> In September of 1967 I looked through the cumulative folders we were going to have in our class for the coming year, that is to say, the next Monday. I read what I already knew—the first grader with the testable high IQ, the remarked bright student, leader, reads at third-grade-level, headed for the big time; and the fourth grader with low-average capability, IQ 89, lazy kid, must-be-pushed-to-achieve, reads-at-second-grade-level, discipline problem, parents co-operative.
>
> The first grader and the fourth grader are the same kid.

I read this once to a group of about forty school administrators. I asked them if they had kids like that, and if so how many, in their schools or school systems. None of them knew. I asked if any of them had ever checked through their files to see whether they had some kids like that. None of them had. Since they didn't even know how many such children they had in their schools, far less who they were, they obviously couldn't even begin to ask themselves how these children got that way, what had blocked or turned off their natural desire and ability to learn.

Parents who find themselves in conflict with schools might find it helpful to ask, somewhere in their educational plan and/or legal brief, a question like Herndon's. Indeed, his question suggests a whole series of questions about what the schools are doing and how well they are doing it. Under some circumstances it might even be useful to raise the questions in the press and other media. Here are some samples:

1. At the various grade levels, how many hours of school time are allotted each week to silent reading, uninterrupted by questions, reading aloud, corrections, or other activities or demands?

2. At the various grade levels, how much time each week are students allowed in the school library? What restrictions are there on the use of the library? What are the rules about borrowing books?

3. In addition to those in the school library, are there books (other than textbooks or workbooks) in the classrooms? At the various grade levels, roughly how many such books are there? What kind of books—novels, poetry, biography, etc.—are they? How are they chosen? When may the students use them?

4. At the various grade levels, how many children are reading below grade level (both national and state)? How many are more than a year behind? Two years? Three years?

5. At the various grades, how many children are reading at least two years ahead of grade level? (Since grade level simply means a national or state average, any parent serious about education would want any of their children much over eight years old to be reading well over grade level.)

6. Of those children in the schools who were reading below grade level two years ago, how many are now reading at grade level or better? In other words, how effective have the schools been at improving the reading of students who were having trouble?

7. Same questions as #4 and #6, only for mathematics.

8. At each grade level, how many children have been designated as having "learning disabilities"?

9. How do these figures compare with the comparable figure for two years ago?

10. Of the children so designated two years ago, how many are now judged to be cured or freed of these disabilities? In other words, how successful have the schools been in dealing with and overcoming these problems.

11. Same as questions #8–10, for "emotionally disturbed."

12. Same, but for "hyperactive" or "hyperkinetic."

13. On the basis of what tests, of what duration, given how often, and administered, scored, and judged by whom, are these judgments about "learning disabilities," etc., made?

14. To what degree are school records, including these test results and judgments, accessible to parents?

15. To what degree is it possible for parents who disagree with any such judgments to challenge them or seek independent confirmation or refutation of them, so as to be able to clear their children's records of possibly incorrect and/or derogatory information?

16. At various grade levels, what percentage of children are being medicated with psychoactive or behavior modifying drugs, such as Ritalin? What medical examinations do the schools give, and how often, and of what kind, and by what doctors, to check for possible harmful side effects of such drugs?

17. What is the policy of the schools about altering students' grades for reasons of attendance or discipline? What percentage of students in the system have had their grades lowered for these reasons?

18. Where grades have been lowered for such reasons, what provisions are there for students and parents to restore the *correct academic grade* to the student's record? What percentage of students in the system, whose grades were first lowered for nonacademic reasons, have had their correct academic grade restored?

THE MEANING OF EQUIVALENT

The law in many states allows for instruction outside of schools, provided that it is "equivalent" to what is given in schools. But what does "equivalent" mean? Schools tend to say that home-schooling families must have as many hours of formal classes per day and per week as the schools themselves. But do the schools really give that much instruction, and is that much really necessary? We find interesting answers to those questions when we consider what schools do about children who, for reasons of sickness or injury, can't come to school.

This question was first brought to my attention by friends who live in a rich suburb with "good" public schools. One winter one of their boys broke his leg and had to wear a hip cast, which made it impractical or impossible to send him to school. The family, who were not unschoolers, told the school they wanted to be sure the boy kept up with his class. The school said, No problem, we'll send around a tutor, which they did, every week—*for an hour and a half*! It was enough.

After we printed this story in *GWS,* a reader wrote from Baltimore:

> I made a telephone inquiry with the Home Teaching office of the Baltimore City Schools and was told that if the student was to be absent, for reasons of sickness, for six weeks or more, a teacher would, upon the signing of a form FH 19 by a doctor, visit and tutor the child at home every day (presumably Monday through Friday) for one hour. I did not inquire about expelled students, only sick ones.

Other readers in different parts of the country have asked their schools how much tutoring they would or do give to sick or injured children. Answers so far have ranged from two to four hours a week. The one hour a day quoted above is the largest figure yet reported. Yet students so tutored keep up with their school classes—that is, after all, what the tutoring is for. If the schools' own tutors need to teach only a few hours a week to keep children up with their classes, why should parents need to or have to teach more than that?

Parents who may be in conflict with their schools may find it helpful to learn what their local and district schools do about homebound children. They might even see if there is some kind of statewide policy on this matter. They could then ask why they should be compelled to do five or ten times more teaching than the schools' own tutors do, and beyond that, point out that since children in schools are getting at best only a few hours of effective instruction per week, their own home education program will be much better than that of the schools.

A DOUBTFUL CLAIM

We have already discussed the claim of the schools that they alone know how to teach children. Most of the time, they make this claim with no reservations whatever. Yet when they are sued in court for not having done what they say they and they alone know how to do, they suddenly become very modest.

A most revealing article on Teacher Malpractice in the *American Educator,* journal of the American Federation of Teachers, said, in part:

> In 1972, parents of a graduate of the public school system in San Francisco brought a $500,000 suit against the school district charging that after a total of 13 years of regular attendance, their son was not able to read.
>
> During his years in school, according to information compiled on the case, he was in the middle of his classes, maintained average grades and was never involved in anything which resulted in major disciplinary action. His parents claimed that during their son's years in the public school they were rebuffed in their attempts to get information on the progress of their son, but were assured by school officials and teachers he was moving along at grade level.
>
> Shortly after the youth's graduation, he was given a reading test by specialists who concluded the youth was only reading on a fifth grade level. . . .
>
> . . . The California State Court of Appeals rejected the parents' claim of the school system's failure to educate their son. The court declared it was impossible for any person, most of all the courts, to set guidelines for "proper" academic procedures which must be followed by all schools and all teachers.
>
> "Unlike the activity of the highway, or the marketplace, classroom methodology affords no readily acceptable standards of care, or cause, or injury. The science of pedagogy itself is fraught with

different and conflicting theories of how or what a child should be taught, and any layman might, and commonly does, have his own emphatic views on the subject," read the court's opinion.

The court was, of course, quite right in saying this. But what then becomes of the claim, which the schools make all the time, that they alone know how to teach children? Parents in conflict with schools might find it very helpful to quote those words from the California ruling.

WHEN SCHOOLS THREATEN TO
TAKE CHILDREN AWAY

Of all the threats that schools make to unschooling parents, the most terrifying (and disgusting) is the threat to take their children away. Indeed, it is hard to credit the intelligence and good faith of school systems that make this threat, as they often have, to obviously loving and competent parents, whose children may in many cases be learning at well above grade level. At any rate, the following quote from the Juvenile Rights section of the 1977 report of the American Civil Liberties Union suggests that parents may have much legal support in dealing with this threat:

> In the past year, the ACLU's Juvenile Rights Project secured a major victory in its struggle to prevent the state from arbitrarily and unnecessarily separating children from their parents. The U.S. Court of Appeals for the Eighth Circuit upheld a lower court decision forbidding the state of Iowa from using its parental termination statute to sever the relationship between Charles and Darlene Alsager and four of their children.
>
> The appeals court ruled that the state cannot "terminate" parents without proving that they are harming their children in *substantial and serious ways* [Author's emphasis]. For that there must be a more compelling reason for separating families than the state's assertion that it is "in the best interests of the child."
>
> Relying on the *Alsager* decision, the ACLU then challenged a Virginia statute which authorized the temporary separation of children from their families in "emergency" situations. The case, *Ives v. Jones,* was successfully settled, and as a consequence the Virginia

law was changed. No longer may children be withheld even temporarily from their parents unless clear and substantial danger to the child is shown. Moreover, parents whose children have been taken under a so-called emergency are entitled to an immediate hearing at which they may have counsel and other due process rights.

The *Alsager* decision also prompted a federal court in Alabama to rule that the state's neglect statute was unconstitutional because of vagueness and amorphous definitions of "child neglect."

The decisions cited here suggest that, in some states at least, the courts may not allow the schools to carry out their threat to take children away from unschooling families. Even though the ACLU and other civil liberties organizations will probably not for some time to come be willing to oppose compulsory schooling on constitutional grounds, they and/or their state and local branches may well be willing to help home schoolers resist efforts by the state to take their children away from them.

On this matter, the Manchester, New Hampshire, *Union Leader,* on October 31, 1978, reported a decision of the New Hampshire State Supreme Court that may be very helpful to unschoolers, not least of all because (1) New Hampshire is a politically "conservative" state and (2) New Hampshire law did not at that time mention home schooling as a legal alternative.

The story reads, in part:

SUPREME COURT
VACATES PARENTAL RIGHTS ORDER

Noting that in an "ideal world, children would not be brought up in inadequate homes," the state Supreme Court yesterday declared that this "is not an ideal world, and to merely hold that inadequate parenting, *absent specific harm to the children* [Author's emphasis], is sufficient to terminate parental rights in the best interest of the child is too vague a concept and places undue emphasis on the parental conduct rather than any harm to the child."

The high court thus vacated a 1977 order of the Merrimack County Probate Court which had terminated the parental rights of a 32-year-old father, identified only as "Robert H.," over his three minor children on the grounds of failure to correct the conditions leading to a finding of neglect.

"We outline the standard to be applied in such cases and re-mand," noted the Supreme Court. It said RSA chapter 170-C was enacted to provide for the involuntary termination of the parent-child relationship by a judicial process which will safeguard the rights and interests of all parties, and that a termination order must be based upon "clear and convincing evidence."

The high court determined that the government must "prove its case beyond a reasonable doubt before the permanent termination of liberty and natural rights of parents guaranteed under the N.H. Constitution, Part I, Article 2, can occur."

"We hold that absent a showing of *specific harm to the children* [Author's emphasis], growing up in a so-called disadvantaged home is not a sufficient basis for coercive intervention. Robert H. may not be a model parent, but he is as entitled to help from the division [of welfare] as anyone else, and maybe more so," said the Supreme Court.

". . . any termination petition under chapter 170-C must be proven beyond a reasonable doubt to meet the requirements of the N.H. Constitution," ordered the Supreme Court.

The high court noted that the father can neither read nor write, suffers serious heart problems, and because of limited job skills, is rarely steadily employed. The children are six, seven, and nine and "they are very much a family unit with strong sibling ties."

The legal point is obvious. If (as is the case) the courts will not allow welfare, etc., agencies to take children from such a parent, or even (as is also often the case) from parents who abuse their children up to the point of causing serious injury, they are not likely, if all the above is pointed out to them in a legal brief, to allow agencies to take children away from otherwise competent and loving parents simply because these parents refuse to send their children to school. As in the case cited above, the burden of proof will be on the state to show beyond reasonable doubt that in such cases the children are being specifically harmed by not being sent to school. This will be exceedingly difficult to prove, particularly if parents go into court well prepared, and well armed with hard questions for the schools.

It might also be a good idea for unschoolers in all states to read their respective *state* constitutions, to see what these may have to say about the rights of parents with respect to their children and their children's education. Some of them, at least, like the New Hampshire Constitution (which I have not read), may be much more explicit about this than the U.S. Constitution. Though we would be very unwise to go into the federal courts with a broad constitutional attack on compulsory schooling as such, this does not mean that we should not make the fullest possible use of anything we can find in state constitutions about parents' rights to influence or control the education of their children.

More recently, the Nebraska Supreme Court has ruled, in *Nebraska* v. *Rice* (quoted in *The United States Law Week,* December 4, 1979) that "the compulsory school attendance law and the statute regarding the neglect of children generally do not pertain to the same subject matter and should not be construed *in pari materia*" [Author's note: i.e., as if they were equivalent]. In short, the state cannot say that parents are guilty of neglect simply because they are, or may be, violating compulsory school attendance laws. This further strengthens the position of parents.

COURT STRATEGY IN GENERAL

A final word on court strategy. As Justice Cardozo pointed out in his enormously valuable book *The Nature of the Judicial Process* (New Haven: Yale University Press, 1921), judges, in making their rulings, take into account a number of things—legal philosophy and principle, legal precedent, the will of the legislature as expressed in the statutes, and *the possible or probable social effects of their rulings.* Thus, as we have shown, parents who have sued the schools because their children did not learn anything there have so far been turned down by the courts, on the grounds that this would very quickly lead to a rush of lawsuits that would bankrupt the schools. We may take it as certain that the courts will not in any foreseeable future make rulings which they think will lead to the quick destruction of the public schools or the end of compulsory schooling. If we ask for such broad rulings, we will be turned down.

Beyond that, either in asking for narrow rulings, or speaking of any we may be able to win, we must be careful not to make large public boasts and outcries to the effect that "this means the downfall of compulsory schooling." In the first place, such boasts would be silly; even if the courts were by some miracle to strike down compulsory schooling, a furious majority of the people would quickly reestablish it, by constitutional amendment if they had to. In the second place, even making such boasts would greatly reduce our chances of getting even narrowly favorable rulings from the courts. In the third place, such boasts tend to terrify the schools, who are already far more terrified than they need be, and whom it is in our best interests to reassure.

15

Legislative Strategy

Early in 1980 I was invited by the Education Committee of the Minnesota House of Representatives to testify at hearings they were holding about home education and private schools. I said that I would be glad to, and sent them in advance a statement of my position. What I said to them could, I believe, be equally and usefully said to any other state or provincial legislatures giving home schooling their attention.

The statement:

> Time being short, let us not waste any of it in arguments about whether the public schools are doing a good job. Such arguments cannot be settled here.
>
> Let me sum up very briefly my position:
> 1. In terms of both the short-run and long-run interests of themselves and of the general public, the schools would be wise to view the growing home education movement not as a threat but as an opportunity and a potential asset, and, rather than resist it, to support it to the fullest extent.
> 2. The legislature itself would be wise, in any education laws it may write, to affirm and support very strongly the right of parents

to teach their own children, and to make it as easy as possible for the schools to assist them in this effort.

3. To try to do the opposite, i.e., to try to make it difficult or impossible for people to teach their own children, would be a most serious educational, legal, and political mistake.

What does the law have to say about all this? Here we must note that "the law" is made up, not just of the laws or statutes, but of the ways in which the courts have interpreted these laws.

According to repeated court decisions, there is here (as in many places) some conflict between the constitutionally protected rights of the parents and the equally protected rights of the states.

The courts have affirmed, in decisions too numerous to cite, that under the police powers delegated to them the several states have a right to demand that all children be educated, and to that end, to write and enforce compulsory school attendance laws.

But the U.S. Supreme Court has also held, first in *Pierce* v. *Society of Sisters,* and later in *Farrington* v. *Tokushige,* that while the state may demand that all children be educated, it may not demand that they be educated in the same way, and that, on the contrary, parents have a constitutionally protected right to get for their children an education which is in accord with their own principles and beliefs. The state, in other words, may not have a monopoly in education, either of schools or of methods. The parents have a right to choice, not just in minor details but in matters of significance.

Subsequent decisions in state courts, in Illinois, New Jersey, Massachusetts, and Iowa, among others, have held that this right of parents to control the education of their children includes the right to teach them themselves. In at least one state the courts have held that the burden of proof is not on such parents to show that they are capable of teaching their children, but on the state to show that they are not capable of doing so.

Some other legal points should be made here:

1. The courts, in upholding the right of the states to compel children to be educated, have upheld this on the sole ground that without such education children would be unfit for employment and would therefore become a burden on the state. It follows that when the states say that a given educational program, whether of parents or of a private school, is inadequate, it must be from this point of view and this one only. The courts have never said, for

example, that compulsory schooling was necessary so that all children would have some kind of "social life." This is a fringe benefit —if indeed a benefit at all. Therefore the states cannot rule out an educational program on the grounds that it does not give students an adequate social life. In this area the states have no rights, and the rights of the parents are supreme.

2. A Massachusetts superior court held recently that the right of parents to teach their own children is located not just in the First and Fourteenth, but also the Ninth Amendment to the Constitution.

3. A Kentucky district court, in a ruling later upheld by the state supreme court, said that before the state could demand, for example, that all teachers be certified, it had to produce evidence to show that certified teachers taught better than uncertified ones. In the court's words, the state was unable to produce "a scintilla" of such evidence. Nor, in all probability, could any other state. Indeed, it would be easy to show that the most exclusive and academically demanding and successful schools, to which the richest and most favored people send their children, have on their faculties few if any certified teachers, or graduates of schools of education.

4. When parents in San Francisco, in 1972, sued the schools because, after 13 years of school their son was reading only on a fifth grade level, the California State Court of Appeals dismissed the suit saying, "Unlike the activity of the highway, or the marketplace, classroom methodology affords no readily acceptable standards of care, or cause, or injury. The science of pedagogy itself is fraught with different and conflicting theories of how or what a child should be taught . . ." and concluded that it was impossible for anyone to set guidelines for "proper" academic procedures which must be followed by all schools and all teachers. How can the schools, when charged with negligence, defend themselves as they did in this case by saying that no one really knows how children should be taught, and in the next breath say that they are the only ones who know?

The point is that if the legislature tries to prevent or even unduly circumscribe the right of parents to teach their own children, such laws will surely be challenged in the already overburdened courts, and will not stand up.

Though you may have been told the opposite, such laws are not necessary to "save" the public schools. The number of people who,

even if it were easy to do so, would want to take their children out
of school and teach them at home, is small. Not many people enjoy
the company of their children that much, or would want to give
that much attention to their interests and concerns, or take that
much of the responsibility for their growth. In places where the
schools have gone to court to prevent people from teaching their
own children, they have told the courts that if they ruled in favor
of the parents they would be "opening the floodgates," "setting a
bad precedent," "starting a landslide." Nowhere have these dire
predictions come true, even in communities in which, after much
publicity, the parents won their case.

The best way for the public schools to save themselves, if they
are in fact in any real danger, is to solve the problems they already
have within the walls of their school buildings. In trying to find
ways to solve these problems, they may in time be very much helped
by what will be learned about effective teaching by people teaching
their own children. They will be further helped by many of these
children who will choose, as some are already choosing, to go to
school part-time for those activities that interest them most. The
example of these independent and self-motivated students will have
a powerful effect on other students and on the schools in general.

Under present Minnesota law, local school boards have an unqualified legal right, if they wish, to allow parents to teach their
children at home. In short, the law, *as it stands,* is sufficient to
permit home schooling. The law may allow local school districts
and law enforcement authorities, if they so choose, to prosecute any
family for trying to teach its children at home, but *it does not require*
them to do so, for at least three reasons:

1. Under the law, school districts may define school attendance
in any way they wish. School districts in many jurisdictions have
instituted different kinds of off-campus study programs (like the
Parkway Project in Philadelphia), or work-study or apprenticeship
programs, or even programs which required students to travel to
other cities or states. In like manner, schools have for generations
been able to extend full academic credit to children of families
living or traveling abroad, or traveling in this country in the course
of business (i.e., families in the circus or theater) and studying from
correspondence courses. No one has ever claimed or could sustain
a claim that in doing this, the schools were somehow violating
compulsory state attendance laws. Nor do the schools, in such
matters, have to defend their definitions of "attendance" to any

other state authorities; in this matter they have absolute discretion.

2. Under the law, the school districts and/or the state may define private schools in any way they wish. There is—fortunately—no absolute requirement that private school teachers be certified. All that is required is that the "common branches" be taught in the English language. As for hours of instruction, it is worth noting that when children who ordinarily attend public schools are for reasons of sickness or injury unable to attend, public schools ordinarily send tutors to the homes of these children, so that they will not fall behind in their schoolwork. How much time these tutors spend with the children varies from district to district. My own limited investigation has shown that this varies from as little as an hour and a half a week to a maximum of four hours a week. It would be interesting for the legislature to check school practices on this throughout the state. Many families using materials from the long-accredited Calvert Institute or similar organizations have reported to me that their children are able to do what the correspondence school calls a week's worth of schoolwork in only a few hours.

3. The law as written gives the school board the right to excuse a child from attending school "if his bodily or mental condition is such as to prevent his attendance at school *or application to study...*" But it is undisputed that many children do badly in school, or fail, or drop out altogether, because they are bored, because the school will not permit them to study at their own level, or because the school has no programs that meet their special interests, capabilities, and needs, or because the competitive and/or threatening atmosphere of the school and classroom prevents them from working up to their capacity. In such cases, and others we might well imagine, it would be legally permissible and educationally wise for schools to grant parents of such children, if they asked for it, the right to educate their children in ways that, being in greater harmony with their interests, temperaments, and styles of learning, would produce more effective results. Nothing in the law as it stands denies school boards the right to do this, or makes them answerable to any higher authority for any exceptions they might grant.

In short, while the law could, and in my judgment should make more explicit the rights of parents to teach their own children, it does not have to be changed in order to permit this. It is only if the intent of the legislature is to make home teaching far more difficult or forbid it altogether that changes in the law are required.

If the legislature wishes to affirm the right of parents to teach their own children, while continuing to exercise its constitutional right to assure that all children are being taught, it could do so very well by passing resolutions which would, in effect, say more or less the following:

1. It is not the intent of the compulsory laws of this state to deny to parents the right to have for their children an education in reasonable harmony with their own deepest concerns and principles, including the right, if they wish, to teach their own children at home.

2. Nor is it the intent of this legislature to authorize any educational authorities to impose on students under their jurisdiction a uniform curriculum, or uniform methods of instruction and/or evaluation. There are and will remain large and legitimate differences of opinion, among experts and nonexperts alike, on the subjects that should be taught to children, on the order and ways in which these are to be taught, on the materials which are to be used, and on the ways in which this teaching and learning are to be evaluated. Only by allowing and supporting a wide range of education practices can we encourage the diversity of experience from which we can learn to educate our children more effectively, and it is the intent of this legislature to allow and encourage such variety.

3. Rather than draw up any set of detailed guidelines to regulate home schooling, or set up some kind of special administrative machinery for this purpose, we would prefer to leave to the local school districts the responsibility for supervising and assisting home-teaching families according to their own best judgment, keeping always in mind the very general purposes noted above.

May I repeat once more, even if the legislature passes such resolutions or their equivalent, it will be a very long time before as many children are being taught at home as are right now truant every day from the schools of our larger cities.

The legislature, at least if it wishes to make home schooling no more difficult than it is today, might be wise to write into law what at least one court, in Nebraska, has already affirmed in a ruling, namely, that the laws governing neglect were not intended to be considered as an integral part of the compulsory school attendance laws, and that the charge of neglect, and the probable consequence of removing children from the custody of their parents, is not to be understood as a natural and legitimate penalty for failing or refusing to send the children to an accredited school. Some considerations:

1. School personnel may say that a threat this severe is needed to guarantee compliance with compulsory school attendance laws. But this violates a very fundamental principle of the common law, perhaps nowhere made explicit but very thoroughly understood, that the penalty for an offense must be proportional to the offense. In the light of this principle, no local government would be able, for example, to punish parking violations with prison sentences, on the grounds that without such severe punishment they could not secure complete compliance with the law.

2. When legislators passed laws saying that the state could, for neglect, remove children from the custody of their parents, what they had in mind was children who were starved, or left naked, or were brutally beaten and tortured, or locked in closets, or chained to furniture. They did not have in mind the children of conscientious and devoted parents whose only crime was that they did not approve of the kind of education offered in the local schools. To lump such parents with gross abusers of children, as schools have quite often already done, is a most serious perversion of law and justice.

3. It should be added that even people convicted of the most serious crimes—assault, grand larceny, manslaughter, even murder —are not automatically deprived of the custody of their families. If and when such criminals finish their sentences, their families and children, at least if they choose to do so, are waiting for them. To say that violent criminals may be fit to raise their children but that people who want to teach them at home are not is again a serious perversion of justice.

It must be categorically said that if it were true (which I dispute) that the compulsory attendance laws could only be enforced by such severe and cruel penalties—for loving parents, the most severe of all penalties—there would be something inherently wrong with those laws. At any rate, this way of enforcing them, or of settling or rather foreclosing arguments about what kind of education is best for the children, ought in the name of justice and equity to be removed from the schools' hands.

What is true of the laws of Minnesota, i.e., that they permit (though they don't require) any school district to allow parents to teach their children at home, is equally true of the laws of all other states, for at least two and in many cases all three of the reasons given above. I know of no court cases in which the compulsory school attendance laws of a state have been used to restrict in any way the right of local school districts to establish any kinds of academic programs they wish, whether on-campus, off-campus, job-related, independent research, or whatever. As long as school districts have the support of the voters in their districts they can do what they want. The notion, apparently believed by quite a few superintendents, that one day a state attorney might prosecute a local school superintendent and/or school board for allowing some parents to teach their children at home is absurd.

In the same way, local school districts can, whenever they want and for whatever reasons they want, allow exceptions to the laws about attending school. State laws saying that parents must supply some kind of statement from a doctor put a burden on the parents, not the schools. In other words, they say that unless the parents produce a statement from a doctor, the schools do not even have to consider their request for an exception. They do not mean, and would not be construed to mean, that the schools are forbidden to consider exceptions unless these are supported by a doctor's report.

In my statement to the committee, I suggested that if the legislature wished to give additional encouragement and support to home teaching, they could do so by passing some rather simple and general resolutions. After the hearings, I said in a letter to the administrative assistant that I thought a resolution by the Education Committee itself, rather than the entire legislature, might do almost as well. If school districts merely wish to be reassured that they are not compelled by law to prosecute all home-teaching families, a statement to that effect by the committee would probably give all the reassurance they needed.

The hearings themselves were very interesting. In opening the hearings, the chairman of the committee pointed out that a number of school districts had asked the legislature to "clarify" the law. What this "clarify" meant was soon made clear. Two witnesses, one a district superintendent, the other a county attorney, told about the troubles they had had, trying to prosecute and send to jail and/or deprive of their children a few families that wanted to teach their children at home. They said to the committee, in effect, "Either rewrite these laws, saying in strict detail what is or is not a private school, so that we can easily and quickly prosecute and convict these people, or else do away with compulsory school attendance laws altogether." No doubt school people in many other states will be telling legislators that they must either allow no exceptions whatever to compulsory school attendance laws (except perhaps to rich people), or give up the whole idea.

In my testimony I did my best to persuade the committee that they were not faced with any such choice. To my written statements I added only these points: (1) In more and more jurisdictions, where families had prepared their case with enough care, i.e., made up a detailed educational plan, supported by quotes from educational authorities and many relevant court citations, the courts were increasingly ruling in their favor. (2) The movement for home teaching was part of a growing nationwide movement toward greater self-sufficiency and minimized dependence on large institutions, a movement that from many points of view could only be considered healthy and admirable and that in any case was certain to grow. (3) Trying to crack down on homeschooling families would increase, not lessen, the number and complexity of cases before their courts.

In this last connection the young county attorney had said indignantly at one point that one family was only using the Bible as a textbook. I asked him whether he thought he would have an easier time if he found himself arguing in court before a judge about how good a textbook the Bible was. I added that I thought it would not be hard to make a strong case that the Bible was a great deal better textbook than most of the ones used in schools. Did he really want to get involved in such arguments? The expression on his face as I said this suggested that he did not.

I went on to say that the committee had to understand that no matter how the legislature might change the laws, the people who for various reasons were now taking their children out of school and teaching them at home were going to go on doing so, no matter what. They will fight in the courts as long as they can, delay, stall, and appeal, for years if need be. If finally pinned to the wall, they will simply move to another district or out of the state altogether. The one thing they will not do is send their children back to the public schools. Is it really worth spending all this time, energy, and taxpayers' money to fight a battle that is lost before it is begun? The district superintendent, speaking of the bad publicity his district had received while prosecuting one family, had said at one point, "Even when we win, we lose." Did the schools, and the state, really want this kind of publicity?

One member of the committee asked me a question that, in one form or another, I hear at almost every meeting. It goes about like this, "What would you do about a family that didn't know anything, that didn't want their children to know anything, and that only took them out of school because they wanted to exploit their work, etc., etc." I replied by reminding them of an old legal maxim with which I was sure they were familiar—Hard Cases Make Bad Law. I said that if we write our laws—as we too often tend to—so as to take care of the worst possible hypothetical case that might arise, we are almost certain to have laws that are long, cumbersome, difficult or impossible to enforce, and far more likely to prevent good people from doing good work than bad people from doing bad. I went on to say that there might well be families like the one suggested, but that these people were the last ones in the world likely to be interested in teaching their children at home. On the contrary, they are only too eager to get them out of the house, and at the end of school vacations say, "Thank Heaven vacation is over, I can't wait to get these damn kids back in school." Committee members smiled; they obviously knew such people.

In closing, I said that there were limits to the power of governments, beyond which they could not go without losing their good faith and credit. A good case could have been made, and had once been made, that as a country we would be much better off if no one drank alcohol. But the Noble Experiment failed; people would not let the government stick its nose that far into their private affairs, and refused to obey the law. The only results were a great increase in corruption in government and general contempt for law.

As nearly as I could tell from their expressions and questions, the committee was interested in and responsive to what I had to say. Only one member seemed clearly angered and threatened by my words. The last question was asked by the chairman himself, "Do you mean that if we want to allow people to teach their children at home we don't need to make any changes in the law at all?" I assured him that was what I meant.

If any on the committee were not convinced by what I had said about how determined more and more people are to teach their children in accordance with their own beliefs, the next witness must have convinced them. She was a representative of some association for Christian education, and in her testimony she furiously denounced the public schools (as I had been careful not to). Compared to her I must have seemed a most mild and reasonable person. I like to think that at the end of the hearings some of the committee, at least, were thinking, "Maybe Holt is right, maybe we really don't want to spend the next ten years fighting these kinds of people, maybe we'd be smarter to leave them alone and concentrate on doing what we can to fix up our schools." For Minnesota or any other state, it would be the wiser course.

16

School Response

THE VALUE OF COOPERATION

How should the schools respond to parents who want to teach their children at home? Even in terms of their most immediate bread-and-butter interests—improving their public image, maintaining their budgets and salaries, keeping their jobs, etc.—the schools would be wise to try to help rather than hinder.

As we have seen, many school systems today still oppose home schoolers by every possible means, some even trying to take their children away from them. They seem to fear that if they let one family teach their children at home, every family will want to, and they will be out of business. Given their present troubles and bad publicity, this worry is natural enough. But it is not realistic. Even with full school cooperation and support, it is unlikely that, in a generation, more than 10 percent of the families of school-age children would be teaching them at home. Most school-age children would still be in some school. There are simply not that many people who like or trust their children that much, or would want to have them around that much of the time, or would take that much time and effort to answer their questions and otherwise help them find out what they want to know.

It is not primarily compulsory attendance laws that keep most children in school so much as the fact that almost no one wants them anywhere else. Until recently, the state of Mississippi had no such laws. They are just now beginning to introduce them; so far they only cover children of ages seven to eight or so. Yet from all we know, about as many children go to school in Mississippi as anywhere else—probably more than in many of our major cities, where as much as half of the high school population is often truant.

Some school people say, "If we let people teach their children at home, the rich will all take their children out of school, and we will have only poor children to teach." One might ask, "Well, what's so bad about that? You will then at last be able to give these poor children your undivided attention." But the fact is, at least so far, that very few of the people who are teaching their children at home are rich. Home schoolers, as far as I can tell from their letters, have average incomes or less. Perhaps a majority of them have gone to college, though many have not. Many of them have chosen, for different reasons, to live fairly simply in small towns or in the country. One reason why many of them are interested in home schooling is that they can't afford private schools, even if there were any around that they liked. For a long time to come home schooling will have little appeal to the rich, who will probably continue to hire other people to look after their children.

In short, there is no reason for school people to see home schooling as any kind of serious threat to themselves. Such threats do most certainly exist. The rapidly declining birth rate is one. Page 5 of the summary of the Carnegie Foundation Report *Giving Youth A Better Chance,* tells us, "The number of 16-year-olds in 1990 as compared with 1980 (according to the Census Bureau's intermediate projection) will be as follows: 1980 = 100%; 1990 = 77%. The population of 16- to 21-year-olds will reach its low point in 1994, as follows: 1980 = 100%, 1994 = 74%. An even lower Census Bureau projection, which now appears even more likely, shows the 16-year-old population reaching its low point in 1995."

No one can predict the future, and perhaps in the next decade large numbers of people of child-bearing age will suddenly decide to have many more children. But from all we know about young people today in their teens or early twenties, it seems likely that even more of them than now will decide not to marry, or if they marry, not to have children, or if they have any, to have only one or two. They are terribly worried about their own economic futures, about the rapidly rising costs of rearing and educating children, and about the general uncertainty of the world. The best bet seems to be that our rapidly dropping birth rate will continue to drop for some time, so that within a generation the population of school-age children might well fall to half or less of what it is now.

Beyond this, more and more parents, white and nonwhite, are determined, if they possibly can, to get their children into private schools. In large cities, more and more parochial school students are non-Catholic, nonwhite children. A mother in Chicago writes that her son is the only white child in such a school. Fundamentalist church schools are springing up in all parts of the country. Private school attendance, after declining for many years, has increased rapidly in recent years. There is no reason to believe this trend will stop.

Along with this there is the danger—from the public schools' point of view, at least—of voucher plans. Under these the various governments, instead of giving education money to schools, would give it directly to parents in the form of credits, which they could then use to send their children to whatever public or private school they liked best. Thus many more parents could afford to, and would, send their children to private schools, or start schools of their own. It now seems very likely that within a generation, and even a decade, voucher plans of one kind or another will be voted in by many or most states.

The public schools have reason enough to worry about all these problems. But they have no good reason to worry about home schooling. By opposing it they stand to gain little and to lose much of what is left of their good reputation and the confidence and trust of the public.

An example. A woman, a skilled performing classical musician, teacher, and conductor, moved to a small town in northern Minnesota. Her youngest daughter was herself training for a career as a professional violinist, and had played with professionals in small concerts. Since the school itself had no advanced music programs, and since in school subjects the girl was two or three years ahead of her class, the mother decided to take her out of school and teach her, in music and school subjects, at home. The schools called the mother's home education program inadequate and took her to court. She lost there, but was acquitted by a higher court.

This story from a small Minnesota town was printed in papers all over the country. Two *GWS* readers sent me long news stories about it, one from a paper in Louisville, Kentucky, and the other from a paper in southern New Jersey. Both stories were wholly sympathetic to the mother and the family.

In Providence, Rhode Island, Peter and Brigitta Van Daam, intelligent and well educated, wanted to take their daughter out of public school. They tried in repeated letters and visits to school officials to find out what kind of forms they needed to fill out and what procedures to follow to do this. The school people (perhaps in ignorance) repeatedly told them, *contrary to fact,* that there were no such forms or procedures. When at length the family, weary of this runaround, began teaching their child at home, the schools took legal action against them, and eventually had the entire family arrested and taken to jail. The Van Daams had worked hard to take their case to the public and the media. When the police came for them, all three major TV networks had cameras there. Soon after, on at least one nationwide TV show, millions of Americans could see these obviously intelligent, concerned, and capable parents, with their obviously intelligent small children, being taken to jail.

Such acts only make the schools look arrogant, greedy, cruel, and stupid. No need to cite other examples, of which there are many. In tough times like these the schools simply cannot stand any more of this kind of publicity. Public opinion on education is making a U-turn. Since they were founded, the public schools have enjoyed almost limitless public trust and confidence. People might criticize them in detail, but in principle almost everyone agreed that the public schools were a great thing. The idea of an effective government monopoly in education was accepted almost without question. Now, suddenly, more and more citizens do not believe any longer that the government should have such a monopoly, and many are beginning to ask whether the government should be in the school business at all.

Some claim that it is still only a minority who are turning against the schools, and then mostly for reasons that lie outside the schools themselves. To some extent this may be true. Today's antischool sentiment is clearly part of a larger reaction against all giant, remote, uncontrollable institutions—big corporations, big unions, big hospitals, above all big government itself. Part of it is the response of people to a shrinking economy, to worries about inflation, their homes, their jobs, gas for the car and oil for the furnace. But how much the schools may be responsible for this sudden turning against them makes little difference. The change of opinion is there and growing. In such a time the schools can't afford to do things that will make them still more enemies. Spending time and the public's money to make trouble for parents who want to teach their own children will surely do this.

But this is only the negative side of the picture. The real point I want to make here, and with which I will end this book, is that the schools have a great many things of real value to gain by cooperating fully with home-schooling families. Let me (in no particular order of importance) discuss some of them here.

RESEARCH

The schools have always needed places where people could do research in teaching. Here I don't mean research as the word is usually understood, with experimental groups, control groups, statistics, etc. I mean the kind of research I myself did in most of my years as a classroom teacher, in which I was continually trying out and improving new ways of teaching my students. This kind of research, done by teachers in their own classrooms, based on *experience* rather than experiments, is the only kind that will significantly improve teaching.

But it is almost impossible for schools, or teachers in schools, to do such research. One reason is that when schools or teachers use "tried-and-true" methods that everyone is used to i.e., rote-learning, drill, etc., and these methods don't work, as they usually don't, the public is willing to let the schools blame the students. But when a school or teacher uses a method that people consider new, and it doesn't work, the public blames *them*. So the rule is, to avoid trouble, stick to the old methods, *even* if they don't work.

Furthermore, whenever the schools do persuade the public to allow and the government to pay for some fairly fundamental research, they are always under heavy pressure to show quick results, i.e., higher test scores. The federally funded Follow Through programs were very rarely given even as much as three years to learn how to teach in a new way and to show that it worked; more often they had to produce their results in a year or two. So a really serious project, like finding out what would happen if children could decide for themselves when they wanted to read, with no teaching unless and until they asked for it, has no chance of being tested fairly or at all. A boy I know, by no means unique among children given such freedom and choice, did not learn to read at all until after he was eight, taught himself, and three years later, when tested by a school, scored at the twelfth grade level in reading. In one of these short-term research projects, this boy would have simply gone down in the statistics as a non-reader, "proof" that the experiment of letting children decide when they would read did not work.

For all these reasons, it seems very likely that the one place where we can hope and expect to see some really fundamental and long-term research on learning, on the kinds and amounts of teaching that most help learning, and on the usefulness of different methods and materials, is in the homes of people teaching their own children. They can afford to be patient, to wait a long time for results; they are in complete control of their work, and can change their methods as they wish; they can observe closely; they are free from all the routine distractions of large schools; and they are interested only in results rather than excuses. From these people and their work, all serious schools and teachers, many of them now severely limited and handicapped by the conditions under which they have to work, stand to learn a great deal.

First, let it be clear what they will *not* learn. They will not learn that this or that is the *best* way to teach reading, or addition, or multiplication, etc.; or that certain books are the *best* books for children; or that such-and-such is the *best* curriculum for this or that grade; or that you should always teach this particular subject in this particular order. Home schoolers will not teach the schools what they so yearn to know, the *one best way* to do anything. What they will teach is that there *is* no one best way, and that it is a waste of time and energy to look for it; that children (like adults) learn in a great many different ways; that each child learns best in the ways that most interest, excite, and satisfy her or him; and that the business of school should be to offer to learners the widest possible range of choices, both in what to learn and ways to learn it. If a number of parents report, as they regularly do in *GWS,* that their children love reading books about astronomy or architecture or anthropology or aircraft or atoms or rockets or space travel or microbes, or working with colored pencils or computers or puzzles or violins or typewriters or gardens or tape recorders or whatever, then that is a sign that these books and materials should be in the schools, not so that all children will have to use them, but so that any child who wants *can* use them.

Beyond this, home schoolers may be able to teach the schools some very important general principles of teaching and learning. Right now, there are so few home schoolers that the things they learn from their experience, about which I have written in *GWS* and in this book, can be and are dismissed by conventional educators as rare examples proving nothing. But as the numbers of home schoolers increase, it will be harder for even their bitterest enemies to ignore or deny their findings. When we can show, as in time we surely will, tens of thousands of children who, having learned to read only when they wanted to, and with only as much instruction as they asked for, are a few years later reading two or three or more years beyond most children of their age in schools, it cannot fail to have a great impact on the schools themselves. The people in schools who want to move in these directions will be much encouraged, while the rest will find it harder and harder to oppose them.

FEEDBACK

People doing a task can only do it better when they can find out how well they are doing it. Experiments have shown this time and time again. If we are estimating the weight of objects, and if we never learn whether our guesses are too low or too high, we never get any better. But if we learn whether each guess was too low or too high, and how much, we quickly improve. If you shoot at a target, but can't see where your shots hit, you have no way to improve them.

One of the reasons why schools and teachers usually find it so hard to do their work better is that they get so little good feedback from their students—candid information about how well they are teaching. A good friend of mine, while a brilliant, successful, and on the whole very happy student at a leading university, once told me that he and his friends never argued or disagreed with their professors, either in class discussions or in writing. He said, "The only way to be sure of an A on a paper or in a course is to say what you think the professor thinks, putting it of course in your own words so he won't think you are just imitating him." Since then, many other college students, in conversations, in letters, or in books about how to succeed at college, have said more or less the same thing. Professors who see themselves as telling truths to the ignorant may not care that students act this way. But others care a great deal. They chose to teach so that they might have lively talks with students about matters they all cared about, and are disappointed and hurt to find themselves dealing more and more with students who care only about getting a good (or at least passing) grade. They grow sick to death of hearing, "What do we have to do to get a good mark in this course? Are we going to be held responsible for this? Is this going to be on the exam?" Such questions drive many of them out of teaching altogether.

Teaching fifth grade, I finally learned that my hardest and most important task was to help my students become enough unafraid of me, and each other, to stop bluffing, faking, and playing testing games with me. Only when they were enough at ease in the class

to be truly themselves could they begin to reveal their true interests and strengths, as well as their fears and weaknesses. Only then
could I think about how to build on the strengths and overcome
or avoid the weaknesses. All this took time and patience. Some of
them would not for a long time tell me that they did not understand how to do a problem, or something I had told them or
written on the board. A few never told me; their masks never came
off.

If only to learn to do our work as teachers, we need students
who are not afraid of us, and so not afraid to tell us what they
think, or what they know and don't know. There may be a few
such students in our schools right now, but not enough—we need
many more. And we will have more as more and more children
who are for the most part learning outside of school come to
school for special classes and activities that they are interested in.

AUTHORITY AND LEADERSHIP

Because they don't understand natural authority, the schools are
in an authority crisis. Their coercive authority breaks down more
and more, but it is the only kind they know. They find it hard to
imagine what it might be like to deal with children who were not
in the least afraid of them and whom they had no reason to make
afraid. Words alone won't change this. The schools will only learn
about natural authority from those children for whom they *have*
natural authority, that is, the children who come to school because
they want to, to use it as a resource for purposes of their own.
From them will come much of the kind of leadership that the
schools so badly need.

While teaching fifth grade, I thought often about educational
leadership. For a long time, I had no idea what it was. Slowly I
began to see that the atmosphere and spirit of my classes were
largely determined by the students themselves, above all by two
or three who, whatever might be their schoolwork or behavior,
were in fact the real leaders. Of the five fifth grade classes I taught,
all of which I liked, the last was much the best—the most interesting and active, the most fun for me, the most valuable for the

children. But by all usual standards it should have been one of the worst; only three of the children were really good students, and more than half the class had serious academic and/or emotional problems. What made that class the best was the two children who (without knowing or trying) led it.

One, a black boy, was by far the most brilliant student I have ever taught, and not just school-smart but life-smart, smart in everything. The other, a girl, just as much a leader, was a very poor student, but exceptionally imaginative and artistic, and also smart in the real world. What made these children such a joy to be with, and such a powerful influence on the other children, was not just their obvious alertness, imagination, curiosity, good humor, high spirits, and interest in many things, but their energy, vitality, self-respect, courage and above all, their true independence. They did not need to be bossed, told what to do. Nor were they interested in playing with me, or against me, the old school game of "You Can't Make Me Do It." No doubt they were helped by the fact that I, unlike so many adults, obviously enjoyed and valued those qualities in them that they most valued in themselves. But I did not create these qualities, they brought them to the class. What without these children might have been a miserable year turned out to be the most interesting and exciting year I ever spent in a schoolroom.

A few such children can make an enormous difference to a class or even an entire school. Far more than any principal or teacher, they set the tone of the place. If, on the other hand, the children with the most energy, imagination, and courage are constantly defying the school, and if the only ones who are "good" are obviously the ones who are too scared to be bad, most of the children will admire and envy the outlaws even if they don't dare imitate them. No one can maintain law and order, or authority, or discipline in such a place.

In my fifth grade class the most admired children were not the outlaws. Not that the two leaders were docile teacher's pets, far from it. If they didn't like something I was doing, or wanted to do something else, or thought I was being unfair, they would tell me. But this had nothing to do with a struggle over who was boss. Our relationship was about something else altogether. They were in many ways interested in the world, and I knew more about the world than they did, so they were glad to find out and use much of what I knew. Meanwhile, we enjoyed each other's company. To be sure, the class had its cut-ups and You-Can't-Make-Me's. When they were really funny, as they sometimes were, the other kids might laugh at them, as I did myself. But they were not admired for being cut-ups. Their antics were often a distraction and a nuisance to kids who had better things to do. What was important and admired was being as alive, alert, active, curious, and committed as those leaders. The class discipline that grows out of that kind of feeling is as different as night from day from the discipline in a class where the children say to each other, "If you do that, I'll tell the teacher and you'll get in trouble." Not only is it a great deal more pleasant, it is a great deal more permanent.

The schools desperately need, if only as an example to the others, more of that kind of children, children whose dealings with them are not governed by fear. Such children will bring to the school, not only a different attitude about the world (interesting and exciting), themselves (independent and competent), and the school (useful), but also interests that go far beyond last night's TV shows. Some of these interests, the other children will pick up. My black fifth grader *taught* the other children in that class far more than I did; admiring him, they talked with him as much as they could (which I allowed), and from that talk they learned a great deal. In the same way, home-schooled children who come to school as part-time volunteers will bring with them many ideas, skills, activities, resources, for other children to share. Even if these children make up only a very small percentage of the student body, they will make the school a very different, and much nicer and more interesting place.

MONEY, PUBLICITY, CLIENTS

One reason the schools worry about people teaching their children at home has to do with money. Most school districts receive financial aid from the state—so many dollars per pupil per day. This aid often makes up an important part of the school's income.

So when a family talks about teaching their children at home, the schools think, "If they do, we will lose X hundred dollars a year, which we can't afford, so we'd better not let them." But clearly, if the schools cooperated with the parents, and the children came to school part-time for activities they liked, the school would be able to mark them present, and so would not lose their share of state aid.

In fact, there is no legal reason why a school district, having decided to cooperate with a home-schooling family, could not enroll their children and list them as attending the school, even if they seldom *came* to school. Nothing in any state education laws I have seen says that "attendance" can only mean physical presence in the school building, or would prevent any school district from doing what, for a while at least, the Philadelphia schools did in their Parkway Project, or the Toronto schools in their Metro Project. In these the students spent their days, not in school buildings, but in various institutions of the city itself. No one ever claimed, or could have sustained a claim, that in sending students around the city instead of shutting them up in school buildings these school systems were violating state attendance laws. Other public school systems have very wisely sent children out of the schools to work as apprentices in various local businesses, giving them school credit for the experience. No one ever claimed that this was a violation of the law.

Since the law gives school districts the right to define attendance in any way they and their constituents choose, there is no reason why a school district could not claim that children learning at home, with the school's support and supervision, were "attending" the school. Indeed, the school might claim that it was not only legally but morally justified in collecting state aid for such students, since in some ways they might be getting more individualized attention than the children in the school building. So there is no reason why schools have to see home schooling as an immediate financial threat.

Cooperating with home-schooling families is not only a way to avoid bad publicity, but a way to get good publicity, which most school systems would very much like to have. During an appearance on a local TV talk show I happened to mention briefly that the schools in Barnstable, Massachusetts, were cooperating fully with a home-schooling family, whose children, whenever they wanted, could and did go to the school to take part in activities they liked. This very brief mention brought and is still bringing the school district a number of inquiring letters and phone calls, some even from outside the state, and all very favorable in tone. School folks, like everyone else, like to feel and have others feel that they are at the forefront of progress, blazing new trails, leading the way. Cooperating with home-schooling families is an easy and an authentic way for schools to put themselves in that position. Then why not do it? Why look bad when it is so easy to look good?

Because of the decline of the birth rate, no matter what else they do, schools are going to continue to lose more and more of their clients. To stay in business, they must find new ones. Many seem to think they can solve this problem by making compulsory education begin earlier and go on longer, if possible forever. Educators in many parts of the country are trying to make kindergarten compulsory; some teachers' unions have even proposed that compulsory schooling should begin as early as age two or three. At the same time, educators talk a great deal about a rather sinister idea called Mandatory Continuing Education, which, if they can push it through, will mean that more and more people, having gone to school for years in order to get a job, will then have to keep going to school in order to keep the job. A prominent educator, a very gifted promoter of education (and himself), used to say proudly that he considered himself a "womb-to-tomb" schooler. What he had in mind was, of course, that *other people* would have to spend their whole lives going to school. Not him; he would be running those schools.

This is the wrong approach. It might have sold in the days when everyone but a handful of cranks was behind the schools, or when people were sure that every extra year spent in school automatically meant so many extra dollars on your paycheck. But it won't sell now, in today's growing antischool climate, and our declining economy, where college and even graduate degrees are worth less and less every year. If the schools are to survive and thrive, as a few understand very well, it must be more and more as places that people go to *only because they like to,* because they think of school as a place where you can find out about and do interesting things.

Very few people now feel that way. Even when most people still supported the schools in principle, hundreds of parents, many of whom had even been good students, were telling or writing me that most of their worst anxiety dreams were still school dreams, or that every time they went into their children's school, for whatever reason, they could feel their insides tighten up and their hands begin to sweat. Many kinds of places—concert halls, baseball parks, theaters, parks, beaches, to name a few—make most people feel good as soon as they step into them. They think that something pleasant, interesting, exciting, is about to happen. For their very survival, the schools *need* people who feel that way about them, for in the long run such people are the ones the schools will have to depend on for their support, they are their only true friends.

Some school districts understand this very well. Here are some words from "Declining Enrollments," a pamphlet published by the Center for Community Education Development of the Santa Barbara County Schools (522 No. Salsipuedes St., Santa Barbara CA 93103), which I strongly recommend to any schools or parents who are worried about possible school closings:

> When schools exist apart from the community, they stand as monuments to the School Board and their ability to get bond issues passed . . . as reminders to citizens of the unpleasant past of their own educational experiences . . . as symbols of something to vote against in the future . . . they stand empty, unused, and economically unfeasible, they create a further segmented and fragmented society. On the other side of the coin is the school which is an integral part of the total resources of the community.
>
> There is also what has become almost a classic story of making a building so indispensable that the School Board could not consider its closing. The principal of Fairlington Elementary School in Arlington, Virginia, saw her enrollment drop from 440 to 225. She first turned space over to a play school, then invited the recreation department to use the school for some of its programs and then reserved space for use by a senior citizens group. A community

theatre and several other local organizations soon joined in using the school's facilities. Before long, talk of closing the school ceased, and some began to wonder if perhaps it needed an addition.

An 800-student junior high school in Arlington, Virginia, uses about half its capacity in a district-wide alternative program. The rest of the building is used by a Montessori school (run by the district but with a tuition charge to parents) and adult education courses. A community center has now been added to the site, connected to the school so as to make use of its gymnasium, food service areas and auditorium. In building the center, the recreation department provided a playground and tennis courts, available for use by the school.

Other schools in Arlington house museums, day care centers, drama workshops, recreational programs, alternative educational programs, lunch programs for senior citizens, branches of the public library and youth programs. The major disadvantage is that the district could spend little to remodel the facilities, so the user groups have to make do with what exists.

TEACHER TRAINING

In time, the home schooling movement could become very useful, at least to the more innovative schools of education, as a way of training teachers.

Professors of education have asked me many times over the years how we might improve teacher training. Until recently I have said that as long as we define teacher training as sending people to college to take education courses, nothing could make that process any less harmful than it already is. Young teachers so trained go into the classroom thinking that they know a great deal about children, learning, and teaching, when in fact they know next to nothing—which I would say even if I had taught all their classes. People so taught have nothing in their minds but words. They know no more about children and teaching than people who had lived all their lives in desert or jungle would know about snow-covered mountains just from hearing people talk about them. We cannot, by turning a complicated experience into words, *give* that experience to someone who has not had it. Hearing mountains or children described, even seeing photos or films of mountains or children, is no substitute at all for seeing and climbing actual mountains or working with actual children.

Since student teachers in their training hear and read only words, and have no experience in teaching or otherwise dealing with children to which they can relate and compare these words, they have no sound basis for saying that some ideas seem to make more sense or fit better with experience than others. What they are told about teaching, they tend to swallow whole. Such students, when they first enter classrooms as teachers, come in, so to speak, with a box of gummed labels: "underachiever," "overachiever," "learning disability," "brain damaged," "acting out," "emotionally disturbed," "culturally deprived," etc. Once in the class, instead of looking at what is before them, and slowly learning to describe and judge this experience in their own way, they look for children or events onto which they can stick one or more of the ready-made labels from their box. Thinking that a child labeled is a child understood, they quickly decide that Billy is an underachiever, and Susie is a typical this, and Tommy a typical that. This would be bad even if the labels themselves were good. Thus, even if the word "underachiever" described something real and important, instead of merely a discrepancy between the results of two different kinds of tests (neither worth much), there would be many different kinds of underachievers and ways of underachieving. But most teachers, satisfied with this kind of instant diagnosis, don't take time, or don't know how, to look further. And so these labels, wrong to start with and hastily slapped on, become a part of the official record of schoolchildren, and largely determine how the schools, and beyond that the world, will see them and deal with them.

None of these faults in teacher training are improved by having teachers, usually in their last year of ed school, do some "student teaching" or "practice teaching" in the classrooms of regular teachers in local public schools. What this "teaching" amounts to is mostly watching the regular teacher and helping out with minor chores. Only rarely, usually under the eye of the regular teacher, are the student teachers allowed to teach a "unit" or two of their own. To expect anyone to learn to teach by such methods is like expecting a child to learn to drive a car by sitting in his parents' laps and holding the wheel while they steer it.

When student teachers worked with me in my fifth-grade class, from time to time I used to turn the class over to them. When I did I would always leave the room, first telling the students that while I wasn't there Miss So-and-so was the boss and they had to do exactly what she said, etc. But they knew, and she knew, that I was the real boss; I gave out any serious punishments that had to be given out, and beyond that, the grades which were the true and ultimate reward and punishment. Their fate as fifth-graders lay in my hands, not Miss So-and-so's. I, and not the student teacher, was still holding the wheel.

In any case, whether the regular "cooperating" teachers are in the room or not during this practice teaching, they will always demand a report on it, and will know if it went badly. Since student teachers need good reports from their cooperating teachers, they will not, as many have told me, run the risk of using in their practice teaching any methods that these teachers might not like. They will be thinking not about what will most help the students, but what will get the best report from the regular teacher. Beyond this, they get so few chances to teach, and these so brief, that they don't have time to make a serious trial of whatever teaching methods they want to use, far less find out how to improve them.

Student practice teaching is mostly a sham and a fraud. It gives the students a very brief look at the inside of a real schoolroom, and enables schools of education to say to future employers of their graduates that these graduates have had some "field experience." But that's all it does.

A more helpful way to train people for the work of teaching in classrooms would be to have them *begin* by teaching real classes in real schools, all the while giving them places and plenty of time to talk about their work with other new teachers in the same position, sometimes (but not always) in the company of a sympathetic and more experienced teacher. Along with these discussions, the new teachers could read and discuss a number of books about teaching, child psychology, etc., looking for ideas that might help them make sense of their experience, and so teach better. They would be encouraged to read these books critically, not passively. Perhaps, out of their experience, their discussions, and their reading, they might write some manuals or books of their own. We might then have many more textbooks about classroom teaching "methods" written by people who had actually and recently worked in classrooms.

But even if we could make these changes in the ways in which we hire and train teachers, teaching classes in compulsory schools would not tell them very much about learning. My own work as a teacher began exactly in the way described above. I started teaching without any formal training whatever. I read no books about education until after I had taught for a number of years. I had plenty of time and occasions to talk with other young teachers like myself about our mutual problems, and many of these talks, with my friend and colleague Bill Hull, were the seed of my first book. Yet in all my years in the classroom what I learned was not so much how children learn as how they defend themselves against learning, not so much how they explored and made sense of the world as how they worked out slippery strategies for dodging the dangers of school, the pain and shame of not knowing, being wrong, failing.

What I really learned about *learning,* in its best and deepest sense, I learned partly from my own adult experiences in learning languages, music and sports, but mostly from watching and playing with babies and very young children in their parents' homes. Only as I began to understand how human beings learned when they learned *best* did I begin to understand what was wrong with the classroom and my own and others' teaching. Seeing human learning at its most powerful, i.e., the learning of infants, above all their amazing and always unique discovery and conquest of language, gave me a yardstick against which I could measure all other teaching and learning.

There is no better way to understand human learning than by closely watching babies and infants during those years in which they are learning (among many other things) to stand, walk, and talk, and no better place to do this than in the home, not as a teacher or coldly detached scientist but as *an attentive, concerned, and loving member of the family.* Such an experience, living like an older sister or brother in families with young children, would be invaluable to people who want to be teachers or helpers of learning of any kind. It is the only kind of training for teaching, other than teaching itself, which has any chance of being any use at all.

Looking into the future, I can see a day when at least a certain number of student teachers would have such an experience as part of their training. Of course, there would be problems to work out. Families would have to be paid, not just for the expense and trouble of housing and feeding students but in fair return for the important service they were doing them. Such an experience should not be compulsory; only those students who felt they could learn something important by living in another family with small children should be allowed to do it. Schools of education would have to give generous academic credits for such training. Nor should they demand from students too much in the way of papers and reports, since the whole point is to have the student in the family *not* as a reporter but as a family member. You can't play with little children and take notes at the same time. Any education professors who need piles of paper to prove that their students are learning anything would be better off left out of such a program. I would never have learned half as much from my own experience of living in families with children if I had been required to write papers about them. When I wrote, as I often did, it was only because, I realized later, I had seen something so interesting that I wanted to be sure to remember it, and perhaps to tell others about it.

Student and family would have to agree about how much the student, living as a family member, would be subject to the family's routines and disciplines. Many families would not want students in their homes doing things that they would not allow their own children to do. Families and students would also have to agree on how much of the family housework the students were expected to do, and how much free time they would have and when. There might well be other problems. But any education department that wanted to put such a program into effect could surely find a way to do so.

It will of course be essential to find the right kind of families.

Students will not learn much about the learning of infants and children except in families which like, trust, and respect their children and enjoy watching their learning and helping it if and when they can. Here is where the home-schooling movement might be very useful to schools. People who are teaching children at home, or who would like to, or even think they might like to, are almost certain to be people who treat their children with loving courtesy, and allow and encourage them to explore the world in their own way.

In a few years, and perhaps even right now, we will easily be able to find dozens or perhaps hundreds of families that would be glad, especially if they were getting paid for doing so, to have a student teacher live in their homes as a family member, like an older cousin, for part or all of a school year. Such an arrangement might help to solve another problem, already discussed in this book. Many parents would like right now to take their children out of school and have them learn at home, but feel they can't because they have to work during the day and have no one to stay with their children. A live-in student teacher would solve this problem for them.

This training might very well be valuable, not just to teachers but to future psychologists, psychiatrists, therapists, social workers, and others whose work might someday bring them into contact with children. Some young people might want to do it for a while just to get themselves more ready for having their own children. We hear much about the need for young people to take courses in "parenting." Six months living in a family with young children would be a great deal more valuable than any such course.

Educational institutions, teachers' colleges and others, will be able to give such programs important support, and I look forward to the day when many of them are doing so. But we don't have to wait for them in order to get started. We could begin without them, on a strictly personal basis, and I propose that we do. I therefore ask readers of this book to write me if (1) they are a family that is teaching their children at home, or would do so if they could solve the day-care problem, or that is planning to do so when their children reach school age, and that would like to have a young person (future teacher or otherwise) live in with them for a while as a family member, or (2) they would like to live in with such a family for a while, preferably for all of a school year but perhaps only a part of it. I would like (only with permission, of course) to list both such groups in the magazine, *Growing Without Schooling.* By this means, and perhaps others, families and live-in volunteers can get in touch with each other and make their own arrangements. Before making these arrangements final, they might want to have a visit and a trial live-in period of a week or two, to make sure they understand and like each other enough to go on with it.

It seems reasonable that if students are doing this as part of a college course, they or the college would pay the family something for their room, board, and cooperation. But if students were doing this on their own, and particularly if they were taking care of the family's children during the day, they might need and want to be paid for this work. In other cases no money might change hands at all. These are matters which students and families could work out among themselves.

CONCLUSION

Having said this much about why I think schools would be wise to give their full support to home-schooling families, I have to make two things clear. First, I do not claim that supporting home schooling is going to be a quick solution to the school's problems. For these there are no quick solutions. It took the schools many years to get into their present bad position, and even after they come to understand how and why they got into it, it will take them many years to get out. Secondly, I am not proposing home schooling *so that* the schools will change their ways and/or solve their problems. I would like to see both these things happen, and believe that home schooling may in time help them to happen. But that is not why I am for home schooling. It is an important and worthwhile idea in its own right.

To repeat once again the idea with which I began this book, it is a most serious mistake to think that learning is an activity separate from the rest of life, that people do best when they are not doing anything else and best of all in places where nothing else is done. It is an equally serious mistake to think that teaching, the assisting of learning and the sharing of knowledge and skill, is something that can be done only by a few specialists. When we lock learning and teaching in the school box, as we do, we do not get more effective teaching and learning in society, but much less.

What makes people smart, curious, alert, observant, competent, confident, resourceful, persistent—in the broadest and best sense, intelligent—is not having access to more and more *learning* places, resources, and specialists, but being able in their lives to do a wide variety of interesting things that matter, things that challenge their ingenuity, skill, and judgment, and that make an obvious difference in their lives and the lives of people around them. It is foolish to think that through "education" we can have a society in which, no matter how low may be the quality of work, the quality of learning and intelligence will remain high. People with dull and meaningless jobs are hardly likely to lead active, interesting, productive lives away from those jobs. They are much more likely to collapse in front of the TV set and take refuge from their own dreary daily life in a life of fantasy, by imagining for a while that they are one of those rich, beautiful, sexy, powerful, laughing, fast-moving, successful people on the screen.

I have used the words "home schooling" to describe the process by which children grow and learn in the world without going, or going very much, to schools, because those words are familiar and quickly understood. But in one very important sense they are misleading. What is most important and valuable about the home as a base for children's growth into the world is not that it is a better school than the schools but *that it isn't a school at all.* It is not an artificial place, set up to make "learning" happen and in which nothing except "learning" ever happens. It is a natural, organic, central, fundamental human institution, one might easily and rightly say the foundation of all other institutions. We can imagine and indeed we have had human societies without schools, without factories, without libraries, museums, hospitals, roads, legislatures, courts, or any of the institutions which seem so indispensable and permanent a part of modern life. We might someday even choose, or be obliged, to live once again without some or all of these. But we cannot even imagine a society without homes, even if these should be no more than tents, or mud huts, or holes in the ground. What I am trying to say, in short, is that our chief educational problem is not to find a way to make homes *more* like schools. If anything, it is to make schools *less* like schools.

Whatever we may call the activity I have tried to describe in this book, it will go on more quickly, easily, painlessly, and productively if the schools will cooperate with it rather than trying to resist it. In these last chapters I have tried to say why I think they would be not simply generous but wise to do so, as some are already doing. (For a list of schools or school districts that are helping and supporting home schooling families, see Appendix and also the magazine *GWS.*)

When John Merrow interviewed me for National Public Radio, I told him why I thought schools would be wise to support home schooling, and about listing all school districts doing so. He said, "Aren't you being a bit naïve?" Well, I certainly would be if I thought that large numbers of school districts were going to do this in the next year or so. I don't at first expect many of them to take this path. But the path is there for those who are willing to take it. Our list of supporting school districts is still very small. But, like the home-schooling movement itself, it is growing and will continue to grow, and for the same reason—because it makes sense, and because it works.

Appendix: Resources for Home Schoolers

GROWING WITHOUT SCHOOLING

Growing Without Schooling is, as we have said, a bi-monthly magazine for people, about people, and to a large extent by people who have taken or would like to take their children out of school, so that they may teach them, i.e., help them learn, in the home and in as much as possible of the adult world that surrounds the home.

The letters and articles we have quoted in this book give a fair sample of what the magazine is like. In addition, there have been and will be letters and articles about many other subjects, including:

(1) Addition, multiplication, and other kinds of math.

(2) Learning to read, and helping others to learn.

(3) Art—drawing, painting, art materials, etc.

(4) Music—buying (or making) instruments, and learning or helping others learn to play them (including piano, violin, cello, etc.). Also, something about how to write music.

(5) Family economics and accounting, and ways of involving children in them.

(6) Handwriting and calligraphy, i.e., italic handwriting.

(7) Spelling.

(8) Writing, of many different kinds.

(9) Computers, and their uses with children, in and out of the home.

(10) Many other arts and sciences, as people bring them up.

(11) Foreign languages and ways to learn them.

(12) Ways in which children can, if they choose, take part in adult work.

(13) Adult workplaces to which adults may bring their children.

(14) Ways in which children can visit other families, perhaps on an exchange basis.

(15) Learning Exchanges—low-cost ways in which people can exchange and share needed skills and information.

(16) Live-in baby sitters and other arrangements that may make it easier for people, including working families, to teach their own children.

(17) Reviews of books, both about and for children, and other kinds of learning materials, some that we sell here, some available elsewhere.

(18) Information about other ways of teaching one's own children, whether by starting schools or whatever.

(19) Information about extension courses, and ways of getting credits, diplomas, and degrees without having to go to school or college campuses.

(20) Latest information about laws or proposed changes in laws, court rulings, legal approaches and strategies, etc.—*GWS* is something of a miniature law review on this subject, probably the most complete available.

(21) News, as we get it, of home-schooling activities in other countries—most of our news so far has come from the U.S. and Canada, but we hope to hear more from others.

(22) Any other ideas that we or our readers may think of that may help children grow up in and into the world.

Earlier in the book we briefly mentioned the *GWS* Directory. This is a list, by states, of names and addresses of people who have chosen to list themselves, so that other people interested in home schooling will feel free to get in touch with them. People in the Directory may or may not have children, and if they do, may or may not be teaching them at home. But in one way or another they are sympathetic to the idea of home schooling, and willing to talk to others about it and to help them do it. Most of these families that have children also list the names and ages of the children, so that other families with children of the same ages may get in touch with them, or so that the children may get in touch with each other—quite a number of children have made pen pals in this way.

On the last page of this book you will find information about how to subscribe to *GWS*, or to send for a sample copy.

CORRESPONDENCE SCHOOLS

American Home Academy, RFD 2, Box 106 C, Brigham City, Utah 84302

American School, 850 E. 58th St., Chicago, Ill. 60637

Bethany Homestead Christian Resource Center, R.F.D. 1, Box 220, Taylor Rd., Thompson, Conn. 06277; 203-928-0453

Calvert Institute, 105 Tuscany Rd., Baltimore, Md. 21210

Christian Liberty Academy, 203 E. McDonald, Prospect Heights, Ill. 60070

Home Study Institute, 6940 Carroll Ave, Takoma Park, Md. 20012

International Correspondence High School, Scranton, Pa. 18515

International Institute, P.O. Box 99, Park Ridge, Ill. 60068

Moody Correspondence School, 820 N. La Salle St., Chicago, Ill. 60610

Mt. Vernon Academy, 184 Vine St., Murray, Utah 84107

Oak Meadow School, P.O. Box 1051, Ojai, Calif. 93023

Our Lady of Victory School, P.O. Box 5181, Room 11, Mission Hills, Calif. 91345

Pensacola Christian Correspondence School, 5409 Rawson Lane, Pensacola, Fla. 32503

University of Nebraska Independent Study High School, 511 Nebraska Hall, Lincoln, Nebr. 68588

For a directory of correspondence schools, write *National Home Study Council,* 1601 18th St. N.W., Washington, D.C. 20009.

PRIVATE SCHOOLS ENROLLING OR HELPING HOME STUDY STUDENTS

Dean Point School, Box 266, Nehalem, Oreg. 97131

Halvi School, 124 N. Paredes Line Rd., Brownsville, Texas 78520; 512-546-1449

Holt School, Box 866, New Providence, N.J. 07974

Home Based Education Program, 1289 Jewett St., Ann Arbor, Mich. 48104

Home School, 849 Drake St., Cambria, Calif. 93428; 805-927-4137

John Holt Learning Center, 8446 S. Harrison St., Midvale, Utah 84047

Jonathan's Place, 4301 Harrison, Kansas City, Mo. 64112; 816-753-5392

Santa Fe Community School, P.O. Box 2241, Santa Fe, N.Mex. 87501

Upattinas School, R.D. 1, Box 378, Glenmoore, Pa. 19343; 215-458-5138

LAWYERS WILLING TO HELP HOME SCHOOLERS

THEODORE H. AMSHOFF, JR., Amshoff and Amshoff, Attys at Law, 3142 First National Tower, Louisville, Ky. 40202

HELEN BAKER, 2555 Kemper Rd., #406, Shaker Hts., Ohio 44120 (legal advice only—cannot take private cases)

ROBERT BAKER, On the Square, Sarcoxie, Mo. 64862

TOM DIGRAZIA, Bates Law Office, 2400 E. Morgan Ave., Evansville, Ind. 47711

JOHN EIDSMOE, 110 N. Mill St., Fergus Falls, Minn. 56537; 218-736-5493

DAVID MANDEL, 1350 Avenue of the Americas, New York, N.Y. 10019

PHIL STUDENBERG, 234 E. Wauna, Klamath Falls, Oreg. 92601

SHELLY WAXMAN, 30 W. Washington St., Ste. 1115, Chicago, Ill. 60602

SCHOOL DISTRICTS COOPERATING WITH HOME SCHOOLERS

Calif.—San Juan Ridge Union School District, 18847 Tyler Foote Rd., Nevada City 95959; Marilyn DeVore, Administrator.

Mass.—Barnstable Public Schools, 230 South St., Hyannis, Mass. 02601; Jane Sheckells, Curriculum Director.

Rockland Public Schools, Rockland 02370; Supt. John W. Rogers.

Southern Berkshire Regional School District, Sheffield 01257; Director of Guidance, Paul Shafiroff.

Vt.—Woodbury School, Woodbury; Marilyn Hill, Principal.

This list, with additions as they come in, will appear in each issue of *GWS*. About this list, we wrote in *GWS* #17:

. . . There are of course many more schools that are cooperating with parents than are listed here, but they are not yet willing to make it public.

We will only list these school districts under the following conditions:

1) The family has to be not just satisfied but *pleased* with the cooperation the schools are giving to their home-schooling efforts.

2) The schools themselves have to be pleased with the relationship with the family.

3) The family has to be happy with the idea of asking the schools whether they want to be included in this list. If they feel that listing the schools, or even asking the schools if they want to be listed, may endanger their good present relationship, then they shouldn't ask.

4) The schools themselves have to be happy about being included in the list. If they are uneasy about it, or fear that it may get them in trouble with someone, we'd rather not subject them to that risk.

. . . By the way, we would also like to hear from schools that would *like* to help home schooling families but have not been able to do so because no families have yet asked them.

PROFESSORS WILLING TO HELP
HOME SCHOOLERS

LARRY ARNOLDSEN, Box 10, McKay Bldg., Brigham Young U., Provo, Utah 84602

DAVID N. CAMPBELL, Dept. of Education, 5B14 FQ., University of Pittsburgh, Pittsburgh, Pa. 15217; 412-624-1266

DR. STEPHEN J. CORWIN, 1179 Weybridge Rd., Columbus, Ohio 43220

MARIO FANTINI, PH.D., Dean of the School of Education, University of Massachusetts, Amherst, Mass. 01003

RICHARD KING, Faculty of Education, University of Victoria, Victoria, B.C. V8W 2Y2

DR. HAL LENKE, 106 N. Cortez #5, Prescott, Ariz. 86301

DR. PAUL NASH, Dept. of Education, Boston University, Boston, Mass. 02215

PROF. ALBERT SCHATZ, 6097 Sherman St., Philadelphia, Pa. 19119

ORGANIZATIONS

Alberta Home Schooling Information Service, 514 7th St. N.E., Calgary, Alberta, Canada T2E 4L6

Alternatives in Education, Rte. 3 Box 171 A, Spencer W.Va. 27276

Canadian Alliance of Home Schoolers, Box 640, Jarvis, Ontario, Canada N0A 1J0

Center for Independent Education, 747 Front St., San Francisco, Calif. 94111

Citizens for Educational Freedom, Washington Bldg., Ste. 854, 15th St. & New York Ave., Washington, D.C. 20005

Education Otherwise, 18 Eynham Rd., London W 12, England

EVAN-G (Committee to End Violence Against the Next Generation), 977 Keeler Ave., Berkeley, Calif. 94708

Florida Association for Schooling at Home (FLASH), 1455 90th Ave., #45, Vero Beach, Fla. 32960

Hewitt Research Center, Dr. Raymond Moore, Director, 533 Tudor Rd., Berrien Springs, Mich. 49103

Home Education Resource Center, 337 Downs St., Ridgewood, N.J. 07450; 201-447-4044

Homesteaders News, Box 193, Addison, N.Y. 14801

Independent Family Schools Resource Center, R.D. 1, Smyrna, N.Y. 13464; 607-627-6670

Manitoba Association for Schooling at Home, 824 Barry Ave., Winnipeg, Manitoba R2C 1M1

National Association of Home Educators, Star Route, Smithton, Mo. 65350

National Association for the Legal Support of Alternative Schools, Box 2823, Santa Fe, N.Mex. 87501

National Coalition of Alternative Community Schools, 1289 Jewett St., Ann Arbor, Mich. 48104

National Parents League, 4195 S.W. Cedar Hills Blvd., Portland, Oreg.

New Jersey Growing Without Schooling, 2 Smith St., Farmingdale, N.J. 07727

Ohio Coalition of Educational Alternatives Now (OCEAN), 66 Jefferson Ave., Columbus, Ohio 43215

Options in Education, 2025 M. St. N.W., Washington, D.C. 20036

If you write to these organizations, please enclose a self-addressed stamped envelope.

OTHER ALLIES WE NEED

LEGISLATORS

The education lobbies—teachers' unions, NEA, etc.—are working hard (and spending freely) in a number of states to get laws passed that would make it virtually impossible for parents to teach their children at home. We need as much help as we can get from friendly or at least neutral legislators to sidetrack or defeat all such efforts. It is therefore extremely important for home schoolers or would-be home schoolers (and often their children) to get to know their elected representatives (state and national), at least by mail but preferably in person.

CERTIFIED TEACHERS

In many states a family can teach its children at home without further argument or trouble if it has the support and help of a certified teacher, and in all states such support will probably greatly strengthen a family's position. We would like to hear from certified teachers who are willing to help in this way.

DOCTORS

As many letters in Chapter 1, "Why Take Them Out," clearly showed, many children's *physical* health is clearly damaged by the experience of school, with its constant boredom, anxiety, and threat of humiliation and pain, either at the hands of adults or of the child's fellow students; and taking children out of school has often produced quick and striking improvements in their health, even in their actual growth. We need to find doctors who can see this and who, if they see it, will say so in writing. In many cases, this may be all that is needed to get children out of school, and in all cases it will surely be helpful.

PSYCHOLOGISTS

In the same way, we need to find people who can see, and having seen, will say for the record that it will be much better for children's psychological and emotional health to do their studying at home, not because there is anything wrong with them, but because if they stay in school very long, there surely will be.

REPORTERS, EDITORS, TV, RADIO, AND OTHER MEDIA PEOPLE

The press and other media have been virtually without exception friendly to home schooling and home schoolers; I cannot recall a single interview or report that was hostile. But it will be important during the coming years for home schoolers to keep the media well informed of what we are doing, to answer any questions they may have about our work and progress, and to make as many allies among them as we can.

SOURCES OF ALLIES

Mother Earth News, Box 70, Hendersonville, N.C. 28791, which now has a circulation of about a million and a readership much larger than that, is beginning to organize local chapters. Since the magazine strongly encourages self-reliance, and has recently published a couple of feature articles strongly favorable to home schooling, home schoolers may find in these local chapters many friends and allies.

Another good place to look for support may well be the La Leche League, International, an organization devoted to the breast-feeding of young children. Address: 9616 Minneapolis Ave., Franklin Park, Ill. 60131.

For similar reasons, the Association for Childbirth at Home, International, and all other organizations devoted to more natural methods of birthing and rearing, may also be good sources of support. A very good magazine on this subject is *Mothering,* Box 2046, Albuquerque, N.Mex. 87103.

THIS PAGE IS GOOD TOWARD ONE FREE ISSUE
OF THE MAGAZINE *GROWING WITHOUT SCHOOLING*.

Check one:

_____Please send me a free sample of GROWING WITHOUT
SCHOOLING.

Please send a free issue, and I enclose a check or money order (U.S.
funds) for a subscription to GROWING WITHOUT SCHOOLING:

> _____ 6 more issues, $15.

> _____ 12 more issues, $24.

> _____ 18 more issues, $30.

> Group subscriptions also available.
> Rates subject to change.

_____

NAME

_____

ADDRESS

_____

CITY   STATE   ZIP

Remove page and send to:

GROWING WITHOUT SCHOOLING
308 Boylston Street
Boston, Mass. 02116

Index

Martin, Judge James G., IV, 285
Maslow, Abraham, 147
Massachusetts
  education laws, 99
  state court decision on rights of parents, 315, 316
Math, 127, 305
McCahill, Judy, 24, 130–133, 172–173, 208–209
McElwain, Bill, 195
Mead, Margaret
  and Balinese, 166
  Blackberry Winter, 132–133
Medical exemptions, 115, 120
Meek v. Pittenger, 279
Meigs, Judge, 285–286
Merrill, Dr. Frank, 22–24
Merrow, John, 347
Meyer v. Nebraska, 278
Michigan v. Nobel, 290–294, 295
Milstein, Nathan ("Violinist Par Excellence"), 224–225
Mingins, Candy, 198–199
Minnesota education laws, 314, 317–318, 320–321
Mississippi education laws, 326
Money
  children handling, 183–185
  and school systems, 335–336
Moore, Raymond
  Better Late Than Early, 14
  School Can Wait, 14
Morgan, Charlie, 258
Morrison, Johnny E., 283
Mother Earth News, 357
Mull, Gary, 258
Murdock v. Pennsylvania, 293
Museum, as resource, 169, 170
Music, learning, 222–225
Muslim family, 25–26
Myles, Gail, 179–181
Myth of the Hyperactive Child, The (Peter Schrag and Diane Divoky), 20

Nagel, Ed, 113
Naked Children, The (Daniel Fader), 230

National Educational Association, and testing, 303
Nature Heals (Paul Goodman), 249–250
Nature of the Judicial Process, The (Justice Cardozo), 312
Nebraska ruling on child neglect and home schooling, 319–230
Nebraska v. Rice, 312
Neglect, child, *see* Child neglect, and home schooling
Neill, A. S. *(Summerhill)*, 139, 201–202
New Alchemy Institute (Massachusetts), 256–257
New Hampshire State Board of Education, and *Home Study Guidelines*, 301
New Hampshire Supreme Court, and child neglect case, 309–310
New Jersey
  education laws, 75, 88
  home study legalized in, 75
  state court decision on rights of parents, 315
New York education laws, 92
No More Public School (Hal Bennett), 108
Nobel, Peter and Ruth (v. Michigan), 290–294
Ny Lille Skole (New Little School, in Denmark), 189

Office work (volunteer), 268–270
Ontario education act, 287, 289
O'Shea, Ms., 33–34
Ovshinsky, 61–62

Parochial school, 7
Paul v. Davis, 278
Peckham Family Center (London), 188
Peer groups, 49–50
People v. Levisen, 298
Perchemlides v. Frizzle, 277–282, 294
Piano: Guided Sight Reading (Leonard Deutsch), 222–223

The Author

JOHN HOLT, author, educator, lecturer, and amateur musician, has written nine books, including *How Children Fail* and *How Children Learn*. His work has been translated into fourteen languages. Recently he has become the leading advocate of home schooling and the editor as well as publisher of a magazine for home-schooling families, called *Growing Without Schooling*.

Of his own educational background, John Holt has this to say: "I have come to believe that a person's schooling is as much a part of his private business as his politics or religion, and that no one should be required to answer questions about it. May I say instead that most of what I know I did not learn in school, or even in what most people would call 'learning situations.'"